K·I·S·S

DK

The Only Guides You'll Ever Need!

THIS SERIES IS YOUR TRUSTED GUIDE through all of life's stages and situations. Want to learn how to surf the Internet or care for your new dog? Or maybe you'd like to become a wine connoisseur or an expert gardener? The solution is simple: Just pick up a K.I.S.S. Guide and turn to the first page.

Expert authors will walk you through the subject from start to finish, using simple blocks of knowledge to build your skills one step at a time. Build upon these learning blocks and by the end of the book, you'll be an expert yourself! Or, if you are familiar with the topic but want to learn more, it's easy to dive in and pick up where you left off.

The K.I.S.S. Guides deliver what they promise: Simple access to all the information you'll need on one subject. Other titles you might want to check out include: Weight Loss, Selling, the Internet, Gardening, Pregnancy, Astrology, and many more.

GUIDE TO

Feng Shui

STEPHEN SKINNER

Foreword by Master Wu Hsien Sheng

A Dorling Kindersley Book

LONDON, NEW YORK, MUNICH,
MELBOURNE, DELHI

DK Publishing, Inc.

Senior Editor Jennifer Williams
Line editor Matthew X. Kiernan
Copy editor Gretchen Uphoff Fruchey
Category Publisher LaVonne Carlson

Dorling Kindersley Limited

Project Editor Julian Gray
Project Art Editor Justin Clow

Managing Editor Maxine Lewis
Managing Art Editor Heather McCarry
Category Publisher Mary Thompson
Production Heather Hughes

Produced for Dorling Kindersley by **Cooling Brown**
9–11 High Street, Hampton, Middlesex TW12 2SA

Creative Director Arthur Brown
Senior Editor Amanda Lebentz
Art Editors Pauline Clarke, Elly King
Editors Alison Bolus, Patsy North, Helen Ridge

First American Edition, 2001

00 01 02 03 04 05 10 9 8 7 6 5 4 3 2 1

Published in the United States by DK Publishing, Inc.,
375 Hudson Street, New York, New York 10014

Skinner, Stephen, 1948-
    KISS guide to feng shui / Stephen Skinner.-- 1st American ed.
            p. cm. -- (Keep it simple series)
    Includes index.
    ISBN 0-7894-8147-2 (alk. paper)
    1. Feng shui.   I. Title. II. Series.
BF1799.F4 S579 2001
133.3'337--dc21

                                                    2001002719

Color reproduction by ColourScan, Singapore
Printed and bound by MOHN media and Mohndruck GmbH, Germany

See our complete product line at
www.dk.com

Contents at a Glance

CONTENTS

PART ONE Understanding Feng Shui

CHAPTER 1 What Is Feng Shui?   22

CHAPTER 2 Who Does Feng Shui and Why?   36

PART THREE The Feng Shui of Interiors

PART FOUR The Feng Shui of Exteriors

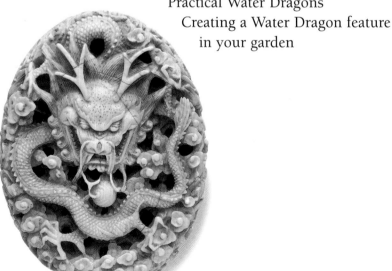

PART FIVE *Remedies and Formulas*

Foreword

I FIRST MET STEPHEN SKINNER in Hong Kong in 1976. He was researching feng shui. At first I could not believe that any European could possibly be interested in, or believe in, something as essentially Chinese as feng shui. But over the months, as I got to know him, I realized that he was one of the few people I knew, including many of my Chinese friends, who really cared about feng shui and genuinely wanted to know how it worked.

We traveled together, stood ankle-deep in mud on new building sites, and walked through old Chinese cemeteries in the New Territories and deeper into southern China. We worked together on sites as friends rather than Master and pupil. He was a natural at finding the true pulse of the dragon in amongst even the most complex tangle of hills.

Never did I dream that Stephen would be so instrumental in bringing feng shui to the West. When he showed me his first book on feng shui, written in the year we met, I was surprised and delighted, although I chided him for confusing the lunar New Year with Li Chun!

When Stephen returned to Hong Kong more than 20 years later
and showed me his magazine Feng Shui for Modern Living,
I could not believe that the Western world was ready for such a
treatment. I was wrong. When the magazine was also printed in
Chinese, I felt that Stephen had closed the circle, and brought feng
shui back to where it belonged, but seen through Western eyes.

With the present book now in your hands, I see that Stephen has
taken yet another big step in bringing the world of the lo p'an,
the lo shu, and the lung shui to the attention of the whole world.
I wish him and this book the very best of luck.

Master Wu Hsien Sheng
Hong Kong
May 18th, 2001,
4th month, Year of the Golden Snake

Introduction

ONE OF THE PERPLEXITIES that everyone experiences upon getting into feng shui is the question: "Which school of feng shui should I learn and use?" The answer is "every one," because they all address a different part of the same problem. In this guide, I have tried to cover traditional feng shui as practiced by traditional Chinese Masters in the East, but have not attempted to cover some of the variants that have arisen in the West in the last 20 years. Black Hat Sect Tibetan feng shui (or, as its exponents prefer, BHS or BTB feng shui) is one such variant. It has its roots in the excellent work of Professor Lin Yun, but it is really a simplified version of Eight Mansion feng shui, which is covered in chapter 17.

Looking at the main schools in a rather oversimplified way:
● You should learn Form School feng shui, not just because it is the oldest, but because the point of the Form School is to find the best site and then to accumulate ch'i most efficiently, tapping into a "dragon vein."

● What sort of ch'i you accumulate depends on which way the building or house faces, and for that calculation (and other more complicated ones) you need to use Compass School feng shui.

● To see if a house is good for you personally, you need to use the East Life/West Life formula.

● To work out the interior layout, you might also use the East Life/West Life and the Eight Mansion formulas.

● To attend to your wealth, you should consider Water Dragon formulas.

Now this may seem like an awful lot to have to learn, but believe me, the more you know, the clearer it gets. Usually, you'd need to refer to several books to find out about the different schools of feng shui listed above — fortunately, this book covers them all. Perhaps for the first time you will have a real overview of this amazing practice, rather than just a part of it.

I wrote my first book on feng shui in 1976. In the past 25 years, I have seen some truly marvelous things happen as a direct result of using feng shui correctly, from the level of major corporate headquarters, right down to one-room apartments. I hope that your eyes light up in the same way that mine did when I first saw the incredible changes that can happen within a very short time after an effective feng shui change . . . we are talking about days.

I hope that as you voyage through this book you will come to love feng shui as much as I do, to wonder at the apparent complexity that becomes elegant simplicity. Furthermore, I will feel that my work has been worthwhile if you try out just one of the formulas. It is better to make a few mistakes than not to make any progress at all. Just remember to try out the things you have learned on yourself — not your friends!

STEPHEN SKINNER

地理先生

What's Inside?

THE INFORMATION IN THE K.I.S.S. Guide to Feng Shui *is arranged to help you learn more about the concepts behind feng shui as you progress through the book so that the theory makes perfect sense and practice comes naturally.*

PART ONE

In Part One, I'll explain what feng shui is and how it works. I'll also go into feng shui's history, from its earliest beginnings thousands of years ago up to its present-day popularity in the West, where it has been embraced by celebrities and corporate giants.

PART TWO

Now you'll learn about ch'i and how it is affected by alignments, the Earth's magnetism, the Compass Directions, and the five Elements. I'll also cover other fundamental building blocks of feng shui, like yin and yang, the eight Trigrams, and the *lo shu* magic square.

PART THREE

This part of the book is concerned with the feng shui of interiors, so that you can get straight down to doing some practical feng shui in your own home or office. I'll look at the feng shui of specific rooms and interior alignments, and how they affect ch'i energy.

PART FOUR

Here I'll focus on Form School (or exterior) feng shui. I'll show you how to use the four Celestial Animals, explain the importance of water and give you a powerful formula for increasing prosperity and wealth, and look at the feng shui of the rest of the garden.

PART FIVE

In this very practical part of the book I'll take you through the Eight Mansion formula, the *pa kua* and the *lo shu*, explain various practical changes ("remedies") that you can apply to your home or office, and show you how to use the East Life/West Life formula.

PART SIX

Finally, I'll introduce you to some slightly more advanced feng shui, such as formulas connected with time and the calendar, and the Heavenly Stems, Earthly Branches, and their combinations. Learn about your Four Pillar horoscope and get to grips with the feng shui compass (*lo p'an*).

The Extras

THROUGHOUT THE BOOK, you will notice a number of boxes and symbols. They are there to emphasize certain points I want you to pay special attention to, because they are important to your understanding of feng shui. You'll find:

Very Important Point

This symbol points out a topic that deserves careful attention. You really need to know this information before continuing.

Complete No-No

This is a warning, something I want to advise you not to do or to be aware of.

Getting Technical

When the information is about to get a bit technical, I'll let you know so that you can read carefully.

Inside Scoop

These are special suggestions that come from my own personal experience as a long-time practitioner of feng shui.

You'll also find some little boxes that include information I think is important, useful, or just plain fun.

Trivia...

These are simply fun facts that will give you an extra appreciation of feng shui in general.

DEFINITION

Here I'll **define** words and terms for you in an easy-to-understand style. You'll also find a glossary at the back of the book with all the feng shui-related terms, including guidance on pronunciation.

INTERNET

www.dk.com

The Internet is a great resource for feng shui enthusiasts, and I've included some web sites that I hope will add to your knowledge and practice of feng shui.

PART ONE

UNDERSTANDING FENG SHUI

FENG SHUI CAN BE USED to modify your home and office surroundings so that their inherent energies *benefit you* and your family rather than work against you. Feng shui has been around for thousands of years and is taken seriously by millions of people, many of whom feel that they owe some of their wealth, health, and happiness to its *careful practice*.

What used to be a closely guarded secret, reserved only for Emperors and their retainers, has now become popular with everyone from Madonna to Donald Trump. Although feng shui is not a spiritual practice, we will discover how it shares its roots with the three main religions of China, and we will meet the main feng shui Masters of antiquity.

Chapter 1

What Is Feng Shui?

IN THIS CHAPTER I hope to answer many of the questions asked by people new to feng shui: How do you pronounce it? Is it a science? Is it a religion? Where do I start? Does it work? What makes it work? There is still quite a difference between the way feng shui is perceived and practiced in the East and the West, and it is important to establish exactly what feng shui is not, so that we don't start on the wrong foot on our journey of discovery. I will define the mysterious energy – ch'i – that flows through and energizes the human body, the surface of the Earth, and the changing patterns of the weather, and show how these different forms of ch'i interact with each other.

In this chapter...
✔ *What does feng shui mean?*
✔ *Wind and water*
✔ *Human ch'i*
✔ *Luck isn't chance*

WEATHER PATTERNS ARE THE MANIFESTATION OF WEATHER CH'I

What does feng shui mean?

"FENG SHUI" CERTAINLY SOUNDED like strange and foreign words *back in the 1980s. Now, thanks to heavy media exposure and a tide of books, most people know that feng shui has got something to do with the effect your home and surroundings have on your happiness, health, and prosperity.*

Let us look at what feng shui actually means. In Chinese, the words "feng shui" simply mean "wind water." This gives us a hint that this subject is connected with the natural elements. Also, we know that both water and air are fluids, so "flow" is part of the meaning of feng shui. Lastly, these two things, air and water, are absolutely crucial to human survival.

When put together using these interpretations in a single term, they refer to the energy behind life; not just the life of the body, of plants, and of animals, but also of the very earth under our feet. This energy, or ch'i, also lies behind the complex day-to-day circumstances of our lives and our interactions with other people. That is a harder idea to accept, but I will come back to it later.

This is a simple demonstration of the way the Chinese language conveys meaning and an indication of the subtlety of Chinese thought, which may seem strange to the average Westerner.

■ **Feng shui** *is concerned with nature, the elements, and the energy behind life itself, which the Chinese call ch'i.*

To a Chinese brought up traditionally, feng shui is a series of do's and don'ts, which their grandmother probably imposed upon the family to help preserve its cohesion and prosperity.

In the last two decades of the 20th century, feng shui came to town in the West – in Europe and the US. Here, people have embraced the original principles of feng shui and have created extraordinary reverses of fortune and wonderful living spaces. However, its practitioners and devotees have built upon the original art and science, and now the title "feng shui" appears attached to such disparate things as shampoo, purses, makeup, and even food. This is perhaps unfortunate, since few in the West can now clearly see what feng shui really is. The art itself has not changed, but the popular definition has widened. Here I would like to take you back to some of the real feng shui, as it is understood and practiced by real Masters in the East.

FENG (WIND)

What feng shui is not

Feng shui is definitely not a recent New Age religion, but a long-practiced technique with a huge body of practice and theory behind it.

SHUI (WATER)

Here is a list of other things feng shui is not:

- A religion of any sort (although its theories sprang from the same roots as Taoism).
- A form of integrative psychology.
- A branch of interior decorating (although there is some cross-over in its application).
- Magic (real work is required, as feng shui is not just the hanging of a few wind chimes at random).
- A cure-all (no, it won't cure everything, just as acupuncture, for example, is only successful with some medical conditions).
- Easy (no, you have to follow its rules very precisely).
- A spiritual practice (despite modern attempts to make it seem so, feng shui is essentially practical, not spiritual).
- Just intuitive (certainly a Master may apply some intuition, but a student must do their calculations first before attempting to use intuition).
- A fad (no fad has gone on for so long; even in the West it has been popular for 25 years – too long a time for a fad!)

What feng shui is

Feng shui is not related directly to spiritual development or religious inclinations, any more than the study of geography is related to spirituality!

Ironically, in Chinese the words *ti li* apply to both the practical science of geography and to feng shui. In fact, I originally approached feng shui from the point of view of my then profession as a lecturer in geography.

Feng shui is a practical technique for manipulating ch'i energy, invented by the Chinese to improve their prosperity, marriage prospects, career luck, family cohesion, the luck of their children, their respect in the local community, their ability to pass exams, and their health.

We all know friends who have large, bright apartments or houses and great jobs, for whom opportunities seem to fall like ripe fruit into their hands, and all with barely any perceptible effort. We also know friends who live in dull, cramped, cluttered environments, for whom life is always a struggle, and who move back two paces for each pace they take forward. Their homes seem as congested as their luck. Maybe we even envy the first kind of friend and feel compassion for the second.

The question is, which came first? Did the luck of the first friend mean that he can afford a great home to live in, or did the advantages of a bright, positive environment enable him to reach a little bit farther, to take advantage of opportunities that might otherwise have passed him by?

■ **According to feng shui,** *a bright, positive environment that promotes the correct flow of energy, or ch'i, has a beneficial impact on our lives and on our luck.*

PRONUNCIATION

How do you pronounce feng shui? Well, there are as many ways of pronouncing it as there are Chinese dialects. The standard Mandarin pronunciation is close to "foong shway," but in Hong Kong, where a dialect called Cantonese is spoken, the pronunciation is closer to "fun soo-ee" (to rhyme with chop suey). In Amoy, it is pronounced "hong soo-ee."

One thing is for sure, the pronunciation "feng shoe-ee" that has become common in the West was never used in China. However, "feng shoe-ee" gets instant recognition in the US, where a more correct Chinese pronunciation usually does not.

In Thailand, feng shui is pronounced close to "hong jew-ee," and in Vietnam these same words are spelled and pronounced "phong thuy."

So stick with "feng shoe-ee" if you want to be understood in the West, or with "foong shway" if you want to sound like you are more aware of its roots. If you are staying in Hong Kong, drop back to "fun soo-ee."

Feng shui says that the opportunities come when the environment is right. Feng shui is the art and science of making the energy environment so supportive that one's attitude, opportunities, and luck change for the better.

Is feng shui a science?

Feng shui has been built over thousands of years from the experience of successive generations of Masters carefully measuring, recording, and matching the outcome of each feng shui change against their original intention. This is the method of science. There is no difference between this and the physics observations made by Isaac Newton, or the electricity experiments of Benjamin Franklin. In fact, the prime instrument of feng shui, the compass, is in every sense a precise scientific instrument.

Now before any of you say, "Ah yes, but it's not being used in a scientific way," let me remind you that the compass used by mariners and trekkers is only a simpler version of the feng shui compass. And the use of the compass for navigation came long after its use in feng shui to orientate graves and homes. So who is scientific now?

Trivia...

Although the involvement of feng shui in health may seem controversial, many feng shui systems see it as an extension of Chinese traditional medicine. Here "curing" the yin/yang balance of the immediate home environment is as important as prescribing herbs or using acupuncture to balance the yin and yang in the body and restore it to health.

■ **A feng shui** *Master studies a lo p'an, or feng shui compass, while his assistant makes notes, in this detail from a Ch'ing dynasty (1644–1912) painting. A scientific tool, the lo p'an is even more complicated than modern surveying equipment.*

Feng shui is a science in the same way that medicine is a science. Every practitioner will not always get the diagnosis right, and even then may not prescribe the right cures, but those cures are based on a body of experimental, and many times repeated, knowledge. A feng shui Master will not get his diagnosis right every time, and sometimes his "cures" will be misplaced, but this does not invalidate feng shui as a science.

If a doctor makes a wrong diagnosis, he doesn't throw out his textbooks. Don't forget that medicine was not always taught at universities, and as recently as the 16th century it was considered more of an art – or even a trade, like cutting hair – than a science. In fact, surgeons were frequently referred to as "barber-surgeons" because they often did both jobs! Feng shui practitioners were sometimes priests, but never barbers!

While medicine achieved scientific respectability in the West only 400 years ago, feng shui in China has been considered a science for at least 2,600 years! A people as pragmatic as the Chinese would have scrapped it long ago if it didn't work.

Wind and water

THE ESSENCE OF FENG SHUI is the containment of the right sort
of life energy, called ch'i, within the home or office in order to improve the luck
of the occupants. This can be done by the moving of external elements in the
landscape, or the manipulation of alignments, elements, and decor within the
building. The theory pays particular attention to the positioning of water: rivers,
lakes, streams, and even the local drainage system in your backyard.

Part of the theory behind feng shui says that water carries ch'i energy with it, and if that
energy can be carried by streams or rivers into the home/office and accumulated there,
then well and good. On the other hand, if the shape of local waterways is such as to
carry this energy away from the building under consideration, then the prosperity of
the occupants of that building will be diminished (see chapter 15 for further details).

A breath of fresh air

Wind is another fluid part of our
environment. It, too, can carry
energy. As everyone knows, living
among gentle summer breezes is
delightful and uplifting. Living in
an area of constant strong winds,
however, such as southern
France where the mistral blows,
is very unsettling. Finally, being
in an area of totally stagnant air,
such as a mangrove swamp,
weighs you down. The ideal air
environment is, of course, gently
circulating breezes that, in terms
of feng shui, accumulate energy
in your vicinity. Fierce winds or
musty air are a big no-no.

■ **Stagnant ch'i occurs** *where air or
water is still or slow-moving, such as in
a mangrove swamp. According to the
Chinese, stagnant ch'i can cause fatigue
and may compromise the immune system.*

WE ARE ALL MADE OF "FENG" AND "SHUI"

Wind and water are very important to human health. In fact, we are all "made of feng shui." Our bodies are 60 percent "shui" (water) by weight, and we inhale and exhale many times our own volume of "feng" (wind or air) during the course of a day. If we are deprived of "feng," we die in minutes; if deprived of "shui," we die within days. No other substances, not even food, are so essential.

So, the ancient Chinese were on to something when they deduced that both these substances together carry the life energy, or ch'i. Not only do these two fluids carry ch'i, but they also make up the bulk of the ecosystem on the surface of the Earth. We are also bathed externally and internally by them: They are all around us. We are living at the bottom of an ocean of air (the atmosphere), which we breathe, and we rely on the rain that falls from it for the water we drink.

Why do we feel so good after a shower or a swim? The resultant feeling is certainly due to more than just the removal of a microscopic layer of dirt. The water running over our skin changes something else in our makeup, just possibly our internal human ch'i.

Feng shui is concerned with the quality of the ch'i energy that wind and water carry, and how it can be modified to our advantage. So now you know why it's called "feng shui."

■ **Water running** *over the skin changes our bodily ch'i, which is why a shower makes us feel rejuvenated.*

Human ch'i

CH'I ENERGY (which we will look at later in greater depth) runs through the human body. Any acupuncturist will confirm that the energy flowing through the acupuncture meridians is real. So real, in fact, that the practitioner missing the meridian by as little as a quarter of an inch makes a considerable difference to the outcome. Even the patient, if they are sensitive enough, can feel the warmth that comes only from hitting the ch'i meridian exactly right. Miss the meridian, and you don't get that unique warm feeling. Think about it the next time you visit the acupuncturist.

Practitioners of *ch'i kung* (or *qi gong*, as it's also spelled) can demonstrate the accumulation and use of this ch'i energy. It's well known that many of the almost superhuman effects demonstrated by martial artists rely upon the accumulation of ch'i at certain points in the body. For example, breaking a brick requires much less effort if the blow is delivered after ch'i has been accumulated in the hand. Without the ch'i, you may instead break the hand.

■ **Martial artists** *are able to accumulate ch'i energy and unleash its force in order to perform amazing physical feats.*

Seeing human ch'i at work

In the 1970s, I spent some time in the New Territories of Hong Kong with a feng shui *hsien sheng* (professional practitioner) looking at various topographical formations. With him, I saw some remarkable examples of human ch'i at work. One unforgettable example occurred after dawn as we explored a particularly interesting valley of my choosing. We came to a clearing that contained a pool about 10 feet across, fed by a small stream. My friend sat down cross-legged and, instructing me to watch the pool carefully, proceeded to do some *ch'i kung* breathing exercises some distance from the edge of the pool.

I noticed that on the bottom of the pool there were some large, smooth, flattish rocks that could be seen through the perfectly clear water. After perhaps 20 minutes, the water remained icy cold but started to move, like the first hint of seething that you see in a pan of almost boiling water. The rocks stirred uneasily, and, moving with a slight back and forward motion, proceeded to rise and fall in slow motion, tumbling over each other. I turned, and Wu put his finger to his lips in a gesture of silence. After about 5 minutes, the rocks settled slowly back on to the floor of the still clear pond, and a thin wispy mist rose from the surface of the pond. No word was exchanged, but I knew that I had just witnessed a demonstration of the power of human ch'i.

Human ch'i might, in fact, turn out to be part of the link between feng shui changes and their effect on people. We are each "imprinted" with the ch'i of our time and date of birth. The condition of the ch'i tides at this time (like the stars of Western astrology) stay with us for the rest of our lives. There is a whole art devoted to interpreting these birth ch'i conditions, and it is normally referred to as the Four Pillars of Destiny (see chapter 22 for more detail). Ch'i waxes and wanes, like a tide, from year to year, month to month, day to day, and hour to hour. Technically, the Stems and Branches of the year, month, day, and hour of birth delineate the particular tides active at that moment in time.

Why do it? What can it do?

Feng shui can help increase your business opportunities, improve your social life, and enhance your marital prospects. It can also smooth life's little wrinkles, the ups and downs of fate.

Feng shui has been credited with doing all manner of miraculous things, but what it is really best at is freeing up energy, increasing your luck, making many more opportunities arise, and/or making you more able to grasp them.

But it can't suddenly make you win the lottery: It can't change the mathematical odds on a dice roll.

So how do you do it? To do feng shui successfully, you don't necessarily need to:

- Believe in it, or change your religion.
- Hire a Master (although that can help).
- Make great changes in the structure of your home/office building.
- Have your home and its contents blessed.

However, you do need to:

- Draw an accurate plan of your home/office using compass readings and measurements.
- Think things through carefully and logically, following the rules of feng shui.
- Identify the type and qualities of energy in the home/office.
- Make changes or install "remedies" to improve or channel these energies.

Going with the flow

Feng shui enables you to "go with the flow." The *Taoist* view of the world is that needless upstream struggling is pointless when you can swim downstream with the whole river flow, the flow of the universe, behind you, working for you. "Better a Taoist than a salmon," was the motto of one old practitioner I met in Thailand.

DEFINITION

Taoist *is derived from the Chinese word* Tao, *which means "the Way."*

Of course, you might say, "How do I know which way the river is flowing? How do I know if I'm knocking my head against a brick wall, or if I'm just about to walk through an imaginary obstruction, arriving just where I had been hoping to be?" Feng shui, with its Taoist roots, tends to ease your way into the most profitable channel, the correct "way," so that you spend more of your time doing the latter than the former.

Tao is both your way through the trials and tribulations of life, as well as the way in the sense of a path or an energy flow. Taoism has been called the "watercourse way," hinting at its roots in the flow of the universe as reflected in the flow of rivers, which is an important facet of feng shui.

Instead of finding yourself always battling against your surroundings, whether in your home life, your love life, or your career, you may find that the correct placement of a sometimes insignificant feng shui "remedy" can have the most unexpected results.

This flow also translates into easing the flow of business and personal relationships. Casual meetings turn into major business relationships or precipitate a significant career advancement. Partners and colleagues suddenly seem more helpful, and you feel more in control of your life.

■ **An informal or chance meeting** *could lead to an important business partnership or a major career move, with the help of feng shui.*

Luck isn't chance

LUCK AND CHANCE ARE TWO completely different things. Chance, according to the Oxford English Dictionary, is the "way things happen of themselves." Luck, on the other hand, is "good or ill fortune, fortuitous events affecting one's interests, [or a] person's apparent tendency to be (un)fortunate."

In short, chance is mathematical, like the chance of winning the lottery, but luck is personal. Luck, according to feng shui, is also cultivatable, but chance isn't. That's an important distinction. When people ask me, "Will feng shui improve my chances of winning the lottery?" I reply, "Feng shui helps you accumulate more personal luck, but it can't alter the mathematical odds of winning the lottery." Luck is an abundance of opportunities, not a distortion of the mathematical laws of the universe.

The Trinity of Luck: t'ien, ren, ti

In the Chinese view of life, we all have three kinds of luck. This is often called the Trinity of Luck.

The first is Heaven Luck (*t'ien choy*), the luck we were born with. That is, were we born with a "silver spoon in our mouth" or were we born in the poorest slums, the meanest back streets? A Western astrologer might also recognize the concept of Heaven Luck as that mapped out in our birth chart. If our Heaven Luck is good, we can sometimes coast through life with our feet up. We all know individuals who do this – though it is rather a waste of their good Heaven Luck.

Ch'i is directly and closely related to luck. In Chinese, another word for "luck" is yun-ch'i, which literally means "moving or working ch'i."

Heaven Luck cannot be relied upon to be consistently good or bad but changes as the configuration of the Heavens changes. A good astrologer, either Western or Chinese, can make some sense of these changes over the course of a life. A Chinese astrologer will work from the so-called Four Pillars of Destiny chart of the individual to give often remarkable predictions of the future fluctuations of an individual's Heaven Luck during the course of his or her life. A Western astrologer will also be able to plot "transits" forward in time (see chapter 22 for more on the Four Pillars).

We can also improve on our Heaven Luck by our own efforts, called Man (or Human) Luck (*ren choy*). We all know of people who have made something of themselves, despite having overwhelming handicaps. These individuals have been exercising their Man Luck.

For most people, that is the sum total of their luck, and their lives are a confusing patchwork of Heaven and Man Luck, changing seemingly randomly. Hence "luck" is usually seen as random in the West. Not so in the Chinese view of the universe.

The third Luck is Earth Luck (*ti choy*), something of which the West knew very little until recently. Earth Luck is none other than feng shui, an art or science imbedded deeply in our surroundings here on Earth. Earth Luck can modify and distinctly improve the vagaries of life. We can set objectives, and then manipulate our Earth Luck to help achieve them.

We are all stuck (in a sense) with what Heaven Luck we have been served, but with feng shui, or Earth Luck, we can take full advantage of the good times, and to a large extent neutralize the bad luck of the lean times.

■ **We can't change the luck,** *or horoscope, we were born with, but we can influence our lives with personal effort, or feng shui.*

Heaven Luck is the strongest, but Man Luck and Earth Luck are both within our grasp to change. Tell me more!

A simple summary

✔ Feng shui is connected with ch'i energy.

✔ Ch'i flows through the physical universe and through our bodies.

✔ We are related much more closely to the energies behind Nature than we realize.

✔ We can take a Taoist view, and work with these energies.

✔ There are three types of "luck." Heaven Luck is the "horoscope" you were born with; Man Luck is your own responsibility; and by directing and accumulating ch'i, you can improve your Earth Luck.

Chapter 2

Who Does Feng Shui and Why?

ENG SHUI IS NO LONGER the exclusive preserve of emperors and their families, nor is it restricted to the Chinese communities of the world. It is now practiced by millions of people in the West, and since the early 1990s many major Western corporations and celebrities have adopted it and incorporated it into their lifestyles. With the arrival of practitioners and feng shui Masters in the West, it is important to know how to distinguish those who really know their art from faux practitioners of interior decorating. It is also important to know when to call in a professional, and when you can do it yourself.

In this chapter...

✓ Celebrity and corporate devotees

✓ Practitioners, new and old

✓ When to call in a pro and when to do it yourself

FENG SHUI ADVICE HAS ENSURED A BRIGHT, SPACIOUS INTERIOR IN THE TRUMP TOWER IN NEW YORK CITY

Celebrity and corporate devotees

TYPICAL CELEBRITY USERS OF FENG SHUI *in the US include Madonna, Donald Trump, Steven Spielberg, and Deepak Chopra. In the UK, famous followers of feng shui are Virgin Atlantic CEO Richard Branson, Body Shop founder Anita Roddick, pop star Boy George, and Jerry Hall.*

Buildings and corporations that have had feng shui applied to them in the US include:

- Trump Tower, New York City
- MGM Grand Hotel, Las Vegas
- Bank of America
- Dreamworks
- Bank of Canada

- White Sox Stadium, Chicago
- Creative Artists Agency, Beverly Hills
- selected Borders bookstores
- Citibank
- Aveda

Internationally, such buildings include:

- Hyatt Hotel, Singapore
- Sime Darby, Kuala Lumpur (with disastrous results)
- Cathay Pacific Airlines, Hong Kong
- Sydney Harbour Casino and Hotel, Sydney
- Crédit Lyonnaise, the French bank that uses feng shui to predict the movements of the Hang Seng stockmarket index, Hong Kong

- HSBC's original head office building in Hong Kong
- Mandarin Hotel, Hong Kong, and Mandarin Hotel, Makati, Manila, Philippines
- The original Budweiser brewery in Budvar, Czech Republic
- Dickson Concept, Hong Kong (the company that owns Harvey Nichols in London and Barneys in New York)

Many other buildings in Taiwan, Singapore, Philippines, Malaysia, Thailand, Indonesia, and Hong Kong have benefited from feng shui advice, but not all large corporations wish to have the public know of their involvement.

In Hong Kong it is seen as a benefit for the public to know that your building has received a feng shui once-over, but in the West there is still a lingering fear that shareholders might see it as a waste or as a superstitious use of corporate funds.

Of course, there are many organizations that did not consult a feng shui expert, such as Lloyd's of London, which has had massive financial problems since it moved into new premises in Lime Street. The modern Lloyd's building's main problem is that its design breaks many major feng shui rules. Another example that could have had great feng shui, given its proximity to the river, is the Dome in London. Unfortunately, that building turned its back on the river, and faced its entrance in the opposite direction.

■ **In Singapore,** *both the small-scale colonial buildings in the foreground and the modern skyscrapers beyond have profited from the beneficial feng shui of the river around which Singapore has been built.*

Practitioners, new and old

TWENTY YEARS AGO *there were few feng shui practitioners in the West, and almost all were Chinese. Now, in Europe (especially in the UK and in Austria, which has more practitioners per head than any other country in the Western world), Australia, South Africa, and the US there are any number of practitioners. A good practitioner is a worthwhile investment. After all, what price can you put on your luck, your health, your wealth, and your happiness? Get these things right, and the fee will soon return to you. Unfortunately, not all these practitioners have been trained to the same level.*

In the US, consultations are sometimes as cheap as $100, but just as you might not expect great work from a $100 surgeon, such consultations have more in common with cheap interior decorating advice than serious feng shui. These consultations often use an oversimplified fixed system of feng shui, which ignores compass directions. You pay your money, and you take your chances. It is understandable that you may not wish to pay out a large fee unless you are sure of the reputation of the practitioner.

How to pick a Master

Unfortunately, there are no universally recognized qualifications in the feng shui world for a *Master*, but I do have advice on how to pick one. In the tightly knit communities of Southeast Asia, it usually becomes rapidly apparent who the Masters are because of their good reputations and the rich clients who ask their advice on a regular basis. A few of the more traditional Masters may even appear to be of modest means. On the other hand, a Master who is obviously successful and well off is a better advertisement for the profession. Just as you would tend to go to a healthy doctor rather than an ill one, so the same applies to feng shui.

A second way to judge a Master is his lineage. In other words, who was his Master? Here, I mean a Master that they studied under as an apprentice for some years, not just one whose 3-day course they attended. In the West there is no lineage system, and a number of practitioners now claim to have learned from this or that Master. You should check if this means they attended a weekend seminar or studied actual practice with the Master for several years, and went out regularly on site with them.

DEFINITION

*A **Master** is a practitioner who has reached a level of proficiency recognized by his peers and has been confirmed as a Master by his own teacher. In the East, such a title is never lightly given and never ever self-assumed. A Master will often, but not always, have his own school and pupils. Unfortunately, very few real feng shui Masters live in the West. A Grandmaster, incidentally, is one who numbers at least one Master among his pupils.*

■ **Master feng shui practitioners** *are in great demand in the Far East, and are consulted by many large corporations before any proposed construction goes ahead.*

The third check on the quality of work is client referral. Just as in the selection of a builder you might rightly ask for some client or previous job references, so a feng shui practitioner should be happy to give the names of satisfied clients. Ask them if and how their life changed after the consultation. If it didn't change, then think again before hiring that particular practitioner.

Lastly, ask the practitioner a few simple questions, in the spirit of natural curiosity. Their answers may be very revealing. Any no's to the following list of possible questions throw the professionalism of the practitioner into some doubt.

 Do you provide me with a written report?

If the answer is "no," then that suggests a sloppy approach and an unwillingness to have his or her changes monitored against actual results. The report may be done at the time of the feng shui survey, or more likely done afterwards.

 Do you use a *lo p'an*, or feng shui compass?

If the answer is "no," or the compass is carried only for show, then the practitioner does not know his or her art in any depth. I once saw a practitioner produce a *lo p'an* to impress a client, and promptly orientate it so that the northerly point faced south, while appearing to take precise note of its "deeper meanings."

 Do you take my birthdate and time into account?

A practitioner who does not need these facts is not considering how the home/office affects you, and is therefore going to provide a diagnosis not of its benefit to you, but just of its general feng shui ambience.

 Can you tell me what kind of feng shui you practice?

If the answer is "I simply use my intuition," then you would be safer employing a physician who used his or her intuition to select drugs than a feng shui practitioner who may "intuitively" destroy your luck for the next 20 years. Answers that include the words Form School, Compass School, Flying Star, *San He*, *San Yuan*, or *Tun Chia* would all be acceptable traditional feng shui indications.

Someone who starts by recommending you purchase various "cures" before he or she has done any calculation may simply be more interested in selling products than actually doing the precise analysis of your luck.

The purpose of feng shui

If the practitioner offers to bless various things or your home, you have to use your judgment. If you wanted your home to be blessed, maybe you should have hired a priest. A sincere blessing does no harm, but someone who offers his or her blessings instead of real feng shui technique is either in the wrong profession or is not a trained practitioner. Having your feng shui done wrongly might lead to disaster, but having a real Master do your feng shui is an investment that should pay handsome dividends.

Make no mistake, the ancient Chinese looked upon feng shui as a very practical art.

For the ancient Chinese, the purpose of feng shui was to secure prosperity, many children, respect, and longevity for the client. It was in no sense a spiritual practice. It has only been since feng shui's adoption by Western writers that spiritual interpretations have arisen.

Despite the fact that some of the most practical inventions in the world, such as the compass, gunpowder, and paper (to name but a few), come from the East, the Victorian view that the "wisdom of the East" is predominantly spiritual persists. For this reason, the West seems to have difficulty in accepting the sexuality of the Indian *Kama Sutra*, or the practicality of Chinese books on the art of warfare, as typically Eastern. Feng shui is another example of a practical art, which, while having its basis in Chinese cosmology and symbolism, is not a spiritual practice, per se.

What you need to know

How much should you pay for a consultation? For commercial premises, feng shui is generally charged by the square foot or square meter. But for domestic premises it's more usual to charge by time, or have a fixed visit fee.

Some practitioners charge the same hourly rate as an architect, or approximately US$120 an hour. After all, the architect only makes sure the building stays up, but a good feng shui Master makes sure the building makes you money. Which would you prefer?

In the US, the difference in fees between Masters and practitioners is perhaps even more marked, but the principles of charging a fixed fee for the job is more popular. Practitioners have been known to charge as little as $100–200, but for this you cannot expect a proper survey, with all the necessary calculations. Domestic feng shui charges in the US can go as high as $2,250 for a home.

Trivia...

In Singapore, one of the best known and busiest Masters, Master Tan, charges: S (Singapore) $1,388 (US$800) for a three-room apartment; S$1,488 (US$860) for a four-room apartment; S$1,588 (US$900) for a five-room apartment; and S$1,688 (US$975) for an executive apartment.

Estimating fees by the square foot is usually restricted to corporate practitioners who may also be architects, or to the more old-fashioned Chinese practitioners.

In the UK, a top Master may charge as much as £27 per square meter (roughly $40 per square yard), although this is the very top end, and £12 ($18) would be more usual. If charging by time, £750–1000 ($1100–1500) a day plus traveling expenses would not be unusual for a Master. His pupils are more likely to charge £350–500 ($500–750) per visit.

Some practitioners attempt to charge a fee that is related to the increase in turnover or profit of a business. Although this is initially an attractive idea, this type of fee is undesirable because it involves the business in a rather unhealthy ongoing relationship with the practitioner. I believe you need a professional survey, not a new (and possibly greedy) sleeping partner.

Also, there is the matter of the school of feng shui in which a Master has been trained and which one would be most suitable for you. I hope that by the time you finish reading this book you will have a much clearer idea of what each school has to offer, and should be able to judge for yourself.

The right school for you

As a general rule, if you were choosing and laying out a virgin site, a classically trained Form School Master would be an advantage. If the house were being built for a specific person, a practitioner who can calculate the Four Pillars and relate them to the house layout would be useful. Where the work is primarily indoors, with little opportunity to make real change, you would benefit from someone familiar with the Elements, the rules of the Eight Mansion system, and interior alignment. If you wish to determine which rooms should be used for which function, an Eight Mansion School Master could be the one for you. If detailed work or changes over a period of time are important, a Flying Star specialist might be best. But don't worry too much: a good practitioner should be able to handle all these aspects of his or her job.

■ **Practitioners from** *different feng shui schools have their own areas of expertise, but they all rely on precise calculations.*

When to call in a pro and when to do it yourself

OF COURSE, ONE OF THE AIMS OF THIS BOOK *is that after reading it you should be able to make a reasonable job of doing your own feng shui. Everybody should be able to check for obvious feng shui boo-boos, and correct them. More than that, you should be able to make simple enhancements, using, for example, the Eight Mansion School of feng shui. Often this is enough to get things flowing your way.*

If you are thinking of improving the feng shui of your business, it might be as well to get a second opinion, after you have done the basic calculations yourself. After all, it is your livelihood you are trifling with.

If you call in a professional, don't be afraid to ask him or her for reasons for each of the recommendations made. You should expect a written report, just as you would get from a surveyor or realtor.

■ **It's always** *a good idea to seek expert advice if you are using feng shui for your business. Make sure you understand the reasons for your practitioner's suggestions.*

When to do it and how to go about it

Don't do change for the sake of change. There is always a possibility that you may make some change incorrectly. Feng shui should not be fooled with for fun.

If everything is going all right and life is a breeze, then my suggestion to you is: Don't change your feng shui.

If, on the other hand, there are things that definitely need changing or improving in your life, then, as long as it is something that feng shui deals with, there is no reason why you shouldn't carefully make some changes. I recommend that, if you are new to feng shui, you make only one major change at a time, and let a week pass in which to determine the outcome. Do not go mad with your new-found knowledge and change everything at once.

In fact, if you are serious about your feng shui, it's a good idea to keep a feng shui diary. Then, when you record what really happened, you can check your work and not kid yourself that it worked if it didn't. Or, if you get an unexpected result, it's possible to trace the cause.

■ **Keep a diary** *of any changes you make and the improvements you expect to see as a result. Then record what really happens, so you can judge whether the changes have been successful.*

How to energize your opportunities

For this example we'll use a simple feng shui formula called Eight Mansions feng shui (more about this in chapter 17). You don't really need to follow the method at this point. This is just a quick illustration of how you might go about using feng shui.

1. Work out which aspect of your life you want to change. You know . . . romance, money, your children's exam successes, or whatever.

2. Determine which part of your home or office relates to this sort of energy. For example, study and education, and specifically exam passing, relate to the northeast corner of your home.

3 Discover which of the five Chinese Elements is involved. In this case, the Element of this sector of your house is Earth. This means that the correct "cure" for the problem relates to Earth.

4 Position something that will increase Earth energies in the northeast sector of your home. You might, for example, use some large crystals.

If these are placed correctly, you should see distinct changes in your children's study habits, or whatever results you were trying to achieve, within a week or so.

This is not meant as an explanation of the method (that will come later in chapter 17). It is simply an outline to give you a taste of the reasoning and method behind feng shui.

A simple summary

✔ Feng shui is much more widespread than you may have realized, with all sorts of well-known people and corporations using it.

✔ To choose the right practitioner or Master, check their reputation, lineage, client references, and their answers to a few simple questions.

✔ Enquire if the practitioner provides a written report, uses a *lo p'an*, uses your date of birth, and what school of feng shui he or she practices.

✔ Check whether fees are charged by the job, the hour, or the square foot or square meter. Then compare these charges with those of other practitioners.

✔ Check your own feng shui, even if you plan to call in a Master.

✔ Know which school of feng shui is best suited to your home or office.

Chapter 3

A Look at Feng Shui's History

IN THIS CHAPTER we are going to look at a short history of feng shui, beginning with its constituent symbols, which are at least 6,000 years old. The *I Ching*, the great classic Chinese text that dates back to at least 2800 BC, is perhaps the oldest of feng shui's roots, and its symbols still form a key part of feng shui. To understand something as interwoven with Chinese culture as feng shui, we also need to look at the three main teachings that were important in ancient China: Taoism, Confucianism, and Buddhism. Of these, Taoism alone had similar roots to feng shui in its observation of natural forces.

In this chapter...

✓ How long has feng shui been around?

✓ The roots of feng shui

✓ The I Ching

✓ The "Three Teachings"

TAOISM, CONFUCIANISM, AND BUDDHISM (WORSHIPPED AT THIS THAI TEMPLE) SHARE FENG SHUI'S ROOTS

How long has feng shui been around?

SOME AUTHORITIES CLAIM *that feng shui is over 6,000 years old, and it is true that some of the symbols used in feng shui may well date back that far.*

The oldest traces of feng shui symbolism that have been found so far are in a neolithic grave excavated in Henan province in China (in 1988) and date from about 4000 BC. The grave is oriented facing south, with a rounded head (symbolic of *t'ien*, Heaven or the sky). The northern end of the grave is square (symbolic of *ti*, Earth). On the eastern side there is an image of a dragon, with an image of a tiger on the west, representing two of the four Celestial Animals of feng shui (see chapter 13). The constellation the Big Dipper (very significant in Chinese astrology and also in feng shui) is traced out at the center of the grave.

Seeing stars

You can't really say that this discovery confirms feng shui was around in 4000 BC, but you can say that some of the main symbols of feng shui were in use by then. This means that feng shui symbolism predates any of the formal religions of China: Confucianism, Buddhism, and even Taoism. So, in one sense, feng shui may be 6,000 years old. Another early artifact that demonstrates the continued use of feng shui symbolism is a box lid dating from 430 BC, which was unearthed at Leigudun in Sui, Hubei province. The sides of the box lid are occupied by a tiger and a dragon, which are the feng shui (and astrological) symbols of west and east. But, most significantly, the center carries a rough circle of the 28 lunar Mansions (*hsiu*), which usually form the second largest ring on almost all feng shui compasses. They surround the word *dou*, which stands for the Big Dipper constellation.

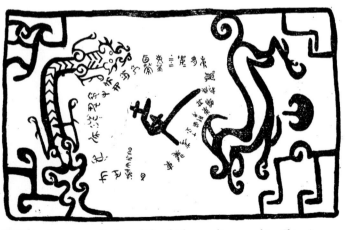

■ **This drawing of a box lid,** *which was discovered in China's Hubei province, shows the Green Dragon (left) and White Tiger (right), with the Big Dipper (center) and the 28 lunar Mansions, or* hsiu.

By the Spring and Autumn period (770–476 BC), the elements of feng shui had been brought together, and it is highly likely that by this time it existed as a distinct discipline.

It was not called feng shui then. *Kan yu*, which means "cover and support," was one of the old names in use then. The name *Kan yu* reflects the idea that this subject dealt with the above–below relationship between Heaven and Earth.

The saying most commonly associated with Hermes Trismegistus, one of the founding fathers in the West of Hermetic thought, was "As above, so below." This exactly reflects the Chinese view that changes in the Heavens caused changes on Earth.

INTERNET

www.fengshuigate.com/
index.html

Dr. Stephen Field's Feng Shui Gate contains a number of worthwhile essays on the origins of feng shui.

Feng shui was first explicitly mentioned as a practice in a text dated to the early Ch'in dynasty (221–206 BC).

So, there you have it! Feng shui may well be as old as 6,000 years, but it is certainly at least 2,600 years old.

The roots of feng shui

TO UNDERSTAND THE HISTORY OF FENG SHUI, *we must first look at the history of its roots, and set it in the background of Chinese culture. There are three main background strands:*

 The *I Ching*

 Chinese religion

 The Chinese attitude to their ancestors and their graves

Only when all three of these strands have been pulled together is it possible to look at the succession of Masters who make up the history of feng shui. The deepest root of all is the *I Ching*.

The I Ching

THE FIRST STRAND, *and one of the earliest landmarks in the history of feng shui, is the invention of the eight Trigrams (see chapter 8). These were supposedly discovered by Fu Hsi, a legendary emperor reputed to have reigned from 2852 to 2737* BC. *These Trigrams form the oldest parts of the* I Ching.

These eight Trigrams are a very important part of feng shui, and we shall see how they work in chapter 8. The *I Ching* (also spelled *Yi Jing*) is a great Chinese classic book that contains a series of 64 short passages, one for each of the 64 possible 8 x 8 combinations of these Trigrams.

By one account, another "layer" of this book was written by King Wen, the founder of the Chou (Zhou) dynasty of 1027–221 BC, while he was temporarily imprisoned. His son, the Duke of Chou, also had a hand in creating another "layer" of this extraordinary

■ **The first Emperor** *of the Ch'in dynasty (221–206* BC*) began building the Great Wall of China. He also destroyed many books written in earlier times, but preserved the* I Ching, *because he considered it one of the greatest classics.*

KEY DYNASTIES FOR FENG SHUI

Chinese history is usually measured by dynasties or periods when the country was ruled, loosely, by the same dynasty or family. See the Appendix for a full chart of the dynasties and their dates.

For feng shui the key dynasties were:

1 Chou (1027–221 BC) when the *I Ching* was probably written.

2 Han (206 BC–AD 220) oldest books on feng shui known.

3 Chin (AD 265–420) a golden age for feng shui (Kuo-p'o, father of feng shui).

4 T'ang (AD 618–906), when feng shui flourished under Yang Yun Sung (Form School).

5 Sung (AD 960–1279), when most of the elements of feng shui were gathered into one system, and Wang Chih was patriarch of the Compass School.

Feng shui remained popular through the Ming (1368–1644) and Ching (1644–1911) dynasties. After the establishment of the Republic of China (1912), it was suppressed in 1927 and again in 1966–76 during the "Cultural Revolution," along with much of the knowledge of traditional Chinese culture. Its practice continued in areas where "overseas Chinese" settled, like Hong Kong, Singapore, Malaysia, Vietnam, and Australia.

book. Thus, the *I Ching* in its earliest form was written in the Chou dynasty, when it was called the *Chou I* (or *Zhou Yi*) or "Changes of Chou."

It was one of the few classics to escape the book burning of the first Ch'in Emperor (*c.* 221 BC), who consigned to the flames any books that he did not consider either great classics or eminently useful (like medical or agricultural texts). Even in modern-day China, where feng shui is frowned upon, *I Ching* studies are considered a very acceptable scholarly preoccupation.

The "Three Teachings"

CHINESE COSMOLOGY AND RELIGION *interweave with much of Chinese culture, so feng shui has been partly influenced by all three of China's great religions, but predominantly by Taoism. It is important to distinguish where religion ends and feng shui begins, so let's take a quick look at the three main religions of China that have had a profound effect on the way in which the Chinese view the world.*

■ **This 18th-century painting** *shows Confucius and Lao Tzu (left), founder of Taoism, welcoming the infant Buddha into their midst, symbolizing the acceptance of Buddhism in China.*

The three main religions of ancient China were Confucianism, Buddhism, and Taoism, although they were so entwined that, even today, a Confucian temple might easily have images of the Buddha or of some of the eight Taoist Immortals, and vice versa. For this reason they were sometimes called the "Three Teachings." To a large extent, in the popular mind these three religions have become one, and an ordinary Chinese might pray to any of the gods with equal sincerity as the need arises.

Confucianism is very much concerned with the nuances of human relationships, and is therefore representative of Man. Buddhism is concerned with the cycles of reincarnation and the heavens of the afterlife, and therefore characterizes Heaven. Taoism is concerned with nature, with the rivers and the mountains, and with earthly sexuality and immortality. It is a religion of Earth par excellence.

Each religion is as important as the other – your focus must be on the balance between Heaven, Earth, and Man. It is no surprise that the Chinese see these as complementary, not conflicting.

An easy way to remember in outline what the Teachings emphasized is to recall the great triad of Heaven, Earth, and Man.

Because feng shui is concerned with the Earth, I will therefore be more concerned with Taoism in this book. But let's look at all three religions in turn.

Confucianism

The founder of Confucianism was Kung fu tze. Try saying that very fast and you have an idea why early translators wrote his name as "Confucius." The "-ius" was added by the translators as a sort of honorific Latin ending to show respect. Confucius lived from 551–479 BC during the Eastern Chou dynasty, but it was not till the Han dynasty (206 BC–AD 220) hundreds of years later that his teachings were actually adopted by the government of the day.

During most of the dynasties, Confucianism has been seen as the state religion. Confucianism stressed the individual's responsibilities to their parents, their family, and to the Emperor of the state.

If ever a religion contributed to China's high regard for state and family loyalties, then Confucianism was it.

Confucianism included a series of sacred rites that had to be performed by the Emperor throughout the year as the seasons changed, to ensure the regularity of connection between Heaven, Earth, and Man. (We will come across the importance of the connections between these three levels of the Universe later.) The Emperor was supposed actually to move from apartment to apartment around the eight sectors of his palace as the seasons changed. This ties in with feng shui, which divides your home into eight sections plus a central ninth, like a "tic-tac-toe" game (see chapter 8).

Confucianism also promoted ancestor worship. Such veneration simply stressed your place in the genetic chain, stretching from your distant forefathers, through you, your children and grandchildren, and on to their distant descendants. Early feng shui made a point of improving the feng shui of the graves of immediate forefathers, as an aid to improving one's own feng shui.

■ **Sculptor Liu Shih's monument** *to the founder of Confucianism, Kung fu tze, can be found in New York's Chinatown.*

■ **In some Western countries,** *where the state provides for elderly parents, there is less emphasis on family responsibility. In the East, the belief in filial responsibility means that relatives are cared for by their family.*

This was done not only out of filial piety (respect by children for their parents), but also out of a conviction that good feng shui can be influenced by immediate ancestors, emphasizing the unity of the family in a time dimension. These ideas are very alien to us in the West but they form a very important part of the theoretical basis of feng shui.

In the West (with the possible exception of the Mormons), we tend to think of ourselves as separate people, rather than as part of an extended family. This could be a result of the decline of religion in the West, the adoption of state responsibility for aging parents, or modern sociological trends. But it does not alter the fact that there are subtle bonds between family generations, the so-called "ties of blood," which are "stronger than water," as the saying goes. Just as twins can be aware of things affecting each other, so there are bonds vertically between family members, between one generation and the next, that are more than just those of genetics or psychology.

A notable exception to Confucianism as the state religion was the end of the T'ang dynasty (AD 618–906), whose rulers were predominantly Taoist. Indeed, in this dynasty, feng shui really flourished, with such Masters as Yang Yun Sung coming to prominence before AD 888.

Confucianism cosmology sees the world as being made up of two things: First form, pattern, and rules, or *li*, and, second, the life that animates these forms, *ch'i*. All physical and psychological phenomena are made up of *li* and *ch'i*.

Human beings must work to reclaim their original goodness by "dusting the mirror," clearing away the impure ch'i to see their true li and discern their connection with the cosmos. So, clearing away stagnant ch'i by feng shui practices is of much greater importance than simply altering the interior decor!

Buddhism

Buddhism is an Indian religion, so originally Buddhism was regarded by the Chinese as a foreign religion. The founder of Buddhism was an Indian prince called Siddhartha Gautama (566–486 BC), who was a close contemporary of Confucius. But the Mahayana tradition of Buddhism did not spread to China until the Han dynasty (206 BC–AD 220) and did not really take root until after this dynasty. The Sui dynasty (AD 589–618) and the early T'ang dynasty (AD 618–906) were a golden age for Buddhism in China.

Buddhism was not the source of feng shui.

However, in AD 845 an Imperial decree ordered the destruction of more than 40,000 temples, with the result that 260,500 Buddhist monks and nuns were forced to leave the haven of these monasteries and work in the outside world. After that, Buddhism never recovered its former power and influence in China.

In Tibet, which was at various times a tributary state to China, Buddhism and the Bon religion grew up side by side. During the Yuan (Mongol) dynasty (AD 1260–1368) and the Ching (Manchu) dynasty (AD 1644–1911), Tibetan Buddhism, or "Lamaism" as it became known, was strong in China, and Tibetan Buddhist monasteries were built in Beijing (Peking).

■ **The Potala Palace** *in Lhasa, Tibet, has been home to every Dalai Lama, the spiritual leader of Tibetan Buddhism, since the 7th century. The current Dalai Lama was exiled from Tibet after an uprising against occupying Chinese troops in 1959.*

Despite the attempts of various modern commentators to associate Tibetan Buddhism with feng shui, the truth is that feng shui is not a Buddhist practice. In fact, it has been frowned upon by many orthodox Buddhists. Feng shui is a uniquely Chinese practice with similar roots to Taoism, which also later permeated Tibet.

India has its own tradition of building alignment and layout called Vastu Shastra. In concept, there are parallels with feng shui, but when the basic practice is observed, these two are seen to be quite different, even contradictory, traditions.

Some scholars have suggested that feng shui originally came from India, but this has not been proved. In my opinion, any thought that Vastu Shastra might have developed into feng shui, or vice versa, should be left in the unproven category.

Taoism

Taoism is where we should look for most of the religious roots of feng shui, although the symbolism of feng shui is much older even than Taoism. Traditionally, Taoism was founded by the 6th-century BC sage Lao Tzu (also spelled as Laozi). Modern thinking seems to doubt that such a person ever lived, although the study of Taoism is often

■ **Taoism is concerned with nature,** *and early Taoists regarded mountains as holy sites where religious energy accumulated and was relatively undisturbed by outside forces.*

referred to as Laozi studies. At any rate, the Taoist classic, which was held in highest reverence and of which Lao Tzu was supposed to be the author, was a small text called the *Tao Teh Ching* (the classic of the *Tao*, also spelled as the *Dao De Jing*).

Basically, the *Tao Teh Ching* advocates the idea of going with the flow, blending with the *Tao*, and not struggling against its relentless flow. Taoism flourished from the 6th century BC to the 5th century AD. During the 2nd to the 5th centuries AD, Taoism was *the* religion of the Chinese people, as distinct from Confucianism, which was primarily the Imperial religion. Buddhism at this time was still seen as a foreign import. Some T'ang Emperors actually claimed direct descent from Lao Tzu himself. Not surprisingly, the T'ang dynasty (AD 618–906) was also a great flowering period for feng shui.

Trivia...

The Tao Teh Ching is one of the most perplexing books in the world, and has been translated into English more than 30 times. Editions even include one made by the early-20th-century poet, mountain climber, and magician Aleister Crowley, edited by the present author. The Tao Teh Ching appears to be a very simple text, but is in fact very subtle and complex.

A simple summary

✔ The symbols of feng shui date back to 4000 BC.

✔ Feng shui's oldest written roots lie in the Trigrams of the *I Ching*, which date back to 2800 BC. This book is perhaps the greatest classic from ancient China.

✔ Originally, feng shui was called *Kan yu.*

✔ The "Three Teachings" – Taoism, Confucianism, and Buddhism – all originated in the 6th century BC. Feng shui is most closely allied to Taoism, but predates all three religions.

Chapter 4

Gods, Graves, and Feng Shui Masters

IN LOOKING AT the Chinese attitude to their ancestors, we will see that the orientation of the houses of the living and that of the tombs of the dead form part of the same practice. It was the rules surrounding the orientation of grave-sites that developed into Form School rules for house feng shui. We will look at early feng shui Masters, from Kuan Lo and Kuo P'o to Yang Yun Sung and Wang Chih, and trace the development of feng shui through several reforms and periods of disinformation, right up to its history in the 20th century.

In this chapter...

✔ Houses in common: ancestral feng shui

✔ Early Taoist Masters

✔ Different schools of feng shui

✔ Feng shui in the 20th century

CHINESE FAMILY GRAVES USUALLY FACE THE SAME DIRECTION, ACCORDING TO FENG SHUI PRINCIPLES

Houses in common: ancestral feng shui

CONCERN FOR THE WELFARE *of ancestors is the third strand making up feng shui. The ancestors were so much a part of Chinese thought that the Chinese word for house,* chai, *can be used to describe the houses of the living (or ordinary houses and offices) or the "houses" of the dead – graves. Originally feng shui was very much concerned with the careful siting of graves. These were considered more important than the houses of the living, since they affected the feng shui of the ancestors, and hence greatly affected the feng shui of their currently living and future descendants.*

Yin and yang chai feng shui

Yin and yang (as we will discover in chapter 7) mean many things, like female and male or dark and light, but here we are concerned with their use in distinguishing *yang chai* (bright or ordinary houses) from *yin chai* (dark houses or graves). Now, before you think I'm getting morbid, the Chinese have a long tradition of respect for their ancestors. This extends to ensuring that the final "resting place" of the immediate

ancestors has as good feng shui as possible. In ancient times, it was possible to set up tombs on land not necessarily designated as a cemetery, and single tombs will often be found out in the countryside by themselves, not in ordered rows in a cemetery. There are many stories about how the feng shui of a particular gravesite propelled the descendants of the ancestor

■ **The Chinese** *would often place the bones of their deceased relatives in pots in a hillside awaiting final burial in a site with good feng shui. As a result, ancestral remains are today found dotted all over the countryside.*

buried there to riches, power, and fame. This vision of family life extending backward into history and forward in time is important to the development of feng shui. We will discover that many of the early Masters wrote primarily about the rules for gravesites (*yin chai*) rather than for homes or offices (*yang chai*).

In many ways it is much more psychologically healthy to see yourself as part of an almost infinite chain of ancestors, with your descendants marching forward into the future, than to see yourself as a single unit, alone in a largely unfriendly world. Perhaps the old virtue of respect for one's parents might not be entirely lost if this perspective were still part of our world view.

Although there are 6,000 Chinese family names in existence, almost 90 percent of the people in China and Taiwan share just 100 family names. Yes, that's right — just 100 names. Can you imagine what a nightmare the telephone directory must be?

Specific family names often originate from a specific region in China. Because of this, and because of the almost obsession with ancestors, it is possible to trace Chinese family history and ancestors quite a long way back.

One Singapore company is using modern technology to help people with Chinese ancestry trace their roots as far back as 1,100 years. Their data goes back to the Sung dynasty (AD 960–1279). At that time, family names and records were first formalized and kept in ancestry booklets called *chia-pu*.

Approximately 96 percent of the world's Chinese people are covered by just 110,000 *chia-pu* titles. Remember, that's over a billion people.

Grave positioning

Gravesites are ideally positioned on a gently sloped and well-drained hillside, looking downward to water – a river, lake, or even the sea. The site should be enfolded on either side by low hills and backed by a much higher hill. Breezes should be gentle, and the site should be protected from strong winds, which can blow away the accumulating ch'i.

The soil should be healthy and well drained. The site should ideally face south or perhaps southeast or southwest, according to complex feng shui calculations for the burial date and for the birth date of the deceased.

INTERNET

www.chineseroots.com

This web site lets people build a family tree by tapping into a database that has records of births and marriages in China. Over the last few hundred years? No, over the last millennium! This free service may be the largest site specifically for Chinese genealogy.

The grave itself is often surrounded by an "armchair," or crescent-shaped stone or cement wall, which protects it from behind. From the air, a cluster of such graves is an amazing sight, many of them facing the same direction but differing by a few degrees over time. There might even be one or two eccentric graves, products of a maverick feng shui Master or of special feng shui considerations, pointing in a totally different direction.

■ **Chinese graves** *are often protected by a crescent-shaped stone or cement wall, giving them the appearance of an armchair. They tend to be found in clusters on hillsides, facing roughly the same direction.*

From these ideal grave positions sprang the theory behind house positioning. So, historically, *yin chai* (gravesite) feng shui preceded *yang chai* (home and office) feng shui. Although there is not much call for *yin chai* feng shui in the West, it is important to know where the roots of modern feng shui lie. Respect for ancestors was part of a complex cosmology that saw changes of luck, not just from day to day, but in the context of 180-year cycles and many generations.

Early Taoist Masters

THE ART AND PROFESSION OF KAN YU *(the old name for feng shui) was well established by the early Han dynasty (206 BC–AD 220). Kan yu is usually interpreted as "the Way of Heaven and Earth," a suggestive title that implies that the imprint of Heaven's ch'i affects the ch'i of the Earth. The main theories of this time concerned yin/yang and the five Elements.*

It is now time to meet some of the illustrious Masters of feng shui. I'll begin 19 centuries ago with the quaintly named Ching Wu, or Master Blue Raven, who wrote a manual on burial feng shui during the late Han dynasty (206 BC–AD 220).

Kuan Lo (AD 209–256) lived in turbulent times and wrote *Master Kuan's Ti-Li Indicator*. This is particularly interesting because to this day *ti-li* means both "geography" (the same as you learn in school, or would if you went to school in China) and feng shui. This book was, however, stuffed with feng shui, and so it seems that the techniques of feng shui and a serious study of landforms were, in that era, one and the same.

Trivia...

It was said that through the manipulation of ch'i, Chu-kuo Liang could make mists and fog rise from the ground to hide the movement of Liu Pei's armies. He knew the secret of Earth ch'i: this enabled him to find and manipulate the hidden portals in the Earth and thus to expel vapor at the critical moment. Using this method, he hid his lord's troops till the last moment and ensured victory. There is more than a hint of the real power of feng shui in this story.

The *chi-men tun-chia* (the Mysterious Gate and Hidden Time) style of feng shui was introduced by Chu-kuo Liang during the Three Kingdoms period (AD 220–265). Chu-kuo Liang was an advisor to Liu Pei, the Lord of the Liu kingdom, and a Taoist magician. The *tun-chia* system has had a great impact on the development of feng shui to this day, but very little about it appears in English. It combined the *pa kua* with the Nine Palace theory.

Kuo P'o – the father of feng shui

The term "feng shui" may have been first used by Kuo P'o (AD 276–324) in his book *Tsang Ching,* or "The Burial Classic." This small book dealt almost exclusively with *yin chai* feng shui, the form of feng shui concerned with gravesites. However, his principles are universal and contain much of the basis of the Form School of feng shui. Kuo P'o is sometimes called the father of feng shui and is reputed to have written a number of other feng shui classics, one of which is cutely titled *The Corners of the Seas Revealed by the Mysterious Virgins of the Nine Celestial Spheres.* Kuo was called upon by the Emperor to select burial sites, and he was also a scholar and a master of various other arcane arts.

In the 5th century AD, Wang Wei (415–443) issued *The Yellow Emperor's Dwellings Manual.* This gave feng shui a sort of ill-deserved antiquity, since the Yellow Emperor, or Huang Ti, was supposed to have ruled *c.* 2697–2597 BC. Versions of this book still exist, but at least one modern feng shui Master, Joseph Yu, considers the material "either fake or containing a lot of material not suitable for today's world." I partly agree with him, but there is still much value in this classic book.

The Taoist arts, including feng shui, flourished during the T'ang dynasty (AD 618–906), which was a golden age for feng shui.

INTERNET

www.astro-fengshui.com

Joseph Yu's site is well worth a visit for his forthright views on the origins and current state of the different schools of feng shui.

During the T'ang dynasty, the Emperor T'ai Tsung appointed a commission of ten scholars to sift real from bogus feng shui. They published a 100-chapter report. Nothing changes!

It was during this period that the feng shui compass, the *lo p'an*, was established in its modern form – with at least 17 rings, at least one of which had the 24 Directions or Mountains. The most famous feng shui Master of the T'ang (or any other dynasty) was undoubtedly Master Yang Yun Sung.

Different schools of feng shui

THERE ARE TWO MAIN SCHOOLS OF THOUGHT in traditional *feng shui from which all others are derived: the Form School and the Compass School. The two schools of feng shui started in different parts of China.*

Some say that the Form School originated in south China, where the landscape around Guelin has hills and mountains that rise straight up from a winding alluvial plain, and whose fantastical shapes look as if they really must have some inner significance. If you

■ **The unusual landscape** *of Guelin in southern China, with its steep hills rising from flat plateaus, is thought to have inspired the Form School method of feng shui.*

know what to look for, you cannot visit Guelin without coming to the conclusion that the special shapes, or forms, of the landscape do have a very real effect upon us.

The Compass School, on the other hand, probably started on the flat plains, where the direction of ch'i flow was not so obvious. This is, however, rather an oversimplification. There is more truth in the assertion that Form School feng shui was designed to find sites in the open country, particularly gravesites, while Compass School feng shui was more concerned (as its alternate name of Houses and Dwellings Method implies) with homes in villages, towns, and cities. Certainly in the city of Hong Kong, Compass School feng shui is more important than Form School.

The Form School

Yang Yun Sung (AD 840–c. 888) is perhaps the most famous feng shui Master. He worked as the Imperial court feng shui Master for the Emperor Hi-Tsung from AD 874–888. He was born in Kiangsi province in China, and his books were the first to really codify Form School feng shui (see chapters 13 and 14 for more information on this school).

Yang Yun Sung wrote a number of books and also had some later titles attributed to him. None of them is currently available in English, but there are plans afoot to publish translations in the near future.

His most famous work is the *Han Lung Ching*, or "Classic of the Moving Dragon." Other books include the *Ching-Nang Ao-Chih*, or the "Secret Meanings of the Universe," and the *I Lung Ching*, or "Canon for the Approximation of Dragons," for use where the terrain is not sufficiently vividly outlined to discover dragon lines by observation. Here "dragons" refer to both water and earth dragons whose veins carry the precious ch'i.

Finally, the *Shih-Erh Chang-Fa*, or "Method of the Twelve Staves," has become a classic for determining where the very best spot supplied with the best quality ch'i is to be found.

In Chinese texts, the Form School has often been referred to as the Kiangsi Method, in honor of Yang Yun Sung, who was born in Kiangsi province. The Form School is also called Kanchow Method or Luan t'i, the "mountain peaks and vital embodiment School."

Trivia...

Yang Yun Sung is said to have had the nickname, "Yang who helps the poor," because he devised simple feng shui strategies to overcome poverty. It is not recorded if this was on an individual basis or as an adjunct to town planning, although his work clearly concerned material, not spiritual, poverty.

INTERNET

www.fengshui.net

Visit this web site for details of translations of the feng shui classics.

Form School feng shui was particularly popular in the mountainous Chinese provinces of Kanchow, Kiangsi, Kwangsi, and Anhui. The Compass School had more adherents in the flat provinces of Fukien and Chekiang, and now in modern Taiwan, Hong Kong, Singapore, and Malaysia.

The Compass School

The Compass School relies upon very precise calculations and measurements of direction. Its prime tool is the feng shui compass, or *lo p'an*, (sometimes spelled *luopan*), which I will look at in more detail in chapter 23. One of the Compass School's first patriarchs was Wang Chih, who lived during the Northern Sung dynasty (AD 960–1127). He emphasized the five Elements, the Planets, and the Trigrams. For him the important indicator was the relationship between the Elements and Trigrams – which destroyed which, and which supported which. He also figured that yang hills should face a yang direction and yin hills a yin direction, taken from the point of view of the building being analyzed. All this is neatly summed up in his *Canon of the Core*, which gets right to the heart of these practices.

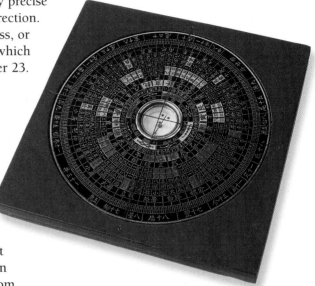

■ **The south-pointing *lo p'an* compass** *was developed by early Chinese feng shui practitioners to help calculate Compass School orientations, and is still in use today.*

The Compass School is also called the Fukien School, in honor of its patriarch Wang Chih, who came from Fukien. Its method is reflected in its other names:

- *Fang wei* – the Directions and Positions School
- The Method of Man
- Houses and Dwellings Method
- *Tsung miao chih fa*
- The Ancestral Hall Method
- *Li ch'i chia*, or *ch'i* Pattern School
- Min School

We will look at Compass School feng shui in greater detail in chapters 22 and 23.

During the Yuan dynasty (AD 1260–1368), Chao Fang, a Compass School devotee, wrote in detail about the *lo p'an*. He contrasted the two Schools, explaining that "in the Form School the principles are clear, but the practice is difficult . . . with the Compass School the principles are obscure but the practice is easy."

Feng shui and the Emperors

In many eras in Imperial China, feng shui was a closely guarded secret, with its benefits originally restricted to the Emperor and the immediate ruling class. Certain points in China's history reflect how guarded feng shui was. During the T'ang dynasty (AD 618–906), the Emperor attempted to purify feng shui texts of errors, but the first Ming Emperor (AD 1368–98) actively encouraged the manufacture of deliberately misleading feng shui textbooks in order to keep the real secrets out of the hands of the populace at large. Such misleading books are, unfortunately, still in circulation. To ensure his monopoly on this knowledge, he also had many feng shui practitioners executed.

Under the Ming dynasty (1368–1644), Taoist diviners were persecuted, and feng shui became more of a lay practice. The result of this was an upsurge of books and ideas about feng shui, many of which were not necessarily written by real Masters. In the same dynasty, the *San Yuan* style of feng shui was established, which divided time into 180-year segments divided into nine 20-year cycles.

The last Chinese dynasty, the Ch'ing (1644–1911), saw a move away from popularization and an attempt to revert to the pure pre-Ming feng shui. The idea that the feng shui reading should be matched with the Four Pillar (*pa tzu*) horoscope reading of the client was introduced in this dynasty. The theory of auspicious hours and days was also heavily promoted in this era.

Flying Star feng shui

The Compass School also deals with the time side of feng shui in the form of Flying Star feng shui. This is a style of feng shui that is not as old as Form School and original Compass School, but is very popular currently in Hong Kong. One excellent book on feng shui refers to Flying Stars as the Floating Stars, which conveys the idea of how they move from one part of the home or office to another from year to year, month to month, even day to day. Flying Star feng shui enables you to predict and control variations in luck across time, to predict specific types

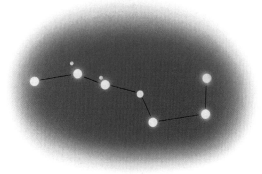

■ **The Flying Stars** *are related to the seven stars of the Big Dipper constellation, plus two invisible stars. These are sometimes known as the Floating Stars.*

of luck for coming months in coming years. In fact, if you asked most Chinese practitioners in Hong Kong, they would say that Flying Star *is* feng shui. They would not be able to conceive of a feng shui consultation that did not involve the Flying Stars.

Other traditional schools not found in the West

One of the most interesting schools is the Tun Chia School. Remember the mists of Chu-kuo Liang (see p. 65)? This school is also called the *chi-men tun-chia*, or Mysterious Gate School, and concerns itself with a concept called "hidden time." Other well-established school names that you might come across, for which there are specific types of feng shui compasses, include *San He* (Three Combinations) and *San Yuan* (Three Period, or Flying Star) feng shui.

THE MISSIONARIES' RESPONSE TO FENG SHUI

The early Jesuit missionaries to China wrote at length about the extraordinary marvels of the longest-running empire in the history of the world. By the mid-1800s, missionaries were writing a lot about China, and among the beliefs they considered was feng shui. Most saw feng shui as an obstacle in their quest to convert as many Chinese to Christianity as possible.

The more practical missionaries realized that as a whole the Chinese were well rooted in their own religion and unlikely to convert even nominally unless subtly bribed, so they spent their time getting to know the culture of their new home instead. Of these writers, Ernest Eitel, writing in 1873, is the most amusing and informative.

■ **The Chinese** *were not to be easily swayed from their religious observances, such as making offerings to agricultural gods, as shown here in a sketch depicting the festival of the Harvest-moon.*

Feng shui in the 20th century

THE LAST EMPEROR OF CHINA *was deposed in 1911, and an era came to an end. These momentous events have been brilliantly portrayed in Bernardo Bertolucci's movie* The Last Emperor. *Already Chinese returning from overseas had, with the questionable benefit of a Western education, begun to ridicule many of the old traditions. Traditional beliefs were seen to be wanting in the face of huge technological and military advances among Western nations.*

With the fall of the last Ching Emperor in 1911, China became much more concerned with material things and with catching up with the industrialization of the West. Feng shui and even acupuncture tended to be seen as marginal. The Chinese could no longer ignore the influence of the West due to the increasing global dominance of Western trade and the subsequent influence of Western culture. Of course, the Westernization of China partly influenced the old ways. Now, in perhaps more subtle ways, Chinese culture is influencing and changing the West, hence this book.

■ **The Forbidden City** *in Beijing was the Imperial residence of the Ming and Qing dynasties until 1911. It was turned into a museum in the early 20th century. The protective lion was one of many feng shui features.*

The suppression of feng shui

In 1927, with the establishment of a Nationalist government in Nanjing, "enlightened" provincial leaders sought to underline their zealousness by suppressing beliefs like feng shui. One such provincial government went so far as to proclaim that, "In the present time of renaissance and scientific enlightenment, these bad traditions not only keep people ignorant but make us the laughing stock among nations."

With the establishment of the Communists in 1949, efforts to discredit "superstition" intensified. Many feng shui practitioners continued to ply their trade from 1949 to 1966. But from 1966 through 1976, the Cultural Revolution began in earnest to sweep away traditional Chinese culture, art, old buildings, libraries, and feng shui manuals. Enormous numbers of *lo p'ans*, other feng shui paraphernalia, and books were destroyed.

The Cultural Revolution caused many feng shui practitioners to flee with their knowledge to Hong Kong, Taiwan, and other overseas Chinese communities.

■ **A carved wooden statue** *of the Chinese deity Kuan Ti presides over the shrine in the Kong Chow Temple in San Francisco, one of a number of cities to which many feng shui practitioners fled during the years of the Cultural Revolution.*

During this period, perhaps the most active places for feng shui were:

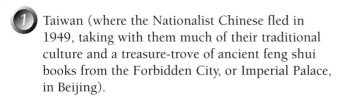

1. Taiwan (where the Nationalist Chinese fled in 1949, taking with them much of their traditional culture and a treasure-trove of ancient feng shui books from the Forbidden City, or Imperial Palace, in Beijing).

2. Hong Kong (where feng shui practitioners have worked for the big property developers ever since).

3. Singapore (although feng shui was for a while frowned upon by the very modern and well-organized Singaporean government).

4. The Philippines (where feng shui was often to be found in local Taoist temples).

5. Malaysia (where much feng shui belief has been kept alive).

6. Other Chinese expatriate communities, such as London, Sydney, San Francisco, and Vancouver.

7. Cochin China, a region that included Vietnam, Cambodia, and Laos (where a variant of feng shui was also practiced).

Trivia...

When the Chinese-language edition of the magazine Feng Shui for Modern Living *was getting its brand registered in China, it was warned that it would be better if it changed its title to something like* I Ching Studies. *The initial trademark registration was refused on the grounds that feng shui is a "superstitious and imperialistic" practice, which is rich coming from a Chinese ministry. The second trademark application stressed the importance of feng shui to Chinese culture and its strong links with the* I Ching, *and this one was more successful.*

The rise of feng shui in the West

After my first book on the subject written in 1976, Western involvement in feng shui was still fairly minimal. The arrival of Professor Lin Yun in the United States from Taiwan via Hong Kong in the 1980s, and the work of his pupil Sarah Rossbach, put feng shui on the map in the US.

Initially, Lin Yun taught a fairly traditional style of feng shui, but soon found, at that early stage, that a simpler form of feng shui was required. Accordingly, he modified a fixed *pa kua* version of feng shui and launched it in 1985 as Tibetan Black Hat Tantric Buddhist Feng Shui.

By allying feng shui with Buddhism, he gave feng shui a cloak of spiritual respectability, and by adding in the mystery of the Black Hat Tibetan Lamaism, he distanced it from its Chinese roots. And "tantric" was the final seductive addition that made feng shui far more popular in the United States than it would otherwise have been.

BHS feng shui

By the 1990s, Professor Lin Yun had a thriving teaching and consulting practice. Without him, feng shui may never have taken off in the United States. His style of feng shui has been abbreviated by his pupils to BTB (Black Tibetan Buddhist) feng shui, although the "Black Hat" part has survived in the other abbreviation for this movement – *BHS (Black Hat Sect)* feng shui.

Feng shui in mainland China

By the late 1980s, architects in the People's Republic of China had begun to wonder about the old feng shui rules that had helped produce traditional building styles. The Chinese media still portrayed feng shui as "unhealthy" and "feudal superstition." But copies of Western books on feng shui by Joseph Needham, Andrew March, Derek Walters, Sarah Rossbach, and myself made their way back to China. Some of these were even translated into Chinese and helped arouse local academic interest.

The first modern mainland book on feng shui was published in Chinese in 1989, with several other academic works following rapidly. Some heavily censored and rather distorted feng shui classics were also reprinted. Professor Cheng Jian Jun and Wang Yude have done much to put feng shui back on its feet in China.

"Intuitive" feng shui

Back in the United States, interest diverged even further from traditional feng shui, and William Spear coined the term "intuitive" feng shui. In fact, he has gone as far as trademarking it. Spear, who previously taught macrobiotics, is another writer who attempted to make feng shui palatable to Western tastes and introduced the idea of "spiritual vision" and intuition rather than complex calculations. Spear also had an effect in the United Kingdom, where he lectured at the East West Center in London in the late 1980s. He was later brought over to lecture in the UK in the 1990s by Gina Lazenby, who founded the UK Feng Shui Society. His book *Feng Shui Made Easy* helped spread his own version of feng shui in both countries in the early 1990s.

Feng shui is a precise technique. Intuition is not a substitute for correct calculation and should come into play only where several technical solutions present themselves to the same problem.

DEFINITION

BHS (Black Hat Sect) *feng shui orientates all houses (or rooms) by the door position. Door positions are supposed to correspond with the most yin northerly K'an Trigram, rather than taking note of actual compass directions, which have always been a central consideration of feng shui.*

Nine Star Ki

Ki is the Japanese spelling of ch'i. Nine Star Ki is not feng shui. It is a Japanese derivation of the Chinese system for determining your annual Trigram (or *kua*) number.

But while the Chinese system takes notice of your sex as well as your date of birth, the Japanese system takes note only of the latter, preferring chauvinistically to calculate female *ki* numbers on the same basis as the male calculations. This means that men will get the same answer using either system, but women will not.

Unfortunately, publishers of books on the Nine Star Ki began to refer to this practice as "feng shui astrology," because the use of "feng shui" in the title significantly increased sales. However, Nine Star Ki is *not* feng shui astrology. If there is such a thing as feng shui astrology, the term should be applied to Chinese Four Pillar astrology (which we will look at in chapter 22).

A simple summary

✔ There is a connection between grave and house feng shui.

✔ Yin feng shui developed into yang, or house, feng shui.

✔ Feng shui Masters were recognized by the first century BC.

✔ The two main Schools of feng shui are the Form School and the Compass School.

✔ Feng shui was suppressed in mainland China by the government, and was virtually destroyed there during the Cultural Revolution.

✔ Feng shui has further developed in the 20th century, primarily outside China.

✔ In the West, simplifications like BTB, Nine Star Ki, and "intuitive" feng shui have increasingly spread.

PART TWO

WATER IS A NATURAL ELEMENT THAT CARRIES CH'I

HOW FENG SHUI WORKS

CH'I ENERGY UNDERLIES all of feng shui practice. Ch'i is a *natural energy* that moves with wind and water. There are different types of ch'i, and the objective of feng shui is to concentrate benevolent ch'i in the buildings in which we live and work. This improves our *health*, *wealth*, and *happiness*.

To do this effectively you have to know what sort of ch'i energy you are dealing with. This depends upon the *time and direction* from which it comes, so you need to know the compass bearings of the building and take account of the times and seasons.

How ch'i moves is also affected by alignments of buildings, streets, and even furniture within the house. This is why feng shui has sometimes been defined as *"the art of placement."*

Chapter 5

Ch'i and Alignments

WHAT IS FENG SHUI REALLY ABOUT? Feng shui is really about five things: Ch'i energy; alignment; the Earth's magnetism; the eight Compass Directions; and the five Elements, particularly Water. Do I hear you say, "What about colors, mirrors, flutes, frogs, windchimes, and intuition?" Well, these things do have a part to play, but it's important to get the big picture first, so that when we get to the elements of home decor, you will know why certain things work and others simply do not! In this chapter I will give a detailed explanation of the first two main aspects of feng shui – ch'i energy and alignments. I will discuss the remaining three aspects – the Earth's magnetism, the eight Compass Directions, and the five Elements – in the next chapter.

In this chapter...

✓ Understanding ch'i

✓ Heaven ch'i, Weather ch'i, and Earth ch'i

✓ The effect of alignments

STREETS DESIGNED ON A GRID SYSTEM CAUSE CH'I TO BECOME DESTRUCTIVE SHA CH'I

Understanding ch'i

CH'I IS A FORM OF ENERGY *that permeates the material universe. It is sometimes spelled qi or even ki, but is always pronounced "chee." Ch'i is what animates, what distinguishes between living and dead matter. Where ch'i has gone stagnant, life energy has dried up. Ch'i can be visualized almost as a curling vapor rising off a morning pond. In fact, the top of the Chinese character looks like layers of mist floating over a liquid. The full character suggests vapor floating over a vat of fermenting rice. This idea of vapor is also reflected in the old-fashioned translation of the word as "cosmic breath."*

CH'I (ENERGY)

Ch'i is not a hard concept to accept. After all, in the 21st century we accept all kinds of invisible forces. We accept radio waves, microwaves, cell-phone transmissions, CB radios, TV waves, X-rays, ultrasound, and cosmic, and infrared radiation without question. Nobody has ever seen or touched *any* of these things, but they are an article of total faith for everyone, because science says so. Like these other invisible forms of energy, ch'i can be appreciated by its effects but cannot be seen, and it's probably only a matter of time before someone devises a way of measuring ch'i.

Ch'i also manifests itself in the body. It flows through acupuncture meridians. Where it is congested or blocked, so illness or disease follows. Martial artists in disciplines like ch'i kung (qi gong) have learned to concentrate it in various parts of the body so it can be felt, to enable the practitioner to do almost superhuman things.

Ch'i acts at every level. Plants and animals need ch'i. On the human level, it is the energy flowing in the acupuncture meridians; at the agricultural level, ch'i energy brings forth fertile crops. For the Chinese, at the human level, this kind of fertility includes the producing of many male children. At the weather level, it is the hydrologic cycle, which ensures the falling of rain (to bring fertility), the filling of streams to irrigate the rice paddies, and the final ascension/evaporation of water vapor, where water rejoins the Dragons in the clouds to cause more rain to fall.

This is both poetry and geography, but a full understanding of ch'i makes many later feng shui problems very easy to solve. For example, the falling of rain is the fertilization of the Earth by Heaven; so, for example, water collected from the eaves of a house is a potent source of *sheng ch'i*, which can be used to advantage in garden feng shui.

■ **Ch'i flows through the landscape** *and through the buildings in which we live and work. Its energy is concentrated and carried by water. Both help to promote the growth of healthy crops.*

How ch'i flows

Ch'i naturally flows in a meandering course. Where it flows gently and accumulates, an abundance follows. Where the flow becomes stagnant, these life energies, and abundance, dry up. Conversely, where ch'i is forced to flow rapidly in straight lines, it becomes destructive. If you visualize it like water, you will not go far wrong in understanding its effects: Neither a stagnant pond full of rubbish nor a roaring rapid is an ideal living environment. Agriculture, life, settlement, and indeed trade – and, in turn, prosperity and wealth – accumulate along mature, slowly flowing, meandering rivers. You only have to think of most of the great capital cities of the world to see that.

Decayed ch'i – bright ch'i

Ch'i goes through cycles like every other natural thing: It is born, it becomes strong, it decays, and it dies. The essence of feng shui is to accumulate the right sort of ch'i at the right point in the cycle. Ch'i can be positive, strong, and energizing. If so, it is called *sheng ch'i*. *Sheng ch'i* is to be encouraged. On the other hand, stagnant energy is called *ssu ch'i* (or torpid ch'i) and is to be avoided at all costs, just as stagnant water should not be drunk, if you value your health. Other ways of describing this is that bright ch'i is yang ch'i, but decayed ch'i is yin ch'i.

Sha ch'i, sheng ch'i, and ssu ch'i

When yang ch'i travels along straight roads, rails, or other alignments, it gathers too much speed. When it finally strikes a building, it is called *sha ch'i*. Such *sha ch'i* is too yang, too energetic, and by the time it hits its target it is destructive and undesirable. There are many conditions of ch'i, but these are the three most important to identify from a practical feng shui perspective.

Balance is important: Ch'i must not flow too fast, especially in straight lines, and ch'i must not be trapped so that it stagnates. If you remember these key rules, you will not go far wrong with feng shui.

TYPE OF CH'I	NAME	CONDITION
Cutting ch'i	*sha ch'i*	overly rapid ch'i or "killing breath"
Yang ch'i	*sheng ch'i*	bright ch'i (the good stuff!)
Yin ch'i	*ssu ch'i*	decayed or torpid ch'i

The whole point of feng shui is to encourage *sheng ch'i*, block or deflect *sha ch'i*, and disperse *ssu ch'i*.

Heaven ch'i, Weather ch'i, and Earth ch'i

THERE ARE THREE WAYS THAT CH'I MANIFESTS: as Heaven ch'i, Weather ch'i, and Earth ch'i.

The three forms of ch'i, Heaven, Weather, and Earth, interact one upon the other. Heaven ch'i has an effect on both Weather and Earth ch'i, and Weather ch'i affects Earth ch'i. Earth ch'i receives the influences of the other two, just as Earth is fertilized by rain and shined on by the sun.

There are modern parallels. For example, scientists have understood for some time that there is a correspondence between sunspots (part of Heaven ch'i) and changes in weather and climate (Weather ch'i) and consequent animal/plant growth cycles, like fluctuating animal populations or changes in tree ring growth strength (Earth ch'i).

Trivia...

Ch'i "is exhaled by the mountains, where the spirits live, as clouds and mist and, therefore, the undulating movement of clouds, mist, or air filled with smoke rising from burning incense is a characteristic mystic representation of Ch'i in Taoist art." This is how ch'i is defined by Laszlo Legeza, author (with Philip Rawson) of Tao, the Chinese Philosophy of Time and Change *(1975).*

Also, variations in the Earth's magnetic field (Earth ch'i) are known to mirror changes in the electromagnetic activities in the Earth's upper atmosphere (Heaven and Weather ch'i). Western science cannot precisely determine the reason for these connections, but the ancient Chinese saw it as perfectly natural that the three different types of ch'i should interact. What's more, they mapped these interactions.

Ch'i in the heavens

Heaven ch'i (*t'ien ch'i*) is sometimes called "guest ch'i," because it descends to Earth, where it is "hosted." It affects Earth ch'i, and may cancel its effects. If you are calculating the compass directions from which Heaven ch'i may arrive, use the Former Heaven Sequence of the Trigrams, where, for quick reference, the Trigram *Ch'ien* (three unbroken bars) is located in the south. You will find more about the Former Heaven Sequence in chapter 8.

Ch'i in the weather

The Weather ch'i mediate between Heaven and Earth, and are called the "moveable ch'i." There are five Weather ch'i:

- Sunshine
- Heat
- Cold
- Wind (feng)
- Rain (shui)

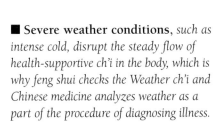

■ **Severe weather conditions,** *such as intense cold, disrupt the steady flow of health-supportive ch'i in the body, which is why feng shui checks the Weather ch'i and Chinese medicine analyzes weather as a part of the procedure of diagnosing illness.*

■ **The occasional downpour is seen as a good omen** *by the Chinese, because rain water (one of the Weather ch'i) comes from Heaven and equates with wealth.*

Taking them in order, *sunshine* changes the degree of *heat* at the surface of the Earth. Modern climatology acknowledges that it is differences in surface heat and *cold* that create warm or cool air masses. As these air masses rise, they cool, and in displacing other air they generate *winds*. Winds, in turn, pick up moisture and, by dumping it again elsewhere, cause *rain*.

So, the ancient list of the five Weather ch'i is in exactly the same causal sequence as the list of climatological factors considered by modern weather forecasters! Note that the last two Weather ch'i are also the stuff of "feng shui."

As we have seen (see p. 65), early feng shui Masters were able to create weather effects like mist at will. This is not an art that has been entirely lost.

The five Weather ch'i are subject to decay like Earth ch'i, and are interpreted by both the Former Heaven Sequence and Later Heaven Sequence of Trigrams (see chapter 8). The fluctuations of Weather ch'i are often described in terms of the "advancing and reverting breath," implying a cyclical existence.

Many feng shui Masters are very aware of the forces of nature and will consider the type of weather on the day they make their site visit as relevant to the consultation.

A feng shui consultant would interpret a rainy or drizzly day, which might put you and me off, as a positive influx of Heaven-inspired Weather ch'i.

An example of this is the rain that fell during the ceremony handing the sovereignty of Hong Kong over to China in 1997, which was interpreted in a very positive fashion by all the Chinese present, and indeed worldwide. Remember that water equates with wealth, and rain just before the launch of a new venture is interpreted as a good omen, not as a nuisance and a dampener as it is in the West. Instead of upsetting the audience, it provoked a smile on many Chinese lips.

From this you can see why in all cultures the greatest magic includes the ability to rain-make, or control the Weather ch'i. Some of the famous Taoist magicians of old were supposed to be able to do just that. Western science, on the other hand, is unable to control the weather (except for simple cloud seeding, which was a Chinese invention anyway) or even to predict accurately its changes for more than a few hours or days in advance. It may be that the old feng shui Masters can still teach us a thing or two.

■ **Weather ch'i** *affects all of us, just as the weather itself does, but in a much more subtle manner. By using the five Weather ch'i, the feng shui Masters can control the interaction of Heaven and Earth ch'i.*

Ch'i on the Earth

Earth ch'i (*ti ch'i*) is sometimes called "host ch'i," because Earth ch'i receives Heaven ch'i when it descends to Earth. Earth ch'i is governed by the Later Heaven Sequence of Trigrams (in which the Trigram *Li* points to the south).

Of course, Earth ch'i is very important to feng shui, since it affects our dwellings and hence also us.

The effect of alignments

AS WE NOW HAVE SOME IDEA of what ch'i is, we can consider how ch'i moves. The nature of healthy ch'i is to meander. In fact, in nature, a stream passing through a uniform bed of sand or a raindrop streaming down a window pane will, if left undisturbed, meander from side to side.

There is something in the energy dynamic of moving fluids that makes their natural and "most efficient" course a meander rather than what you might have naturally thought – a straight line.

According to share chartist theory, the meandering nature is even true of stock prices, which, if following an upward or downward trend channel, tend to meander from one side to the other of this channel. There is obviously an undiscovered law of motion that governs this, since this behavior cannot simply be described in terms of friction or trend channels.

Speeding up on the straight stretch

Earlier we briefly mentioned *sha ch'i*, which is ch'i that has speeded up by following a long straight path, such as a succession of telegraph poles, an expressway, or any other straight alignment.

Ch'i needs to accumulate to be beneficial. This is best achieved when there are suitably sheltered places, uncut by sha ch'i, for the ch'i to accumulate.

If ch'i moves along straight lines, it gathers speed and becomes destructive. Hence, if there are long, straight stretches of road, the ch'i gains speed and is destructive when it reaches the end of this alignment. Such fast flowing ch'i is called *sha ch'i*.

Ideally, a home or site needs to be located where the ch'i meanders, preferably in the inner bend of a river or road.

Inside a building, long corridors so beloved of 1960s' planners are classic cases of a feng shui no-no. Likewise, desks placed in long, straight rows are not conducive to good office feng shui. In homes, through halls need to be broken up by the introduction of strategically placed plants or wind chimes, for the same reason.

■ **A long, straight road** *encourages ch'i to gather speed and become destructive. A town at the end of such a road would become a target for fast-flowing, killing ch'i.*

Streets and railways

One of the first steps in any feng shui analysis is to identify any straight alignments aimed at the house. The classic example is the T-junction. Here, the property at the top of the road forming the stem of the "T" will be badly afflicted by the energy rushing up that road, especially if the road carries heavy traffic. There are ways of partially protecting such properties, but it is better not to buy or live in one if you have the choice. Hedges, high fences, and fountains will reduce but not eliminate the downside of this particular bad feng shui configuration.

Another feng shui no-no is being positioned so that the edge of a curved, raised expressway overpass is aimed like a knife-edge at a home or office. In such a situation it is better to be on the "inside" of such a curve, rather than on the outside "knife-edge."

The knife-edge rule, incidentally, also applies to riverbanks. It's interesting to see how many thriving cities are initially built on the inside curve of a major river. Often, in these circumstances, the suburbs on the "outer" edge of the river bend are the less prosperous ones. In Chicago, the Els (elevated trains) have the same "cutting" effect on adjacent properties as elevated expressways.

Modern cities are full of straight lines and therefore generate lots of *sha ch'i*. These include repetitive roof alignments, particularly along lines of suburban terrace houses. Rows of telegraph poles marching past a house are not much of a problem, but if your house is located at the end of such a row, then the *sha ch'i* so produced is very destructive.

■ **A gently meandering river** *generates just the right flow of ch'i – in fact, many thriving cities and towns have been built on the inside of such curves.*

■ **Like most major cities,** *Paris is full of straight lines. Such rectangular configurations may be the hallmark of Western civilization but they are not conducive to the flow of beneficial ch'i.*

A clear example of the action of this feng shui phenomenon is demonstrated in a number of businesses on Oxford Street, a famous shopping street in London. Many of the properties facing incoming side streets are regularly vacant or constantly changing tenants. This demonstrates the destabilizing effect of the *sha ch'i* being funneled down these side streets.

Poison arrows

"Poison arrows" is the name given to long alignments, which enable ch'i flow to speed up to a point where it impacts upon a person or building, like an arrow. They are also called "secret arrows," because they cannot be seen. Secret arrows can be blocked off with walls, trees, or embankments. The principle is that, if they can't be seen, then they will not cause a problem.

Another possibility is to use a mirror to deflect them back to where they came from. A *pa kua* mirror is a small circular or octagonal mirror surrounded by the eight Trigrams laid out in a specific way, as shown in the Former Heaven Sequence (see chapter 8). Typically, if there are strong poison arrows aimed at the front door, then one solution is to hang a *pa kua* mirror over the center of the door. Such mirrors are usually to be found for sale in Chinese supermarkets or from specialist feng shui mail-order suppliers (usually at a higher price).

Spike-shaped features

Other poison arrows can be generated by spike-shaped features. Church spires were a favorite target for destruction in European settlements in China in the 19th century, because their very aggressive points are supposed to be not just an affront to Heaven, but also very bad feng shui for their long-suffering neighbors.

On a smaller scale, today's satellite dishes are very feng shui-unfriendly items to point in the direction of your neighbors. Conversely, if a neighbor has done this to you, screen off the offending site. This is really a case of what you can't see can't harm you! Alternatively, send the poison arrows back to where they came from with a mirror.

Another cause of poison arrows, which is not often mentioned by books on feng shui, but which is nevertheless important, is simply a disproportionately large building, particularly one close enough to overpower your own home/office. Here, the sheer size is the problem. A building that overwhelms your building also overwhelms your feng shui. This is particularly aggravated if a corner of the building points directly at your home. And it is

■ **The spire** *of London's St Martin in the Fields church is an example of a "poison arrow," which will damage the feng shui of buildings whose entrances it confronts.*

totally disastrous if this corner points at your front door. The alignment or line of sight along a wall of such a building is even more damaging than simply being pointed at by a blunt corner.

One interesting point seldom mentioned is that the reason for corners being damaging from a feng shui point of view is that ch'i flows along the walls of large buildings. At the end of a wall, where it reaches maximum concentration, it over-runs, and continues moving rapidly in the same direction. Any close building in line with this over-run will be affected.

Where two walls meet at a corner, the ch'i flow is doubled and becomes turbulent. This makes the corners of large buildings dangerous from a feng shui point of view.

In all these situations, it is the access point for ch'i that needs to be specially protected. The front door is the most vulnerable, because this is the main "mouth" through which ch'i can enter the home/office. Back doors and windows are to a lesser extent vulnerable to such poison arrows.

Internally, on a much smaller scale, poison arrows can be generated by badly placed or overpowering furniture, and we will look at this later in chapters 9 and 10.

A simple summary

✔ There are five main feng shui considerations: ch'i energy, alignment, the Earth's magnetism, the eight Compass Directions, and the five Elements, in particular Water.

✔ Ch'i energy is described by its state as *sheng, sha,* or *ssu ch'i.*

✔ Geography and feng shui interact in the form of Heaven, Earth, and Weather ch'i.

✔ Ch'i is as much a part of the physical universe as the spiritual universe.

✔ Alignments direct the course of ch'i flow. Forcing it to move in a straight line can change it from *sheng ch'i* to *sha ch'i.*

Chapter 6

The Building Blocks of Feng Shui

MAGNETISM, the eight Compass Directions (plus center), and the five Elements are the remaining building blocks of feng shui. The compass points to magnetic north and south, and is used to identify the other Compass Directions. The eight Directions correspond with four of the five Elements and the four Seasons. It is the interaction of the eight Directions and the five Elements that gives rise to feng shui diagnosis and Element remedies. The Production, Destruction, and Reduction Cycles, which explain how to relate the Elements to each other, are key.

In this chapter...

✓ Magnetism

✓ The compass

✓ The Directions

✓ The Elements

✓ The Production, Destruction, and Reduction Cycles

THE EARTH'S MAGNETISM, AND THE EFFECT IT HAS ON US, IS A CENTRAL CONCEPT OF FENG SHUI

Magnetism

MAGNETISM IS THE THIRD important core concept of feng shui. In some subtle way, ch'i energy, water flow, and the Earth's magnetic field are definitely interlinked. Dowsers have an intuitive grasp of that fact, but increasingly scientific proof of these links is beginning to emerge.

Some physics experiments that were done recently at one East Coast US university look very promising. The researchers stumbled across a force that may well be related to ch'i while trying to prove something totally unrelated concerning gravity.

The Earth's magnetic field

The Earth is a huge magnet with a magnetic field extending well into space, so it is certain that this field affects all life on the surface of the Earth. We already know from medical MRI scanning techniques that a strong magnetic field can affect all the organs in the body, so the much weaker but all-pervading magnetic field of the Earth must also affect our bodies. Of course, it is possible that this natural magnetism might even be to the benefit of the body. I am simply saying that this field has a very real effect on us all.

Biologists are also making fascinating discoveries about the mitochondria. These are the microscopic food processors in the body's cells. Not only are they crucial to the energy supply of the cell, but they also respond directly to the Earth's magnetic field and will line up in a north–south direction. Interesting, isn't it? Somewhere, somebody has to research the connections that exist between that alignment, magnetism, and the body's health and well-being.

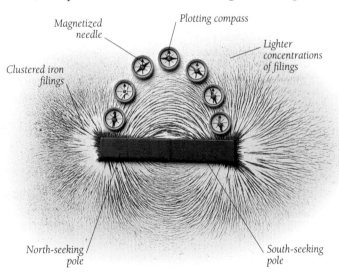

Magnetized needle

Plotting compass

Lighter concentrations of filings

Clustered iron filings

North-seeking pole

South-seeking pole

■ **Magnetism is invisible**, *but lines of magnetic force around a magnet can be demonstrated. Here, temporarily magnetized iron filings swivel to align with the magnet's field, clustering around the poles, where the force is strongest. The compass needles, which are already magnetized, show this effect in a similar way.*

The compass

THE EARTH'S MAGNETIC FIELD *can easily be measured by using a compass. At a basic level, it is enough to have access to a simple trekking or hiking compass, which can be used to tell in which direction your house or office faces. Feng shui compasses are a lot more complex than this, and we will look in detail at the feng shui compass in chapter 23.*

Why do we need a compass? The reason is so you can find out how the building is related to the Earth's magnetic field and to find the eight main Compass Directions. For the purposes of feng shui, we cannot simply orientate ourselves and our rooms from the front door, because we need to set the house or office we are analyzing in the context of the surrounding landscape and its magnetic field. It is also from these surroundings that the vital ch'i affects the house and determines its feng shui qualities. Hence a compass is essential for proper feng shui.

Westerners tend to think that the compass needle points north. In actual fact, the needle points both north and south.

North and south

The only difference between north and south, with regard to the compass needle, is that the north end is marked. The Chinese like to think of the needle as pointing south. Hence, in this book, there will sometimes be statements about the compass pointing south. This does not mean that the needle has suddenly swung round 180 degrees. It simply goes with the Chinese convention of turning their maps around so that south is at the top of the page.

Magnetic north or south is the direction in which the compass needle points, whereas *map* north or south is supposed to point exactly to the North or South Poles, those points where the (imaginary) Earth's axis projects out of the ground, where every line of longitude meets, and where every polar explorer attempts to end up! Magnetic north is a real place, whereas map north, and indeed the whole concept of longitude, are only a mapmaker's convention. Feng shui uses only real magnetic north. Magnetic north appears to vary over time and according to where it is measured. The Earth's axis, and hence map north, also vary over time.

Each generation may take slightly different compass readings when putting up its dwellings, as magnetic north "wanders." Don't let this confuse you. Given that feng shui is about magnetism, in feng shui when we speak of a direction like north, we *always* mean magnetic north – *never* map north.

It's an historical fact that the Chinese discovered or invented the compass in the 4th century BC, a good 1,500 years before compasses were first mentioned in Europe in AD 1190. What is not so well known is that the Chinese used the compass initially on land to find south and to perform feng shui calculations. It was only centuries later that the compass began to be used by mariners for finding their way around the oceans. (Before that, mariners relied upon the sun and star positions or simply sailed within sight of land.)

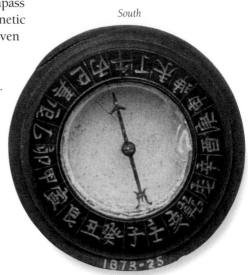

South

North

CHINESE MARINER'S COMPASS

The Directions

MAGNETISM IS USED TO MEASURE DIRECTION, *particularly to find north and south. For the Chinese, however, there are five main Directions: north, south, east, west, and center, in between which are the four inter-cardinal (or corner) points: northeast, northwest, southeast, and southwest. This gives eight Directions plus center. Thus these directions fit neatly in with the five Elements, the eight Trigrams, and the nine cells of the* lo shu *(which we will get to in chapter 8).*

The Directions measured by the feng shui compass, or lo p'an, are magnetic directions. Where there are local variations in magnetic declination, these are not adjusted for by feng shui Masters.

The four winds

The "feng" of feng shui is wind. In feng shui, winds have often marked off the Directions. On old European maps there were "wind-roses" showing the relative strength of winds coming from different directions. Just as in olden times in North America or Europe, winds and directions were identified together. So the cold winds coming from the north, for example, brought with them certain conditions, and that direction became associated with those conditions. Likewise, warm winds came from the south.

WIND-ROSE

In the southern hemisphere, it is the association of climate with the Compass Directions that encourages local feng shui practitioners to switch the Trigrams around. The traditional view is that the Trigrams don't change and that the climatic parallel is only a convenient metaphor.

Don't worry if you didn't understand the above bit about Trigrams. It just means that either you don't live in the southern hemisphere or you haven't reached the point where this distinction matters to you.

The four seasonal Directions

Now, because Chinese thinking, particularly Taoist thinking, is holistic, there are many numerical connections between things that don't at first seem connected to a Westerner. For example, the Chinese correlate the four cardinal Compass Points with the seasons.

How can that be? Well, if you think about it, each of the four Compass Points corresponds with one of the four seasons. For example, in a country like China (which is wholly in the northern hemisphere), the direction of greatest heat is in the south. Hence, summer was associated with the south. Conversely, the direction of the greatest cold was in the north, and therefore that was associated with the season of winter.

In between summer and winter come spring and fall. Spring is associated with the east, because that's where the sun rises, and fall is associated with the west, where the sun sets. So the year follows round from the east (spring) through south (summer) to west (fall) and north (winter), before returning to east (spring) again. These four Directions and seasons have added to them a fifth Direction (the center), which corresponds to the fifth Element, Earth, and its season (which we will discuss in chapter 21).

INTERNET

www.fengshuisociety .org.uk/newsletter.htm

For details of the other views of southern hemisphere feng shui, see the Feng Shui Society's Newsletter online.

■ **The Chinese associate the four cardinal Compass Points** *with seasons of the year. Fall is associated with the west, because that's where the sun sets.*

If you look at it cyclically, the time of day also correlates with the direction. The sun rises in the east at dawn, is at its hottest in the south at noonday, sets in the west at dusk, and is totally invisible in the dark of night at the north at midnight, before rising again at dawn in the east.

Various other cycles fit beautifully on this model. But what is *really* being shown in all this is the waxing and waning cycle of yin and yang. Later we will discover how closely this ties in to various calendar tides, and come to realize how the whole process of daily, monthly, or yearly change is governed by changing relationships between yin and yang. You can even throw in the cycle of human life to see the same process at work.

Parallel cycles

The yin/yang and life cycles are oversimplified in the chart below but they do help explain the parallel between the cycles, which repeat endlessly.

DIRECTION	YIN/YANG CYCLE	SEASON	DAY	LIFE CYCLE
East	Yang born	Spring	Dawn	Birth
South	Yang at maximum	Summer	Midday	Youth
West	Yin born	Fall	Dusk	Middle age
North	Yin at maximum	Winter	Midnight	Old age

The Elements

THE FIVE ELEMENTS are key to understanding and practicing feng shui. They are not elements in the chemistry sense of the Periodic Table of the elements, which lists almost 100 different elements in order of their atomic structure or, more correctly, according to the periodicity of their electron shells. Nor should the Chinese Elements be thought of in the same way as those of the ancient Greeks, who considered that the universe was made up of Fire, Air, Earth, and Water.

Interestingly, there is a parallel in some of the elements making up the list, but there the similarity ends. The Chinese thought of the physical equivalents of the Elements as examples or outgrowths of the underlying energy rather than as the energy itself. The five Elements are:

WATER   FIRE   EARTH   WOOD   METAL

The interaction of the Elements

The way in which the energies of these Elements interact is one of the main keys to feng shui. When I first came across the list of Chinese Elements, I tried vainly to match it with the Greek list of Elements. OK, I thought, Water, Earth, and Fire appear in both lists, but why is Air missing from the Chinese list? This seemed especially crazy since Air is actually part of the words "feng shui." And why did the Chinese consider Wood and Metal to be Elements? Chemically, all these Elements are very mixed.

The answer is that the Elements are not really elements but types of constantly changing energy. For example, in the case of Wood, the Element means the energy of vegetative growth. As Dylan Thomas once so elegantly put it, Wood energy is "the force that through the green fuse drives the flower."

Wood is the energy of spring that drives the sap up the stems of plants and drives the growth of many other things. Sure, wood is part of Wood, but the dead planks of furniture are miles away from the spring energies of vegetative growth. Likewise, Metal is not just mineral metal but also the energies of man-made fabrication. It also refers to that special metal, gold, and the energies that allow it to lubricate business and trade.

Water has a really special place both for man and for feng shui. It is the Element that nourishes the energies of growth, just as water nourishes plants. But it also carries ch'i energy. Rivers and lakes are a highly important part of feng shui, because they both carry and bind, or limit, ch'i energy.

Fire is easier to understand, since even in a Western chemistry context it is seen as a transformation of oxygen plus a carbon-based material into heat energy and gas. As such, it is closer to the Chinese idea that all Elements are a form of transformational energy.

Earth is a special Element. Where there are four cardinal Compass Points but five Elements, the solution is to place Earth neutrally at the center, balancing the others. Earth usually falls into the middle of any scheme relating the Elements to any other feng shui symbols.

Don't confuse the Element Earth with the planet Earth or with the earth you walk on.

In the case of air, it is part of "feng" and "shui," which carry ch'i energy, but it is not considered a Chinese Element in its own right.

THE MEANING OF "HSING"

The Chinese word for Element is *hsing*. This is almost impossible to translate into a recognizable English word. It is one of five types of transformational energy and has sometimes been translated as "moving agent" or "phase," but neither of these translations carries its real meaning. Because of this, we are going to stick with the old translation of *hsing* as "Element." Note the capitalization: This is to distinguish it from the 100 or so elements of modern chemistry. In its Chinese sense, it is even more fundamental than they are.

The key idea to remember is that instead of the Elements being a bucket of earth, a pail of water, or a pile of wood, they are changing aspects of a universal energy behind the manifested universe. Using the names of common things like fire or water to explain the changing energies was a stroke of genius by the ancient Chinese – how else could we conveniently grasp the idea of *hsing*? But you have to be careful not to take it too literally.

The Production, Destruction, and Reduction Cycles

WE HAVE ALREADY MET THE FIVE ELEMENTS – Earth, Fire, Water, Wood, and Metal. It's time now to consider them in greater detail, and particularly how they interact with each other. The five Elements help to sum up various qualities and things that are associated with them. For feng shui, the most important associations are the way the five Elements relate to the eight Directions plus the center.

The Chinese symbols for the five Elements are shown with their associated Directions below. The attribution looks a bit asymmetrical, and the ambiguous position of Earth at the center gets over the apparent difficulty of attributing five Elements to eight Compass Points, but it really works when you get to appreciate it. The secondary Directions are shown in brackets.

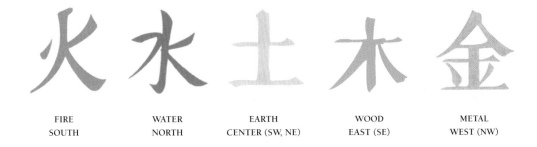

FIRE	WATER	EARTH	WOOD	METAL
SOUTH	NORTH	CENTER (SW, NE)	EAST (SE)	WEST (NW)

There are a number of ways in which the five Elements relate to each other. The two most commonly known are the Production and Destruction Cycles. There are many other cycles, like the Reduction, or Control, Cycle and the Masking Cycle. We will look at only three cycles: Production, Destruction, and Reduction.

Understanding the cycles

These cycles are a convenient guide to the effect that various changes in Element concentration can have on the feng shui of a home or office. A full understanding of them is very handy when it comes to prescribing cures to various feng shui problems. Make sure you understand the first two; you can pass over the third cycle if you like.

How the Elements interact with each other

The five Elements continually produce and destroy each other in a special sequence. This sequence is the key to concentrating, or enhancing, them so that the correct feng shui results occur. If your eyes are beginning to glaze over at this point, hang in there, because a correct understanding of these five Elements is perhaps the most useful thing you can learn about feng shui.

Don't scan through this section: Read it until you feel comfortable with at least the first two Element Cycles. You will find later that knowing these cycles properly will speed up your comprehension of more complicated feng shui.

The use of the Production Cycle of the Elements is to find out which Element helps another Element to grow.

Understanding how the five Elements interact with one another is a key piece of information. It helps you to understand the process of change. More importantly, it enables you to control the process of change to your own advantage – and that, after all, is what feng shui is really about.

Each of the five Elements interacts with each of the other Elements in four main cycles (Production, Destruction, Reduction, and Masking). If you remember that part of the meaning of Element, or *hsing*, is "moving agent," then you should not have much difficulty with the idea that each of these Elements produces one of the others. So not only do the Elements interact, but they also actually produce one another.

One secret of feng shui is that if you want to stimulate an Element, use its "producer." For example, Water produces Wood, so by introducing water (perhaps a fountain) into a room, you automatically stimulate the Wood energies.

■ **Introducing water** *to a room stimulates the production of the Element Wood. Chrysanthemums help produce even more.*

The Production Cycle

To help you remember the sequence of production, I am going to explain it in a very physical fashion, but do remember we are discussing changing energies. This is not difficult if you visualize it as I go along.

- Wood burns to produce Fire
- Fire produces ash, or Earth
- Earth is the mother in which are found veins of Metal
- Metal is a cold surface on which forms dew (Water)
- Water nourishes vegetation (Wood) . . . and so we start again at the top

PRODUCTION CYCLE

Everyone remembers Wood burning to produce Fire. The tricky one here is Metal producing Water. You are not convinced? You must have seen water condensing on cold metal in the early morning light to really appreciate this one. Remember that these images are just a way of remembering this important sequence of energy transformations.

The Destruction Cycle

This operates in the reverse direction and is used if you need to reduce the impact of any Element. The cycle is as follows:

- Water puts out Fire
- Fire melts Metal
- Metal (axes) cuts down Wood (trees)
- Wood puts its roots down into the soil and feeds on Earth
- Earth silts up Water . . . and so we start again at the top

Most of this follows nature, so closely, in fact, that you find yourself thinking in far too concrete terms.

DESTRUCTION CYCLE

A similar secret of feng shui is that if you want to minimize the effects of an Element, use its destroying Element. For example, Metal destroys Wood, so by introducing metal into a room, you limit the Wood energies in that room.

The Reduction Cycle

The Reduction, or Control, Cycle is the reverse of the Production Cycle. In it, the product of any Element is used to wear it out by draining it, just like children can wear out their mother. In fact, the produced Element is often called the child of the producing Element. For example, we know that Water produces Wood. Using reverse logic, Wood drains Water. This is the Control, or Reduction, Cycle.

REDUCTION CYCLE

- Earth controls Fire
- Fire controls Wood
- Wood controls Water
- Water controls Metal (the hard one to visualize)
- Metal controls Earth . . . and so we start again at the top.

Using the Reduction Cycle is much more sophisticated than using the Destruction Cycle. Often you will find a feng shui situation where an excessive Element needs *reducing* rather than *destroying*. Reduction yields other benefits in terms of the strength of the remaining Element.

Another cycle is the Masking Cycle (which we will not look at here in detail), which effectively says that if an Element is being destroyed, you can help it by supplying more of its "producing" Element.

■ **Rusting metal** *shows how Water controls Metal in the Reduction Cycle, which we can understand by remembering that, in the Production Cycle, Metal produces Water by forming dew on a metal surface.*

Using the Element Cycles

Let's try out the theory by asking a question and coming up with four possible solutions.

You have an area of the house that you have decided should be predominantly Wood. But the area is packed with metal filing cabinets, so that the Metal Element is constantly destroying the Wood energies. What do you do?

1 Move the metal cabinets out? But this may not be practical.

2 Replace the metal cabinets with wooden ones? A bit retro from a style point of view!

3 Introduce some Fire to destroy the Metal? This could work – try painting the cabinets red. But this does not do anything beneficial for the Water.

4 Introduce a Water feature.

The last option is the smartest. Using the Production Cycle, Water then produces Wood. Using the Reduction Cycle, Water also reduces the destructive Metal. Two birds killed with the one stone! Much more Wood generated.

Head spinning? I don't blame you! But, now you see how it works, go back and look again at the Production and Destruction Cycles. You will see in chapter 17 the reasons why you might want to change the Element concentrations in a particular part of your house, but for the moment the point is to know how to work it out.

A simple summary

✓ Instead of seeing Directions and Elements as different phenomena, as Western science does, feng shui sees them as closely inter-related things.

✓ Magnetism determines Compass Direction, which determines the eight Compass Points, which are, in turn, related to the five Elements.

✓ The five Elements produce and destroy each other like a living web of fluctuating energies. An important part of feng shui is determining how to influence these energies beneficially.

Chapter 7

Chinese Cosmology

IN THIS CHAPTER we will look at some of the various sets of symbols that make up Chinese cosmology and that together help explain the energies or feng shui. According to the Chinese, all manifestation came from the *t'ai chi* – the origin of all things – which split into yin and yang, the male and female, force and form. These, in turn, generate the Trigrams of the *I Ching*. In turn, two Trigrams together make a Hexagram, which is the basis of the *I Ching*, that almost magical classic that enables you to predict the future course of change. The *I Ching* and its Trigrams are a very important part of feng shui. We'll take a look at the relationship between these Trigrams and what they mean for feng shui.

In this chapter...
✓ The symbols of cosmology
✓ T'ai chi: the Great Ultimate
✓ Yin and yang
✓ Light and dark, male and female

YIN AND YANG, DEATH AND LIFE, ARE APPARENT IN THIS TREE, WHERE LIFE SPRINGS FROM DEATH

The symbols of cosmology

THE SETS OF SYMBOLS *used on the feng shui compass range from the duality of yin and yang, through the five Elements, eight Trigrams, ten Heavenly Stems, 12 Earthly Branches, 24 Mountains, 60 Dragons, 72 Dragons, 120 fen chin (or golden divisions), to the 360 degrees of the compass.*

Now before you shut this book immediately and put it away forever, I want to reassure you that this is not nearly as complex as it sounds. All these symbols simply come from the positive and negative of yin and yang. Each of the above categories fits together in a very neat way. I am going to explain them starting with yin and yang – all the others are related to each other by numbers.

IT'S ALL IN THE NUMBERS

You'll notice as we go along that many of the groups of symbols are multiples of 12, thus:

1 x 12 = 12 Earthly Branches
2 x 12 = 24 Mountains
5 x 12 = 60 Dragons
6 x 12 = 72 Dragons
10 x 12 = 120 *fen chin*
30 x 12 = 360 degrees of the compass

Also, five categories on the feng shui compass are based on arrangements of the five Elements:

1 x 5 = 5 Elements
2 x 5 = 10 Heavenly Stems
12 x 5 = 60 Dragons
24 x 5 = 120 *fen chin*
72 x 5 = 360 degrees of the compass

The same numbers (above) keep coming up. So, if you make sure you know the simple stuff, then the rest will come easily. But let's start at the beginning – in fact, let's start before the creation of the universe.

T'ai chi: the Great Ultimate

THE FIRST NUMBER IS 0, OR ZERO, *which is totally unknowable. But we are not going to get philosophical about that. The next number is 1, the t'ai chi, or Great Ultimate. From this springs the opposites, yin and yang, and from them evolve what the Chinese refer to as "the ten thousand things," which is Chinese shorthand for the rest of the manifested universe. Simple, eh?*

The "ten thousand" symbolically means an infinite number. Although Chinese has words for "hundred thousand" or "million," in everyday use "ten thousand" means "myriad" or "infinite number" – in the case of "ten thousand years" it means "immortality."

There is even a special way of writing the characters for "ten thousand" to look like a meandering watercourse – which is a little feng shui hint.

The *t'ai chi* is the point from which all manifestation has flowed. Even at this abstract level, the lessons of yin and yang show in its symbol.

The t'ai chi symbol

The symbol of the *t'ai chi* looks like two interlocked tadpoles or fish. One is black (yin), the other white (yang). In each is a tiny spot of the opposite color, indicating that in extreme yang is the seed of yin, and in extreme yin is the seed of yang.

T'AI CHI SYMBOL

Their tails also embrace the opposite, showing the interdependence of yin and yang. The symbol is often shown different ways up. It still conveys the same meaning, even upside-down, but traditionally the correct way is to have the "head" of the white yang "tadpole" at the top, as Heaven (yang) is above Earth (yin). It would be, wouldn't it?

It is popularly believed in China that the t'ai chi symbol can even be seen on the mother's placenta at birth.

Yin and yang

I HAVE REFERRED TO YIN AND YANG *already a few times. It's now time to explore what they mean in greater detail.*

The first key to understanding yin and yang is to fathom their cyclical nature. Interpreted through the five Elements, yin and yang transform cyclically one into the other. For example, at the extreme of mid-winter yin, what is born? The seed of yang, or spring.

By understanding the fluctuations of yin and yang, a sage can look at current conditions and from them determine likely outcomes, because the transformations of fate run along mapped paths, along a certain way. Of course, if you are not a sage, then you have to use the *I Ching* to discover future changes. This is the root reason why, at the deepest level, the *I Ching* is so intertwined with feng shui. (For more on the *I Ching*, see chapter 3.)

■ **A snow-covered tree** *in mid-winter (yin) will begin its seasonal regrowth in spring (yang).*

The beginning of the universe

Chinese science starts not with the Big Bang theory but with the division of the first state, or **Great Absolute**, into yin and yang. These are two very different ways of looking at the beginning of the universe, each equally a symbolic representation of what really occurred, each typical of the culture that generated it. The Chinese division of everything into either yin or yang has an immediate practical use, however, that no amount of ingenuity can give to the Western physicists' Big Bang. Yang is a word that includes everything overt, bright, active, and masculine, while yin is a word that conveys the secret, dark, passive, and feminine side of the universe.

Don't ever assume that the items in the list (shown below) are yin or yang. It is the pairing that is important. Yin and yang are relationships between things, where one is yielding and the other forceful, not the things themselves.

A fundamental link

You only have to look at the rings of any *San Yuan*-style feng shui compass, with its 64 Hexagrams of the *I Ching*, to see how inextricably feng shui is intertwined with the *I Ching*. Cyclic transformation is the key to predicting change (using the *I Ching*) or causing change (using feng shui).

Remember that the I Ching predicts change, but feng shui allows you to actually make changes, and that is why the two are so intimately linked.

The second key to understanding yin and yang is that as the nature of anything moves toward the extreme, so it gives birth to its opposite. Therefore, old (or fully developed) yang, if moved farther toward extreme yang, turns immediately into young yin, and vice versa.

Why is this significant? Well, you would normally think that existence wavered evenly between the extremes of yin and the extremes of yang, like a giant sine wave. But it's not like that. When the extreme is reached, the opposite is immediately born.

Yin–yang pairings

Yin and yang are usually explained as pairs of opposites. To get you into the mood, I have listed some of the traditional yin–yang pairs below. Think about them!

YIN	YANG		YIN	YANG
Dark	Light		Shady	Sunny
Cold	Hot		Female	Male
Soft	Hard		Yielding	Firm
Dead	Alive		Valley	Hill
Passive	Active		Night	Day
Even	Odd		Moon	Sun
Waters	Mountains		Earth	Heaven
Tiger	Dragon		Winter	Summer

Light and dark, male and female

IT IS SO EASY TO BE POLITICALLY INCORRECT when examining yin and yang, attributing cold, dark qualities to the female and light, bright qualities to the male. This kind of chauvinism is not intended. The point is that in the manifested universe there is always a negative-to-positive polarity. This is the essence of the I Ching and even of life. If there was no interaction of extremes, no creative polarity, then there would be no movement, no life, no fecundity, no creativity . . . just boring blandness.

If you look at the pairs of words on page 111, you can see that they can be equally well applied to the decoration of the home, the preparation of food, or the delineation of moods, or applied to metaphysics. So when we speak of a room needing more yang, it should now be obvious that you should use hot, positive colors, such as reds, yellows, and oranges. In a yin room, such as a bedroom, cool, passive colors, such as blue, may be needed.

As we know, feng shui is all about balance, so getting the balance of yin and yang right is a large part of the practice. For example, it was considered that the ideal combination of these is two-fifths yin mixed with three-fifths yang. The dynamic balance of yin and yang encourages the effective flow of ch'i, which is the subtle energy nutrient that affects our lives.

Ch'i is manipulated by effective feng shui, and this manipulation is facilitated by an understanding of yin and yang.

Shopping streets and ancient vineyards

It is thought that the words "yin" and "yang" originally referred to the dark and light sides of a hill. Just as the French, and perhaps the Californians, are very much preoccupied by determining the south-facing (yang) and north-facing (yin) sides of hills in a vineyard to decide where best to plant vines, so the ancient Chinese were likewise concerned.

One of the simplest precepts of feng shui comes from this basic observation of yin and yang: It is better to have a home, or business, on the north side of a street facing south than to have it on the south side facing north. This is a very general rule and can be modified by many other feng shui rules, but it is amazing to see how often (in the northern hemisphere, at least) it seems to hold true.

■ **South-facing (yang)** *slopes in a vineyard are always the most desirable, since it is here that the best grapes will be produced. It is thought that the contrasting sides of a hill are the origin of yin and yang.*

■ **Here, in Gdansk, Poland,** *south-facing houses present a sunny yang aspect that is as appealing to those passing by as it is to those living within. The dark yin side, opposite, seems cold and forbidding.*

The right side of the street

Just stop and think about the stores in your home town, for a moment. The main street of the suburb where I live presently exemplifies this. The northern side of the street (facing south, and therefore the sunny yang side of the street) is always thronging with shoppers. The north-facing yin side of the street has less than a quarter of the numbers of passersby, despite it being the side of the fire station, police station, and church.

Many more businesses change hands or fail outright on the yin side of this street than on the yang side. This is possibly a result of the lack of shoppers, but then maybe they migrate to the yang side of the street instinctively. Which came first: The lack of shoppers or the bad feng shui? The answer, of course, is that the bad feng shui came first. On a grander scale, all the well-known shops on Oxford Street, (the main shopping street in London) like Selfridges, are located on the yang side of the road facing south. Very few, if any, well-known brand stores are located on the yin side facing north. In New York it's not so easily explained, because many of the great stores are located on the north–south avenues. This is not as clear-cut a yin–yang situation as the north–south contrast.

Think about the main roads in the big city near you, but take your compass along! Remember to check which way the stores are facing: North-facing is yin, south-facing is yang.

Broken and unbroken lines

The sexual symbolism of yin and yang is carried through into their representation on paper. Yin (female) is shown as a broken or penetrated line:

while yang (or male) is shown as an unbroken or penetrating line:

As we shall see later, these broken and unbroken lines are the paper representations of the (sexual) polarity of all things. These broken and unbroken lines are combined together, three at a time, to make one of the building blocks of feng shui, the eight Trigrams.

A simple summary

✓ Yin and yang are at the basis of the binary structure of feng shui.

✓ The yin is the dark, soft, yielding half of any pair. The yang is the bright, hard, firm opposite half.

✓ Yin and yang join together to make Trigrams, which in turn pair together to make Hexagrams.

✓ Hexagrams make up the *I Ching*, perhaps the most important Chinese classic, which allows change to be predicted.

✓ Feng shui (using the same basis) allows change to be made.

Chapter 8

The Trigrams and the Lo Shu

I N THIS CHAPTER WE TAKE a closer look at the eight Trigrams and how they relate to each other, to nature, and to family values. There are two main octagonal arrangements, called a *pa kua* (sometimes spelled *bagua*) layout. This octagon is the first key figure used to unlock many feng shui puzzles. We will also learn about the second key feng shui diagram, the *lo shu*, or nine-chambered square.

In this chapter...

✓ Trigrams and Hexagrams

✓ The eight Trigrams

✓ Former Heaven and Later Heaven Sequences

✓ The lo shu magic square

EACH FAMILY MEMBER HAS HIS OR HER OWN TRIGRAM AND PLACE AT THE TABLE

Trigrams and Hexagrams

THE THREE LINES DRAWN one on top off the other that make up a Trigram are always counted from the bottom line upward, just as you would if you were piling one log upon another. Each line can be either broken (— —, yin, female) or unbroken (——, yang, male). There are eight ways of stacking these three lines, and hence there are eight Trigrams. The Chinese for Trigram is kua. The Chinese for eight is pa. Hence the eight Trigrams are collectively called the pa kua.

A Hexagram ("hexa" means "six" in Greek) is made up of six lines (either yang or yin) stacked one upon another. Like the Trigram, a Hexagram's lines are also counted from the bottom upward.

Hexagrams

In fact, Hexagrams are often viewed as two Trigrams, one placed on top of the other. For this reason, these Hexagrams are also, confusingly, called *kua* in Chinese. There are 64 Hexagrams, which, according to the Chinese, make up every possible combination or stage of change in nature (or in whatever field of endeavor you work). (See chapter 3 for more on the *I Ching*.)

One of the difficulties of translating Chinese feng shui texts is the word "kua," which means both Trigram and Hexagram, depending on context. I will use kua in this book always to mean "Trigram."

■ **Trigram Li:** *reading from the bottom, Li is made of a yang, a yin, and a yang line.*

■ **A Hexagram** *is represented by two Trigrams, one on top of the other.*

The eight Trigrams

THE EIGHT TRIGRAMS *have many associations. However, the most ancient descriptions of them appear as an appendix in the* I Ching, *which may date back to Confucius in the 6th century* BC, *where they are described in a very strange way. At first, the descriptions don't seem to be consistent, even in the range of information they give about each Trigram, but as you work with them, the character of each Trigram will come to the fore. For simplicity, I have reduced these early descriptions to a table, which is illustrated on the next page.*

Some of the correspondences in the table are immediately useful, like color, season, symbol, and direction. Others will become useful as you learn how to use the Trigrams and fit them together. This is covered in the next chapter.

The eight Trigrams and their relationships

The eight Trigrams are a basic part of Chinese culture. They're found, for instance, as a major cultural symbol on the national flag of South Korea, just as the crescent of Islam appears on other national flags. Korea is, of course, not part of China, but it was an area of Chinese cultural influence.

The five Elements and eight Trigrams were considered totally universal. They formed the theoretical basis behind not just feng shui but also acupuncture, acupressure, tui na massage, Chinese herbalism, astrology, food combining, some martial arts, sexual exercises, and a host of other Chinese arts and sciences, even classical landscape painting.

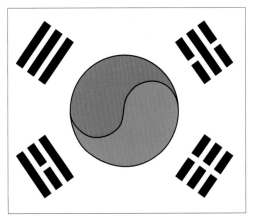

Since a Trigram is a set of three yin (broken) or yang (unbroken) lines, there are precisely eight different ways in which you can combine three yin or yang lines. Therefore, there are eight Trigrams.

■ **Four Trigrams** *are featured in the central motif of South Korea's national flag.*

THE EIGHT TRIGRAMS

TRIGRAM SYMBOL	ELEMENT	DIRECTION		NUMBER	SEASON	COLOR
		*F. H. S.	**L. H. S.			
Ch'ien Heaven	Big Metal	S	NW	6	Late fall	Gold, silver, white
K'un Earth	Big Earth	N	SW	2	Late summer	Yellow
Chen Thunder	Wood	NE	E	3	Spring	Green
K'an Water/Moon	Water	W	N	1	Mid-winter	Black
Ken Mountain	Lesser Earth	NW	NE	8	Early spring	Yellow
Hsun Wind	Lesser Wood	SW	SE	4	Early summer	Green
Li Lightning/Sun	Fire	E	S	9	Summer	Red
Tui Lake	Lesser Metal	SE	W	7	Fall	Gold, silver, white

*Former Heaven Sequence **Later Heaven Sequence

FAMILY	ANIMAL	BODY PART	OTHER ASSOCIATIONS	PINYIN SPELLING
Father	Dragon, horse	Head, lungs	Creative, strength, roundness, vitality, sky, energy, immobility, heavenly sphere, jade, a prince, fruit of trees	*Qian* (pronounced cheen)
Mother	Mare, ox	Stomach, abdomen	Receptive, yielding, nourishment, docility, cloth, cauldron, parsimony, large carts, figures, a multitude, handle	*Kun* (pronounced khoon)
Eldest son	Galloping horse, flying dragon (see also Ch'ien)	Feet	Movement, arousal, motion, development, high roads, decision, vehemence, bamboo, rushes	*Zhen* (pronounced jen)
Middle son	Pig	Ears	Curved objects, flowing water, danger, channels and streams, hidden things, a bow, a wheel, anxiety, a premonition, high spirits, drooping head, thieves, strong trees	*Kan* (pronounced kahn)
Youngest son	Dog, rat, black-billed birds	Hands, fingers	Steadiness, stillness, gates, fruits, seeds, stoppages, paths and roads, small rocks, gates, fruits, cucumbers, porters or eunuchs, finger rings	*Gen* (pronounced ken/gun)
Eldest daughter	Hen/fowl	Thighs	Gentleness, penetration, growth, vegetative growth, length, height, backwards and forwards motion, bald head, broad forehead	*Xun* (pronounced shun)
Middle daughter	Pheasant (or red bird), toad, crab, spiral univalves, mussels, tortoise	Eyes, heart	Clinging, dependence, weapons, drought, brightness, beauty, helmets, spears and swords, dryness	*Li* (pronounced lee)
Youngest daughter	Sheep	Mouth, tongue	Joy, pleasure, serenity, reflections and mirror images, spirit mediums, concubines	*Dui* (pronounced dwee)

The arithmetic of the Trigrams is essentially binary arithmetic. In the early 1700s, Gottfried Leibnitz, the inventor of calculus, recognized that the I Ching was a complex piece of six-bit binary arithmetic. More recently, the Hexagrams have even been compared with the intricacies of the binary code of DNA.

Although the eight Trigrams look similar at first sight, they soon develop their own character as you work with them. The basic definition of each is to be found in one of the appendices of the *I Ching*, and these are summarized in chapter 7 of this book.

Heaven, Earth, and natural phenomena

The main key to the Trigrams is in their titles. Apart from *Ch'ien* (Heaven) and *K'un* (Earth), they are all described in natural phenomena terms, or, in other words, in feng shui terms. These titles are very physical and not mythological, as you might have expected. Each is a very concrete image and they always come in pairs.

After Heaven and Earth come the two heavenly lights, the Sun (*Li* – also Lightning) and the Moon (*K'an*). Then you have two of the Weather ch'i, Thunder (*Chen*) and Wind (*Hsun*). The last two are the two key feng shui landform features, the Mountain (*Ken*) and the Lake (*Tui*). So if we tabulate this, we get two distinct groups which are, of course . . . yin and yang. Suddenly they begin to make sense.

Then, if you put in the Compass Directions using the Former Heaven Sequence (see later in this chapter), you can see that each Trigram forms a pair with its direct opposite.

The Trigrams according to the Former Heaven Sequence

The table below shows the yin–yang split and Compass Directions of the eight Trigrams according to the Former Heaven Sequence.

	YANG			YIN	
S	Heaven	*Ch'ien*	*K'un*	Earth	N
E	Sun	*Li*	*K'an*	Moon	W
NE	Thunder	*Chen*	*Hsun*	Wind	SW
NW	Mountain	*Ken*	*Tui*	Lake	SE

So Heaven and Earth are the Great Yang and the Great Yin in the south and north respectively. Likewise the sun (in the east) faces the moon (in the west) and Thunder (in the northeast) opposes the Wind (in the southwest). Lastly, the Mountain (in the northwest) squares off against the Lake (in the southeast)

Don't confuse the solar heavenly body the Sun with the Trigram that is spelled Hsun (but also sometimes spelled Sun). This is a coincidence, and there is no connection. In fact, to make it easier, we are going to use the older spelling of this Trigram, which is Hsun, indicating more of a "sh" sound at the beginning of the word.

It all adds up to symmetry

So there you have it. Say aloud the pairs again: *Ch'ien–K'un, Li–K'an, Chen–Hsun, Ken–Tui*. Then read down each column: Heaven, the Sun, Thunder, and the Mountain are all stern, strong yang aspects, while Earth, the Moon, and the soft Wind playing across the Lake are all yin and feminine. Easy!

Also reading downward (in the sense of altitude), we go from the Heavenly and its archetypal opposite, through the astronomical Sun and Moon, then the atmosphere (Thunder and Wind), finally to the surface of the Earth with Mountain and Lake.

Isn't that so beautifully symmetrical? See, didn't I tell you that if you got your basic concepts right, the rest would follow?

Now look again at the table opposite. The archetypal things like Heaven and Earth, the Sun and the Moon are all at the four cardinal points. It's easy to see why the Sun is in the east – that is where it rises. The opposite of day is night, so the Moon is in the opposite quarter, west.

■ **Uluru, or Ayers Rock,** *in Australia is a classic example of a mountain with a stern, strong yang aspect.*

The natural phenomena, like mountains, lakes, thunder, and wind, are at the inter-cardinal points of the compass (NW, SW, SE, NE). The Chinese call these the "corner points."

Remember that here we are using the Former Heaven Sequence of the Trigrams, rather than the Later Heaven Sequence. The two sequences are very different, and the usual one found in English feng shui books is the Later Heaven Sequence.

Former Heaven and Later Heaven Sequences

THE EIGHT TRIGRAMS CAN *be arranged in factorial eight ways, or 1 x 2 x 3 x 4 x 5 x 6 x 7 x 8 = 40,320 different ways. Fortunately for us, only two arrangements are used in basic feng shui: The Former Heaven Sequence and the Later Heaven Sequence. (Interestingly, this number, 40,320, is evenly divisible by many of the important feng shui numbers that occur again and again on the feng shui compass, such as 5, 8, 10, 12, 16, 24, 28, 60, 72, 120, and 360.)*

The Former Heaven Sequence, allegedly arranged by the legendary Emperor sage Fu Hsi (2852–2737 BC), is the supposedly ideal arrangement, with everything perfectly positioned as in the table on page 122: It is categorized by yin and yang.

By contrast, the Later Heaven Sequence, supposedly designed by King Wen at the beginning of the Chou dynasty (1027–221 BC), gives the more Earthly and imperfect sequence and is used to map the internal feng shui layout of the home or office. However, if you look at it closely in the same way we looked at the Former Heaven Sequence, you will see how delightfully logical it is.

The Trigrams according to the Later Heaven Sequence

The table below shows the yin/yang split and Compass Directions of the eight Trigrams according to the Later Heaven Sequence.

	YANG			YIN	
NW	Heaven	Ch'ien	Hsun	Wind	SE
S	Sun	Li	K'an	Moon	N
E	Thunder	Chen	Tui	Lake	W
NE	Mountain	Ken	K'un	Earth	SW

The Sun and Moon still oppose each other, but from different quarters, having moved round by 90 degrees. The Mountain (earth) opposes Earth. The Wind is the yin side of Heaven, just as the Lake (water) is the yin side of the Thunder, which brings rain.

Arrangement of the pa kua

Pa kua literally means eight Trigrams, but the phrase has also come to refer to a specific eight-sided figure with the eight Trigrams arranged around its edge.

DEFINITION

The **pa kua** (*or bagua*) is simply the eight Trigrams arranged in an octagon shape, in one of two ways.

The oldest layout, the Former Heaven Sequence, is how the Trigrams are seen on most of the octagonal mirrors so beloved by feng shui practitioners. (See chapter 18 for more about these mirrors.)

The convention of arranging the eight Trigrams in an octagon shape is quite useful in visualizing the eight Directions with which they correspond.

The BHS (or BTB) School of feng shui refers to this as the "stop sign" in remembrance of the octagonal shape of certain road signs.

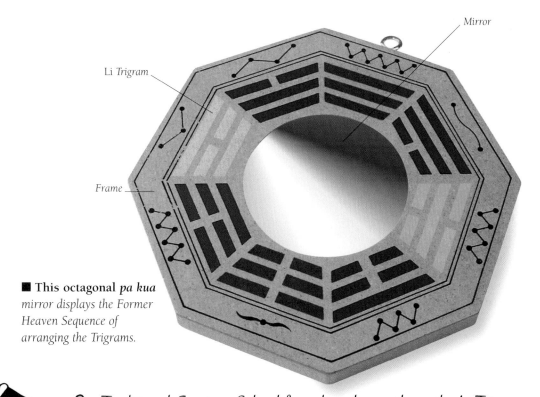

Mirror

Li *Trigram*

Frame

■ **This octagonal *pa kua*** mirror displays the Former Heaven Sequence of arranging the Trigrams.

Traditional Compass School feng shui always places the Li Trigram in the south. But the more recently derived BTB school of feng shui places the Li Trigram furthest from the main door, regardless of actual Compass Directions.

Former Heaven Sequence

The arrangement of the eight Trigrams, or *pa kua*, in these two differing sequences has considerable importance for feng shui. The Former Heaven Sequence, being the ideal version, is applicable to Heavenly matters.

It is therefore used for the feng shui of the ancestors, the feng shui of grave-sites. It is also used to measure the influences of the outside of a building, the part that is open to Heaven.

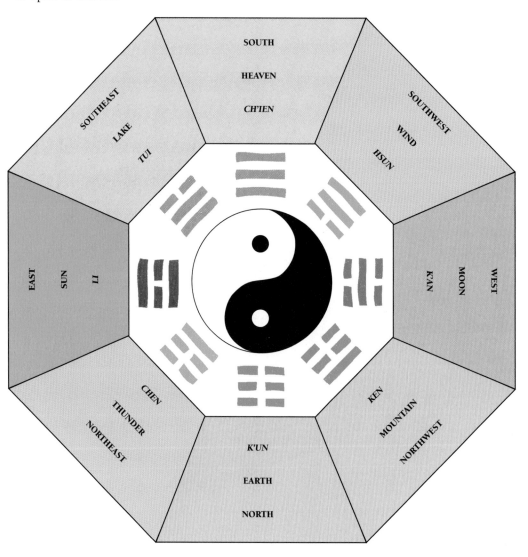

NB: All Trigram lines are traditionally read as if standing in the center looking outward.

Later Heaven Sequence

On the other hand, the Later Heaven Sequence is used for the houses or offices of the living. Specifically, it should be used for determining Directions and locations inside the home or office.

It is therefore the sequence that will concern us most in this book.

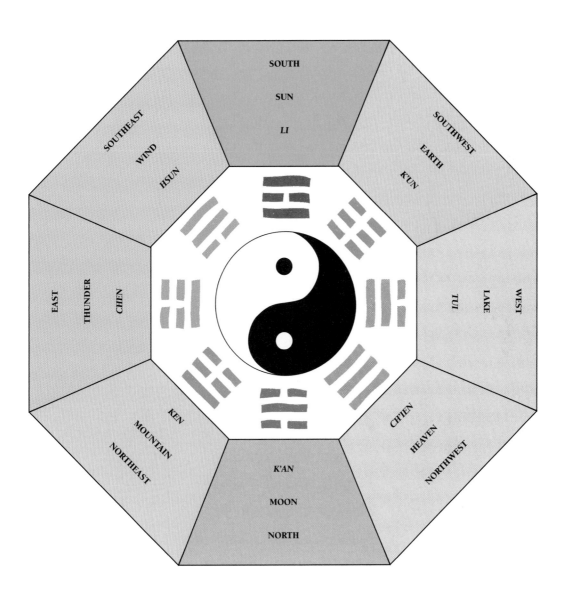

The family and its place on the pa kua

From here on we will be dealing almost entirely with the Later Heaven Sequence. The *pa kua* is a versatile and essential part of feng shui, cosmology, and many other facets of Chinese culture. It will come as no surprise, therefore, that the *pa kua* can also be used to define the ideal family, attributing a Trigram to each family member. This is of practical use when you are trying to determine the effect of a feng shui change on specific members of the family.

All the female (yin) members of the family are arrayed on the right, while all the male (yang) members of the family are on the left. At the very simplest level, these might be used for arranging family members around a table, although without a full complement of six children it might be a bit tricky.

Family members and their Trigrams

In the following table you can again see the principles of yin/yang pairing in action:

	YANG			YIN	
SW	Father	*Ch'ien*	*K'un*	Mother	NW
E	Eldest son	*Chen*	*Hsun*	Eldest daughter	SE
N	Middle son	*K'an*	*Li*	Middle daughter	S
NE	Youngest son	*Ken*	*Tui*	Youngest daughter	W

The lo shu magic square

THE LO SHU MAGIC SQUARE *is one of the oldest and major keys to the understanding of practical feng shui. It is a 3 x 3 tic-tac-toe grid containing the numbers 1 to 9, but in a very special order. The number 9, being the largest yang number, is aligned with the south, while the smallest yang number, 1, is aligned with the north. Remember, odd numbers are yang, and even numbers are yin.*

Let us consider the original "base" *lo shu*, which always has "5" in the center cell. Tradition says that this square dates back to the reign of Emperor Yu (2205–2197 BC). The story of the introduction of the *lo shu* into Chinese culture is an ancient one. The myth says that the *lo shu* was a map engraved on the back of a tortoise that emerged from the

4	9	2
3	5	7
8	1	6

BASE *LO SHU*

river Lo, hence its name, *"lo shu,"* which means "river Lo map." The nine "cells" engraved on the shell of the tortoise were not filled with numbers, but instead contained dots, the total of which added up to the number shown in each cell. The tortoise is a very important feng shui animal.

Symbolic connections

There are all sorts of symbolic connections in this story. The tortoise is symbolic of the north. The sage Emperor Yu, who saw the tortoise emerging from the water, was responsible for taming the great floods in China with hydraulic works, so the *lo shu* in a sense "controls" the Water that is so much a part of feng shui.

A variant of this story says that Fu Hsi (an earlier Emperor, 2852–2737 BC) gave the square to Yu in a mysterious mountain cavern. Think back to chapter 3 and you'll remember that Fu Hsi was the inventor of the Trigrams, and hence the basis of the *I Ching*. So there's a real connection between the *lo shu* square and the eight Trigrams of Fu Hsi – tortoises, water, and feng shui. Think about it!

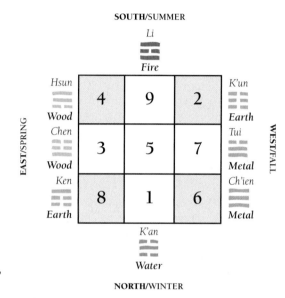

■ **Once the eight Trigrams** *are added to the base* lo shu, *it becomes a key feng shui diagram that can be used to plan the layout of your home or office.*

We can therefore make the *lo shu* square more meaningful by adding the eight trigrams. It will come as no surprise to discover that the nine cells of the *lo shu* neatly coincide with the eight Trigrams arranged in the Later Heaven Sequence, plus a center cell assigned to Earth.

Why is the lo shu square magic?

The *lo shu* square is magic because the numbers placed in its nine cells add up to 15, regardless of the direction in which you add them, even diagonally.

The number 9 represents Heaven and yang. The number 6 represents Earth. So Heaven and Earth in harmony is the sum of 9 + 6 = 15, and each direction of the lo shu adds up to 15.

THE LO SHU IN OTHER CULTURES

As well as in China, the *lo shu* square has been part of traditional magic in Europe, the Middle East, and North Africa for at least 2,000 years. In Arab, Hebrew, and other Middle Eastern magical traditions, there are seven squares, each associated with one of the seven classical planets: Saturn, Jupiter, Mars, the sun, Mercury, Venus, and the moon. (The ancients were not aware of Uranus, Neptune, or Pluto, and often referred to the sun and the moon as planets.)

Each planet had a square, of which the simplest was the Square of Saturn (3 x 3 = 9 cells), and the most complex was the square of the Moon (9 x 9 = 81 cells). Each planetary square adds up to the same number, whichever way you add it (up, down, sideways, or diagonally). These seven planetary squares are called *kameas*.

Fortunately for us, we need be interested only in the simplest square, the 3 x 3 square of Saturn. Make sure you make no mistake: I said Saturn, the god of agriculture and mining, not Satan! This square was also considered to be the square of earth, so here we have an amazing link because, of course, feng shui is very much concerned with energy in the earth beneath our feet.

But even more amazing, each square has a special zigzag path linking the cells in numerical order. Despite this, the zigzag line (one out of many thousands of possible lines) is exactly the same on the square of Saturn in the Middle East as it is on the *lo shu* in China.

It is not easy to say which came first, the Square of Saturn in the Middle East or the *lo shu* in China. Using the dates of its discovery by Yu in China, it is tempting to say that the square is oldest in China. But the mystery remains as to why there are seven perfect planetary squares in the Middle East but apparently only one in China.

A further clue is that, in the Middle East, each cell was associated with a letter, but in China it is not (because the Chinese do not have an alphabet as such). So it seems more likely that the seven squares began their life in the Middle East because that is where the tradition is most complete. Only the 3 x 3 Square of Saturn made the journey along the Silk Route to China.

Then again, Emperor Yu really could have discovered the universal truth of these magic squares independently of the Middle East on the back of a tortoise climbing out of the river Lo.

Using the lo shu with the eight Trigrams

To use the *lo shu* square, simply place it over a plan of your home or office. The *lo shu* square containing "9," the strongest yang number, should be placed over the south side of your home, while the square containing "1," the smallest yang number, should be placed on the northern side of your home. If your home has its main walls pointing to the cardinal points of the compass, then it will fit nicely over the floor plan. If, on the other hand, the corners of your home point to the cardinal points of the compass, the *lo shu* is placed in a diagonal fashion, so that "9" still coincides with the south. You will learn how to interpret this when we do specific feng shui formulas in chapter 17.

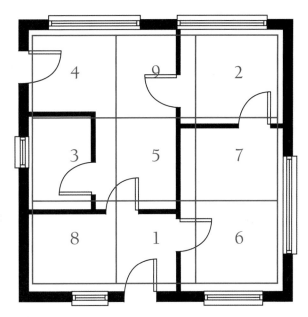

■ **Making the *lo shu* square** *fit the house plan is the key to interpreting the feng shui.*

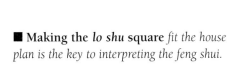

A simple summary

✔ The eight Trigrams, or *pa kua*, have a number of color, Direction, family, and other correspondences.

✔ The two arrangements of the eight Trigrams are: Former Heaven Sequence and Later Heaven Sequence.

✔ The Former Heaven Sequence is used on the outside, but the Later Heaven Sequence is used indoors.

✔ The *pa kua* is arranged as an octagonal allocation of the eight Trigrams to the eight Compass Points.

✔ The family structure is also reflected in the eight Trigrams.

✔ The magic *lo shu* square is a key feng shui diagram that adds up to 15, regardless of the direction in which it is counted.

PART THREE

WOOD IS ASSOCIATED WITH THE EAST AND SOUTHEAST

THE FENG SHUI OF INTERIORS

IT'S NOW TIME TO give theory a rest and get down to some *practical interior* feng shui by dealing with ch'i flow and alignments inside the home and office. We will look at how feng shui *relates to you*, how it can help you in arranging the rooms in your home or office to concentrate the most *beneficial energy* for various aspects of your life.

We deal with the rooms in which you spend a lot of time and look at the effects of water on the feng shui of your home. Corridors and stairs are another important part of the home, as they conduct ch'i through the house.

As well as seeing how color can be used to change the feng shui of the interior, we will look at how feng shui affects business and how to use it to your best advantage in your particular office.

Chapter 9

Feng Shui Inside Your Home

Most Western books on feng shui stress interior furniture and furnishing arrangements. But before we deal with the rules for that, we need to look at the layout of rooms within the house. There are eight different types of home or building, according to the eight possible facing directions: north, south, east, west, northeast, northwest, southeast, and southwest. The auspiciousness of different parts of the house for specific functions, such as bedroom or kitchen, changes according to the direction in which the house faces.

In this chapter...

✓ The layout of rooms within the house

✓ House types and their Trigrams

✓ Doors and windows

✓ The front door – ch'i mouth of the house

AS THE "MOUTH" OF THE HOUSE, THE FRONT DOOR DETERMINES THE TYPE OF CH'I THAT ENTERS

The layout of rooms within the house

NOT ALL ROOMS IN THE HOME are equally important. The rule to remember is that the important rooms are those in which you spend most of your time. Hence these rooms are your bedroom, living room or TV room, study, and dining room. Also important rooms, but for negative reasons, are the "wet rooms" where water is used: your bathrooms and kitchen. These have a special effect on the feng shui of the house. The kitchen also holds a special place in feng shui analysis, not only because it contains live examples of the two Elements Fire and Water, but also because it is where the food, or nutriment, for the family is prepared.

HUO (FIRE)

SHUI (WATER)

Feng shui is fairly specific about the layout of rooms within the home. However, you and I don't always have control over the layout of the rooms in our home. When an architect designs a home or an office, he starts with a blank sheet of paper and can theoretically put specific rooms, like the bedroom or kitchen, wherever he pleases. If, however, the house is already built, then constraints of plumbing and corridor access will force us to use particular rooms in specific ways. For example, it is not likely you would be able to, or would want to, change a bathroom into a bedroom.

We can summarize the basic rules by thinking about the requirements of ch'i in the house:

1 Ch'i should be invited in via an uncluttered and welcoming front door that is at the same time protected from *sha ch'i*.

2 Ch'i should be encouraged to circulate freely around the home, neither stagnating nor rushing through rapidly.

3 Ch'i should be activated where beneficial, but pressed down upon when inauspicious.

Traditional Chinese courtyard houses

The rules regarding where the rooms are placed in the layout of the home are in part based on the old Chinese house style with a central open courtyard. In this layout, the head of the family's bedroom was toward the back of the house. Then children's bedrooms should be ranged on the yang eastern side (where the ch'i is stronger) and grandparents' bedrooms (assuming a multi-generation household) on the west or more yin side, befitting their declining years. On p. 154, I explain the relationship between the various members of the family and their seating position around the dining table. This same arrangement can also be used to select the location of bedrooms for individual family members.

On p. 154, I explain the relationship between the various members of the family and their seating position around the dining table.

DEFINITION

Sheng ch'i is strong and beneficial ch'i energy. More specifically, it can be ch'i that comes from your best direction.

The central courtyard of a traditional house is open to the sky and so receives rain and *sheng ch'i* directly from Heaven. In some modern houses, including Lillian Too's, I have seen this principle adapted by leaving a roof opening to supply natural rainwater directly to an indoor pool. Although some feng shui Masters counsel against the idea of having an interior pool at all, it seems to work very well for her!

It is also a feng shui rule that private rooms, like the bathroom, should be located a long way from the front door. Likewise, semi-public rooms where entertaining occurs should be near the front door. The further into a house you move, the more private the rooms should become.

Trivia...

This all sounds very similar to Roman courtyard houses with their atria and impluvia open to the rain. Courtyard houses have a long tradition in Mediterranean and Latin American countries. It's interesting that a similar approach to housing developed in China and the West.

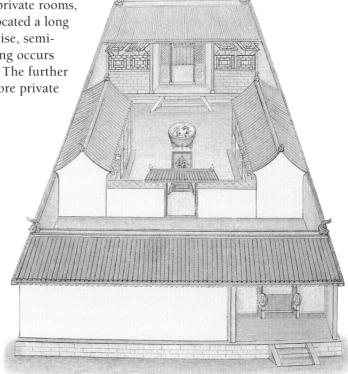

■ **Old Chinese houses** *were built with open courtyards designed to receive rain and beneficial ch'i directly from Heaven.*

If you are lucky enough to be building your own home or office from scratch, consider what each room should be used for, rather than leaving it up to the architect.

In a business, the same feng shui principle prevails, and it is common feng shui practice to locate the office of the CEO a long way from both the main entrance and the service entrance. Common sense you might think, but the common sense option is always worth a second look.

Problem areas

It is a general principle that areas considered troublesome in a house need to be either "pressed down upon" or left as undisturbed as possible. By troublesome, I mean rooms located in the less auspicious areas of the house, or wet rooms. These rooms should preferably not be used as principal living, eating, or sleeping rooms, and they should be left relatively undisturbed, where they will not, in turn, disturb the balance of your luck.

■ **If you happen** *to be building a house from scratch, or perhaps extending your current home, don't just leave the plans up to the architect – think about what each room will be used for, and consider the feng shui implications.*

I know that many of you have to make do with the rooms you already have and may not have all the space you need. But even if you have the luxury to pick which bedroom you can sleep in or which room becomes the home office, don't immediately grab the largest or the one with the best view. Instead, take some time and do a few calculations.

If you are already settled in your home, take a few minutes to see whether swapping a bedroom with another family member might just improve your personal feng shui immensely – and maybe their feng shui, too.

House types and their Trigrams

DEPENDING UPON THE TYPE OF HOUSE or its facing direction, certain rooms are better suited for some functions than others. Locations that have a beneficial configuration should be used as living rooms, dining rooms, or bedrooms, while those parts of your home that have less positive energies should be used less, or used as storerooms or wet rooms. By locating storerooms or closets in these negative areas, they will tend to keep "quiet."

To discover the best locations you will need to judge which way your house is facing. This is usually the direction of the front door, but more detailed rules for judging the facing direction of your house are elaborated on in chapter 20. Depending upon the facing direction, each house is allocated a specific Trigram. So, for example, a house that faces east will be a "*Tui* house," while one that faces north will be a "*Li* house."

If you look at the first line of the table on the next page, a *Li* house should preferably have its living, dining, and sleeping quarters in the E, SE, N, or S parts of the house. On the other hand, its guest bedrooms, storerooms, and wet rooms, like the kitchen and bathroom, will be better placed in the NE, SW, W, and NW parts of the house. This is only a general rule, so don't worry too much if your house is not perfect. There are other more important considerations, which we will examine in the next four chapters.

■ **To work out** *which parts of a house have beneficial or negative energies, and to determine which rooms are best situated where, you must know the direction in which your home faces.*

BEST ROOM LOCATIONS

Once you know the direction in which your house is facing, you can use the following table to help you to decide where different rooms are best situated in your home. The best directions are listed in descending order from left to right.

Facing direction	House type Trigram	Best location for living, dining, bedrooms	Best location for storage, bathrooms, toilets, kitchens
N	Li	E, SE, N, S	NE, SW, W, NW
NE	K'un	NE, W, NW, SW	E, S, SE, N
E	Tui	NW, SW, NE, W	N, SE, S, E
SE	Ch'ien	W, NE, SW, NW	SE, N, E, S
S	K'an	SE, E, S, N	W, NW, NE, SW
SW	Ken	SW, NW, W, NE	S, E, N, SE
W	Chen	S, N, SE, E	SW, NE, NW, W
NW	Hsun	N, S, E, SE	NW, W, SW, NE

■ **In a south-facing** K'an *house, the ideal location for a bedroom is in the southeast portion of the home. Another feng shui principle worth bearing in mind is that windows facing south or southeast should also be larger than those facing north.*

Doors and windows

DOORS ARE ALSO A VERY IMPORTANT consideration, because ch'i energy flows along corridors and through doors. This flow should be gentle and sinuous. It is therefore considered bad feng shui to have three doorways lined up in a row – indeed, two is bad enough. Several feng shui books on the market have illustrated this principle as if the problem were having three doors lined up on the same wall, like in a hotel corridor. This is not the problem.

The problem is where you have three doors opening in succession, so that the ch'i can pass through each in a straight line, encouraging the ch'i flow to increase its speed. Remember that ch'i should circulate slowly in lazy curves, not zip along rapidly in a straight line. In such a situation, try distracting the ch'i to slow it down by hanging a wind chime in its path.

Doors in apartments

Apartments in apartment buildings have an extra feng shui dimension in that they have two "front" doors: the main exterior building door, plus the apartment door. It's important to know which you should consider as the door to determine the facing or sitting direction. Just remember that it is the mouth of ch'i that counts, so obviously it's the outer building door direction that is the most important.

A studio or one-room apartment is a special case because there are no, or few, internal partitions. The studio is a world on its own. Since the front door opens directly onto the main living area,

■ **In a loft or studio apartment,** *the front door opens onto the main living area, giving little protection from sha ch'i. However, when there are few internal walls, a feng shui practitioner has more maneuverability to enhance different sectors of the living space.*

thought has to be given to protecting the studio from *sha ch'i*. Obviously the front door of a studio opens right into the room, so there is very little protection from the direct entry of unwanted energies.

In traditional dwellings, a screen would be erected immediately inside (or outside) the door so that anyone or anything entering would have to proceed around the screen rather than barging straight in.

In traditional Chinese thought, evil influences tended to travel in straight lines and therefore could not manage the maneuver of rounding a screen.

If space is limited, such a screen may well be impractical. Hence the opportunities for controlling the ch'i flow into the studio are limited.

Windows

Windows should help to keep the balance of yin and yang. Tiny windows, like in a medieval castle, are bad feng shui as they tend to keep the interior too dark and gloomy, in other words too yin. At the other end of the scale, huge panorama windows that let in masses of sunlight, flooding a home with heat and light and letting everybody see in, are too yang. The room must be protected, yet it must not be gloomy.

■ **A spacious, light-filled room** *that's relatively free of clutter is uplifting and comforting for its occupants. This room also has the benefit of a peaceful and plant-filled view.*

Remember, for good feng shui there should be about three-fifths yang to two-fifths yin, and this applies especially to lighting.

Another consideration concerns what you can see through the window from the room. If you can see anything that might be overpowering or produce poison arrows, then it's best to screen the window or even regularly pull the curtains. Typical examples of such poison arrows include:

- Huge adjacent blocks of apartments looming over your home.
- The cutting edge of a building directly aligned with your window.
- A roadway coming directly at the window before turning sharply left or right.
- Any one of a number of pointed objects like TV aerials or church steeples.

What you can't see can't hurt you. From a strictly feng shui point of view, the ostrich was right! The reason is that negative visual alignments can't exist if there is no visibility.

Inside doors

Windows and inside doors are entry points for ch'i to the room. An easy way to work out where you shouldn't sit or sleep is to imagine that the ch'i entering the room is like a draft.

If the window and the door are in a line, a draft will blow from one to another. Now you know not to sit in a draft, or at least that's what my grandfather always told me. Likewise, you should not sit in a ch'i draft, especially not with your back facing a doorway or, to a lesser extent, a window.

■ **Positioned between** *an open door and the window, an armchair sits right in the middle of a ch'i draft, which is not conducive to comfort.*

The front door – ch'i mouth of the house

THE FRONT DOOR MATTERS *above most other feng shui considerations. It is through this that the bulk of the all-important ch'i enters the building. Ch'i enters the building in other ways – through open windows and side doors – but the front door is the most important entry point for ch'i.*

The entrance to the whole house, the "mouth of the house," is extremely important in a feng shui diagnosis. Depending on the direction in which it points, the house will "breathe in" a different kind of ch'i. Remember that ch'i is sometimes called "cosmic breath," and here we are examining what sort of cosmic breath enters your house.

When considering the feng shui of a building, try to visualize the path that the ch'i breath takes as it flows through the house. The main entry point for ch'i is, of course, the mouth of the house, the front door. The real reason why the direction in which the front door faces is so important in feng shui is that this direction influences the type of ch'i entering the building. This is also why it's essential to use a compass to determine exactly what type of ch'i this is, in order to make any kind of feng shui diagnosis.

FRONT DOOR FENG SHUI

1 A front door should open onto an uncramped hall space containing no clutter.

2 A front door should never directly open onto a bathroom door.

3 A front door should not open onto a mirror, which will deflect good ch'i entering the building directly out again.

4 There should not be any obstructions that prevent the door opening totally.

5 There should not be a bathroom on the floor directly above the front door, as this will taint the ch'i entering the building.

Ssu ch'i

I will try to make the concept that a house "inhales" ch'i through its front door a little clearer. Try visualizing yourself lying on the ground with a pile of stinking rubbish in front of your face. Now imagine that, like the house, you are unable to move. You can imagine how breathing in these bad odors, day in and day out, will affect your view of the world and indeed your health.

You must also look at the house as if it's a living organism. If its front door is pointed at an alley full of trash cans, the ch'i entering the house will be tainted, or *ssu ch'i*, rather than the bright, energetic *sheng ch'i* that you need for the occupants of the house to flourish. Thinking more along these lines, the front door should not face stagnant water, a graveyard (very yin *ssu ch'i*), or a slaughterhouse.

Even facing a place where many people come and go, such as a sports ground, is bad because it regularly disturbs the ch'i.

There are reasons not to live near a church or temple, because the energy they give off is not conducive to quality home life. Other institutions that are not good to face include hospitals, police stations, bars, funeral homes, and even social security offices. So many confused emotions – so much disturbed ch'i. In a less extreme way, the reason why the East Life/West Life school works (see chapter 20) is that even good ch'i must be a type of ch'i suitable for you. This helps explain why some houses feel good for some people, but bad for others.

The ming tang

One of the simplest things you can do to improve your feng shui is to clear up the area in front of your front door. Ideally, there should be a wide open space, called a *ming tang*, to collect beneficial ch'i and feed it to the house.

The direction in which the door points determines the sort of ch'i that enters the house. We know from chapter 8 that each of the eight Directions is attributed to one of the Trigrams. This tells you what sort of ch'i you can expect to flow from each quarter. The sort of ch'i that enters a door facing

■ **The front of a house** *should have an open area, or* ming tang, *where ch'i can collect before entering through the front door.*

south, for example, is that which is conditioned by the Trigram *Ch'ien*, or Heaven. It is strong, masculine yang ch'i, and the opposite of the ch'i that enters through a door facing north, which will receive the more yin type of ch'i associated with the Trigram *K'un*, or Earth. This is why the direction in which the door faces is most important and especially affects more advanced feng shui like Flying Star feng shui.

■ **A straight paved path** *pointed directly at this house delivers negative energy right to the front door. The gate posts add to the effect of the "poison arrows."*

Remember that the outside of a building is governed by the Earlier Heaven Sequence of the Trigrams, not the Later Heaven Sequence of Trigrams that apply to the interior of the building. Hence in this sequence, Ch'ien is in the south, not Li.

Poison arrows and the front door

The next thing you should do is check to see if any obvious alignments are aimed at your front door forming poison arrows. If such a configuration exists pointing toward the front door, then try to deflect it with something or block it off with a hedge or low wall.

If this fails, and the poison arrow is caused by a major alignment, then hang an octagonal *pa kua* mirror over your door pointing in the offending direction to send back the *sha ch'i* to whence it came. Never just hang these mirrors up for fun, and certainly never hang them inside your home or office.

A simple summary

✓ There are eight different types of homes, and they are classified by using the eight Trigrams.

✓ Each of these types of house has different preferred locations for their good and bad rooms.

✓ Rooms like the living or dining room, study, and bedrooms need to be located in the positive locations, while wet rooms, guest bedrooms, and utility rooms should be located in the negative locations.

✓ An open central courtyard allows for the entry of Heaven ch'i.

✓ Doors and windows can cause ch'i drafts, so make sure your bed or chair is not located in one.

✓ The front door is the main ch'i entry point for the house, and should ideally look out upon an open space, or *ming tang*.

✓ A front door should not open onto a bathroom, obstructions, cramped space, or a mirror.

Chapter 10

Living Rooms, Dining Rooms, Bedrooms

THIS CHAPTER IS CONCERNED more with the yang rooms in the house, those in which we spend a lot of our time and that have heavy traffic from all family members. Living rooms are often the main location for feng shui corrections. Dining rooms are special because food symbolizes the nourishment of the whole family. We consider the special requirements of bedrooms, which are slightly more yin rooms. In each case, we look at the layout of the furniture within the rooms. Finally, we look at children's bedrooms, which have special requirements.

In this chapter...

✓ Living room and furniture placement

✓ Dining room: nourishment for the family

✓ Bedrooms

✓ Children's bedrooms

A COZY FIREPLACE FORMS A BETTER FOCUS TO A LIVING ROOM THAN THE UBIQUITOUS TELEVISION SET

Living room and furniture placement

THE LIVING ROOM *is the focus of family activities, and one of the most used rooms, after the bedrooms, in any house. Often the living room can become the main room for the installation of feng shui-related improvements. The living room thus becomes a microcosm for the whole house, with changes made here affecting the feng shui of the whole household.*

There are some rules that should be observed when considering furniture placement in this or any room:

● Make sure that the general furniture layout is such that there are no cut off corners where ch'i can stagnate.
● Try to arrange the chairs so that no chair has its back to any doorway.
● Look to see if you, and indeed ch'i, can walk easily through the room without bumping into furniture or catching on sharp edges. If not, then streamline the furniture placement.
● Minimize any convex sharp edges that might create secret arrows by draping them or allowing indoor plants to cover them.
● Try to avoid L-shaped furniture configurations. Sharp edges include the convex right-angled protruding corner that will always be found in any L-shaped rooms.
● Make sure that the room is reasonably lit – the living room needs to be more yang than yin.

The living room can also be treated as a microcosm of the whole house – in other words, a little representation of the whole house.

● To open out conversation and interest onto other things, try not to design the room so that the TV is the focus. It's a common modern design habit to focus the room on the TV, just as in past times the focus used to be on the fireplace.
● Try to position the TV and hi-fi on the west or northwest (Metal) sides of the room (the reasons for this will become obvious in chapter 17).
● If there are multiple entrances, thought should be given to the flow of ch'i through the room so that one entrance alone becomes the main one.
● Chairs should not be placed in confrontational positions, such as directly facing each other (except around the dining table). Try to position them at 90- or 45-degree angles to each other.

- Friendly groupings are better than a rigid L-shaped configuration of furniture, or a line of chairs backed against the wall.
- Try to avoid placing chairs under any overhead beams. If you can't avoid beams, attach ch'i conductors like flutes to the beams to allow disturbed ch'i concentrations to drain harmlessly away.
- Try to orientate any chair that is regularly used by specific members of the family to face in one of their four personal best directions (see chapter 20).
- The general yin/yang balance of the room should be checked, so if there is much dark, heavy furniture (yin), this should be balanced by light, bright hangings, wall colors, or lighting.
- A centrally positioned chandelier is very good feng shui, because it introduces much yang light. Also, as it is symbolic of Fire, in the Production Cycle of the Elements it produces Earth, which is the Element of the central area of the *pa kua*.

Changing a sector of the room

Where you find you cannot make an Eight Mansion (see chapter 17) feng shui change on a whole house basis, you can simply use the correct sector of the living room to get over this problem.

For example, if you wanted to install an Eight Mansion feng shui change or remedy in the southwest corner of a house, but find the room in this sector is unsuitable to make the change (like a bathroom), then instead make the change to the southwest corner of the living room.

■ **Bookcases or shelves** *act like knife blades, generating cutting ch'i, so these should be minimized if possible, for example by hanging doors on all open shelves.*

Dining room: nourishment for the family

THE DINING ROOM IS WHERE THE FAMILY EATS. *In the Chinese world, eating well and prosperity are closely linked in a way that does not occur in the West. The multi-course meals of the Chinese banquet are examples of this belief. The larger the number of courses, so, symbolically, the greater the apparent prosperity of the family giving the banquet. Hence the setting for the dining room is an important feng shui consideration.*

This concept is reflected in feng shui practice by a common recommendation to symbolically double the quantity of food by placing a mirror opposite the dining room table. The mirror, however, must not reflect another mirror on the opposite wall, giving rise to infinite and confusing reflections, which in turn confuse the ch'i.

Under some circumstances, ch'i is personified as a way of expressing its actions, but you must never lose sight of the fact that ch'i is a form of energy.

General concerns

- Because the dining room is central to the nourishment of the whole family, ideally it should be a room close to the center of the home. It certainly should not open directly onto the street or onto public areas.
- If the house is multistory, try to ensure that the dining room table is not located directly under a bathroom on the floor above. Obviously it's not good to have the source of the family's nourishment pressed down upon by foul water. To a lesser extent, the dining room should not be beneath a kitchen for the same reason.
- Any paintings in the room should be of food or other good fortune subjects. Paintings of peaches or oranges are considered in Chinese culture to be particularly fortunate. The orange, because of its golden color, symbolizes wealth, while the peach has an overtone of longevity and family fecundity.
- Try to arrange the furnishings on the table so that all members of the family have a clear view of each other. The practice in old-fashioned homes or restaurants of having a heavy centerpiece containing flowers or condiments is to be avoided.
- Try to minimize the potential sources of yin energy in this room; for example, avoid heavy antiques or other darkly colored decoration.

■ **A central light fixture** *is good feng shui, provided it's not too heavy and overbearing. The dining room table should be round, or have rounded corners. Use yang colors to decorate the dining room: Earth tones are appropriate if the room is located at the center of the home, which is associated with the Element Earth.*

- The energy in this room should be predominantly yang (as opposed to the bedroom, which should be predominantly yin). Hence decoration should be with positive yang colors, like red, pink, yellow, orange, or bright green.
- If the dining room is indeed at the center of the home, then this area is also associated with the Element Earth, so yellows and earth tones would be most appropriate in that case.
- If possible, no chairs should point their seatbacks in the direction of the doorway, leaving their occupant vulnerable and unsupported.
- The seat of the main breadwinner, in particular, should have its back firmly against a supporting wall.
- Do not allow the dining table to be oppressed by an overhead beam or large and heavy chandelier.

- The dining room should not open directly onto any one of the wet rooms of the house, for example the toilet, bathroom, or even the kitchen itself. This is because these areas of water drainage can deplete the otherwise beneficial ch'i of the dining room. Of course, common health regulations usually forbid the first two mentioned from opening directly onto the dining room.
- For the same reason, but less importantly, it is advisable for the dining room not to share a common wall with a bathroom.

SEATING FAMILY MEMBERS AT THE TABLE

It is important for individual family members to select the correct seat at the dining room table. This is calculated by reference to the association between individual family members and the Trigrams (see chapter 8).

There is an ideal format that suggests a round or octagonal table, with each member of the household seated in the position occupied by their Trigram in the Later Heaven Sequence. For example, the male head of the household should sit in the northwest, the position occupied by the Trigram *Ch'ien*, or Heaven; the Mother sitting in the southwest where the Trigram *K'un* falls, while the youngest daughter should sit in the west by the Trigram *Tui*.

Another more practical arrangement is to have everyone facing one of their four best directions, especially their *sheng ch'i* if at all possible (see chapter 20).

■ **The dining table** *seating arrangement is very important for Chinese families, with senior members given first choice at the table's "best seat." Seats are often arranged according to the occupants' best directions, as determined by their birthdays.*

Bedrooms

THE BEDROOM IS ONE OF THE KEY ROOMS for feng shui, because we spend about a third of our lives there. As we saw earlier, even at a cellular level, the body responds to the magnetic field of the Earth, and hence the direction of alignment of the bed is particularly important.

Everyone who has slept in different hotels will know that in the morning you can wake feeling much more rested than you ever do at home, or you can wake feeling as if you are fit for nothing. Barring the bed itself, or the state of the air conditioning, this huge difference is often the result of sleeping in a different and sometimes non-beneficial direction. In chapter 20, I will show you how to calculate these *kua* directions for yourself.

If you have a choice of bedrooms, choose one in a part of your home that corresponds to one of your best directions.

Someone with a kua number of two would do well to choose a bedroom in the southwest of their home for rest, or the northeast of their home, as that is their sheng ch'i direction.

A bedroom should be a place of rest, and therefore predominantly yin. As such, the bedroom should not be too heavily activated with feng shui remedies. You should specifically not have water features or too many living plants in your bedroom.

There are a number of do's and don'ts in the bedroom:

- Do not sleep directly under a beam, as it will interrupt your sleep with disturbed descending ch'i, or, if you prefer to have a more psychological explanation, it will subconsciously pose a threat hanging above your sleeping head.

■ **The headboard** *should be positioned up against a wall to provide maximum support. However, it is not beneficial to have it under a sloping ceiling.*

- Don't sleep under overhanging built-in cupboards, as these are very bad feng shui indeed.
- Make sure that you can see the door from the bed, so that it is not possible for anybody to creep up on you unawares. Such a situation is unconsciously disturbing.
- Do not position the bed with your feet pointing directly at the door, a position commonly referred to as the coffin position.
- Do not position the bed so that it is directly between the door and a window, in a straight line, as the resultant rush of a ch'i draft will not be conducive to a good night's rest.
- Make sure you have adequate support behind the bed in the form of a headboard placed firmly against a wall.
- You should not have empty space or a window behind the bed, as this removes its support.
- The door to the bedroom should not line up directly with a staircase as that will mean a strong ch'i flow into or out of the bedroom. In this case, use a very strong uplighter on the ceiling just outside the door and try to keep that door closed.
- Likewise, a bedroom door should preferably not directly face another door across a corridor.

Hang a red and gold double happiness sign written in Chinese calligraphy in the southwest corner of your bedroom to strengthen your relationship or marriage.

DOUBLE HAPPINESS SIGN

- Make sure that you cannot see your reflection in any mirror from the bed, and especially don't have ceiling mirrors above the bed. Despite the *Playboy* ambiance, this configuration can have serious ill effects on your relationship.
- Make sure that no sharp wall or major furniture corners point directly toward the bed. This is often the case in an L-shaped bedroom.
- Any bedroom open shelves should be covered or enclosed with doors as they act like cutting knives aimed at the sleeper.
- Be sure not to sleep with a bathroom door opening directly onto your bed. The water will drain the beneficial bedroom ch'i.
- Try not to have too many yang electrical devices in the bedroom, such as TVs or computers.
- Do not place indoor plants in the bedroom as they are quite yang.
- Do not put water features in the bedroom, as they will tend to disturb sleep, and can also provoke bad luck.
- Your bed should never back onto a closed-up fireplace, as this will certainly drain much of the romance out of your relationship.

Bed positioning

As you will learn in chapter 20, everyone has four good directions and four bad directions out of the eight possible directions: N, S, E, W, NW, SW, NE, and SE. After you have taken the above into account, try to sleep with your head pointing toward your best direction, or *sheng ch'i*. Or, to get a better night's sleep, point your head toward your fourth best direction.

It is sometimes very tempting to put the bed diagonally into a corner just to achieve one of these directions. Don't do this, as the resultant triangular hollow behind the headboard will leave you with no support.

It is much more important that the head of a bed is properly supported and does not have a big gap behind it, than that you should catch one of these directions.

■ **It's bad feng shui** *for a bed to back into a corner, because the hollow provides no support. Close proximity to two windows also places it in a draft, which the Chinese believe can cause headaches.*

Children's bedrooms

A CHILD'S BEDROOM poses an interesting dilemma for the feng shui practitioner. On the one hand, it's a place that will see lots of bright yang play, but, on the other, it should be sufficiently yin to lull the child to sleep at the end of the day. The last thing any parent wants is a hyperactive child late at night.

This can be partly solved by painting the room with light, bright yang colors for daytime use, but arranging the curtains and lighting so that a more yin atmosphere can be created in the evening.

The main light source should not be directly over the head of the bed, although a reading light can be positioned to one side.

In a general sense, placing the child's bedroom to the NE, E, or SE of the house is more yang and therefore more appropriate than to have the bedroom on the NW, SW, or W side of the home.

■ **A child's bedroom** *should be free from clutter, and the headboard of the bed should be firmly up against the wall. The small shelf over this bed is not acceptable as it will make the child feel vulnerable and worry subconsciously that something will fall on him while he is asleep.*

As I mentioned before, specific bedroom locations are associated with specific members of the family. This placing has its roots deep in Chinese tradition, and associates particular members of the family with particular Trigrams, and hence particular rooms. With the exception of the youngest daughter, all the other children are predominantly placed on the central or east (yang) side of the home. This is, of course, a counsel of perfection, and can be followed only if the rooms are available for such a choice.

DIRECTION	ASSOCIATED FAMILY MEMBER
North	Middle son
Northwest	Father
West (a yin direction)	Youngest daughter
Southwest	Mother
South	Middle daughter
Southeast	Eldest daughter
East (a strong yang direction)	Eldest son
Northeast	Youngest son

One of the most important functions feng shui layout can perform in a child's room is to limit the effect of nightmares. Many practitioners have found that the application of basic feng shui rules have often critically changed the child's tendency to have nightmares, and in the case of young children has even cleared up chronic bedwetting.

Banishing monsters

First ensure that nothing presses down on the bed, be it a large lampshade, a beam or, worst of all, overhanging shelves.

Then make sure that the child's lines of sight are unimpeded, that he or she can see the doorway and every part of the room from the bed. This is good psychology as well as good feng shui. Leave no space in which monsters may lurk! Make sure the headboard is firmly against a wall, so the child is well backed.

Don't be tempted to hang heavy pictures on the wall behind the bed: Children are very sensitive to the implied threat that something may fall on their head while sleeping. The foot of the bed should also not point directly at the door, in the so-called coffin position.

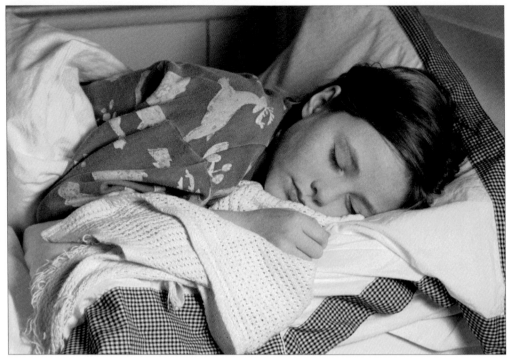

■ **By applying feng shui principles** *to children's bedrooms, you can promote a restful environment at night that will encourage youngsters to sleep more soundly and even limit the frequency of nightmares.*

It is very important that there is no mirror directly visible from the bed so that, should the child wake in the night, he or she will not catch sight of a moving reflection. This is bad feng shui, and may also encourage fear in the half-light of the night.

Although not part of feng shui, clutter is a particularly important issue for children's bedrooms. By their nature, children will tend to create clutter, and the best any long-suffering adult can do is to provide plenty of storage space in the hope that the child will use it. From a feng shui point of view, it is important that this clutter is not stuffed under the bed where it can trap the free flow of ch'i.

Remember, real clutter is the stuff that does not move from week to week. A casual and temporary scattering of toys does not really threaten the permanent feng shui of a room.

You should also, if possible, align the bed so that its head points to one of the four good directions of the child in question, just as you would in an adult bedroom. If the child has difficulty sleeping, or is hyperactive, then use their fourth best direction.

Study aids

If the child also uses the bedroom as his or her study to do homework, place the desk in the NE quarter or face the study chair in that direction if possible, for this is the Education sector (see chapter 17 for more details). If this faces a window, then placing crystals there to deflect the NE light is particularly good as Earth is the Element of the NE sector. Sporting trophies, scarves, and pictures of sports teams are best not hung in this sector as they may prove a distraction.

Although a computer is typically found in many children's bedrooms, it is really too yang for a bedroom, and is best turned off and covered at night.

A simple summary

✔ It is important to arrange the furniture in the living room in a way that leaves no chairs backing onto doors or in the way of *sha ch'i* alignments.

✔ The living room is a feng shui microcosm of the whole house, and may be used for feng shui remedies that can't go in the corresponding house sector.

✔ The dining room affects the feng shui nourishment of the whole family, and should not be adjacent to, or under, a bathroom or kitchen.

✔ Bedrooms have a number of specific no-nos, associated with alignments, bed direction, and the preservation of a more yin atmosphere.

✔ Children's bedrooms need to be particularly well thought out as they are both yin sleeping areas and yang playrooms.

Chapter 11

Bathrooms, Kitchens, Corridors

W E WILL NOW LOOK at the house's wet rooms, the bathroom, washroom, and kitchen – all areas where ch'i may be drained. The kitchen needs special attention as it is the source of family nourishment, and because of the proximity of actual Fire and Water. In a multistory residence it is worth considering the effect of wet rooms above and below key rooms like the dining room. Ch'i flow in connecting corridors and stairs could also be slowed down with feng shui remedies, if necessary.

In this chapter...
- ✓ Wet room downsides
- ✓ Kitchens
- ✓ Bathrooms
- ✓ Storerooms and garages
- ✓ Corridors and stairways

BATHROOMS ARE AREAS OF POTENTIAL CH'I LOSS, AS IT FLOWS AWAY WITH DRAINAGE WATER

Wet room downsides

THESE ROOMS ALL DEAL *with real water, and therefore affect the Water Element quite strongly. As a general rule, where lots of water, particularly soiled water, leaves the house, some of the ch'i will also exit. So, if possible, try to make sure that these rooms correspond to troublesome locations, so that predominantly bad ch'i exits. Energy accumulating in such rooms will be regularly flushed away.*

SHUI (WATER)

This is the origin of the feng shui saying that you should always put your toilet lid down. It's not a bad idea from a hygiene point of view, but putting the lid down will unfortunately not stop the water (and therefore the ch'i) from exiting. Nor will it stop the *sha ch'i*, associated with bad smells, escaping from the toilet.

Drainage directions

Remember that water flowing away from a dwelling also takes beneficial ch'i with it. In a rural environment, a house and its occupants will not flourish if a river passes by a house and then turns in such a way that its occupants can see this constant tide of water streaming away from them. This takes some of their beneficial ch'i with it (see chapter 15 for more on this).

Trivia...

Another harmless and well intentioned, but useless, practice recommended by some practitioners is to put pebbles into drainage holes. Putting rocks into large culverts, or disguising large exterior drainage hoppers is one thing, but regularly replacing the plug with a few pebbles every time the sink is emptied is ineffective and boring to do.

What works at that level also works in an urban environment. Drainage water must not be seen leaving the premises. In most modern houses or offices this is not a problem, but there are some older houses where the drainage pipes all come through and down the external wall in an untidy tangle before dropping into a (sometimes not even grated) drain hole.

Many older houses have visible drainage, and this visible drainage is a definite feng shui defect.

Even worse, the direction of their drainage is visible. We will look at the Water Dragon formula in chapter 15 to determine the correct direction of drainage. But essentially the inability to change this drainage exit position is a big drawback for that kind of house. On the whole, the best thing to do is to disguise the fact that these are drainage exit points. In the East where many houses have their own garden or compound, and where the drains are often considerably larger to cope with monsoon rains, the flexibility to

■ **Water flowing out of the house** *takes beneficial ch'i with it. For this reason, it's best to keep the bathroom door closed at all times.*

redirect the bathroom and kitchen sink drainage so that it appears to exit at the right point is much greater. Of course, at this point, I often hear people say, "Well, that's not fair. I live in an apartment building and can't do anything about the drainage, whereas if I lived in a freestanding villa with its own grounds I could." All I can say is, yes that is true, so you will have to concentrate on those bits of feng shui that you *can* change.

Keeping negative energies at bay

It does not take a genius to figure that you also should not stimulate your wet rooms. But what if your toilet or bathroom falls in the sector associated with romance? Assuming that you can't move it, which most of us can't, my advice is not to stimulate it. Don't suddenly start hanging wind chimes or lighting candles in the bathroom. Why not? Well, apart from being considered crazy by the rest of your family, you don't want to stir up negative energies, especially not in your Romance sector.

Stimulating the bathroom with wind chimes or candles is a big no-no, although sometimes solid-rod metal wind chimes are used to press down upon the water in such rooms.

If the bathroom (specifically the toilet) is located in the Romance sector, lighting pairs of red candles there may energize the sector enough to provide you with a new boyfriend, but he may turn out to be somebody you would never want to meet. No boyfriend is much better than "the boyfriend from hell."

Likewise with storerooms, if the location is bad, leave it alone. Keep the door closed, even put a spring closer on the door to make sure the rest of your family gets the same idea, whether they want to or not.

A piece of advice often given with respect to the bathroom is to make it "disappear." This advice sometimes goes as far as recommending you put a full-length mirror on the door, so it can't be obviously seen. Well, as that could fool some of your guests, it might even fool the ch'i!

Kitchens

THE KITCHEN IS A VERY *special place because it is where the family's food is prepared. As we have seen, food symbolizes nourishment and, by extension, health and wealth. Just as we take care over hygiene when working in a kitchen, so we should take care of the feng shui of the place where our food is prepared.*

There are certain basic rules:

- Preparation surfaces should be located so that the chef should not have his or her back to the kitchen door while working. Surfaces should be kept clean and clear of clutter.
- The kitchen itself should be in a protected part of the house and not be immediately visible from the front door.
- Try to use green in the decor of the kitchen, as Wood works with both Fire and Water, both of which will inevitably be present in a kitchen.
- Don't put up mirrors facing the stove, as the doubling of Fire may pose a real threat of fire to the household.
- A preparation island in the middle of the kitchen is not good feng shui, as the central t'ai chi should remain open and empty.

- The kitchen should not be beneath a bathroom on the floor above, and preferably not under a wet room (bathroom, kitchen, washroom) of any sort.
- The kitchen should not be located in the northwest corner of the house as this is the corner associated with the Heaven Trigram *Ch'ien*, thus resulting in "Fire at Heaven's gate," a feng shui configuration that is very undesirable.

■ **The kitchen is at the root** *of the family's health and wealth, and should always be kept clean and well ventilated. Choose light colors for the kitchen to create a feeling of openness.*

Drains

Paradoxically, because the kitchen is a wet room and therefore drains away ch'i, it is quite good if it is located in the part of the home that corresponds to one of your worst locations. Alternatively it is OK if it is located in one of the eight Aspirations (see chapter 17) that are unimportant to you, for example the direction west (children) for someone who does not have or particularly want children. Of course, this is a counsel of perfection, and hard to organize unless you are building your house from scratch.

Oven mouth directions

One of the most important feng shui rules is connected with the orientation of the oven "mouth." The oven is associated with Tsao Chun, the god of the stove or the hearth. He is a Taoist god, and sometimes called the Kitchen god. His shrine is often just a little niche in the brickwork of the oven. Because of the association with fire, he has an interesting connection with alchemy, as *tsao* means "furnace" as well as "oven."

INTERNET

www.fengshui-paradise.com/murray.html

Cynthia Murray's thoughts on kitchens and feng shui can be found at this site.

■ **A Ching dynasty family** *sets off firecrackers in honor of Tsao Chun. In ancient China, food was often scarce and it was believed that appeasing the Kitchen god would ensure abundance and ward off hunger.*

It was thought that the Kitchen god gave an account of all the doings of the family once a year to the ruler of Heaven, the implication being that the kitchen was the best place to hear all the gossip about family members.

His departure to Heaven is often accompanied by sweetmeat bribes (to make sure he says nice things about the family, or keeps his mouth shut), and his return each year after reporting on the family to the ruler of Heaven is celebrated with a special ceremony.

Ideally, the oven mouth direction should coincide with the kua number of the breadwinner. We will go into the calculation of these numbers in chapter 20. At the very least, try not to have the oven mouth facing any of your four worst directions. The mouth of the oven also should preferably not point out the opened kitchen door.

The oven is symbolic of the Element Fire, and the sink and fridge are symbolic of Water. This means you should be careful in kitchen design that these two don't clash. For example, the sink and stove should not directly confront each other. Similarly, they should not be located next to one another, although at right angles is fine.

The definition of oven mouth is controversial in the case of electric cookers, with some experts claiming it is the entry direction of the plug (or source of fuel). Others take the view that the modern definition of oven mouth should be the facing direction of the door from which the food emerges.

■ **The sink and stove** *should not directly confront each other, as shown here, because they represent the conflicting Elements of Fire and Water.*

Bathrooms

WATER IS A SIGNIFICANT PART of feng shui, indeed "water," or "shui," is half the meaning of the phrase. The designing of exterior waterworks, especially ponds and fountains, has always been an important part of feng shui.

In fact, early practitioners involved hydraulic engineers in redirecting the course of whole rivers, often imposing some amazing and unnatural patterns on the rivers in an effort to build up and accumulate good ch'i. The reason for these exercises is that water carries ch'i. But not only can it carry it to a site or help store it when it is there, it can also carry it away.

Feng shui practitioners working on gardens or landscapes were always careful that the eventual exit point of water, where the river disappears, should be invisible from the home.

■ **If you have mirrors in the bathroom,** *make sure they do not reflect the toilet, since this will simply serve to double the amount of negative sha ch'i generated.*

These principles carry into the other wet rooms of the house, where drains do carry away ch'i. Hence you have to be very careful that the exit points of drains are not open or visible. The extension of this rule is that bathroom doors should always be kept closed.

Of the several wet rooms, the bathroom is considered the worst, as bad smells have always been associated with toilet *sha ch'i.*

The general principle is that bathrooms should ideally be in a location where they do the least damage. In fact, there is positive benefit in having the bathroom in a sector that you want to deplete rather than energize.

For example, it might be acceptable to have the bathroom in the west, which is the sector associated with children, if the residents in the home did not have children and were not interested in having them.

■ **Keeping the toilet lid down** *will, unfortunately, not prevent beneficial ch'i from draining away. The toilet should not face a door, as this will encourage* sha ch'i *to spread throughout the house.*

You should instead concentrate upon making the bathroom "disappear" by keeping the toilet lid down, keeping the door closed, and generally de-emphasizing this room.

Bathroom do's and don'ts

General rules connected with bathrooms include:

- Don't have the toilet positioned so that it is visible from the front door. This is a very bad feng shui configuration.
- Toilets should, for preference, not be located in the northwest or southeast sector of any home or office. Location in the southeast, for example, may drain accumulated prosperity.
- Try not to have toilets positioned on an upper floor directly above anything except another toilet or a seldom-used storeroom. Otherwise, the *sha ch'i* may affect the room below.
- If your bathroom adjoins your bedroom, you must be very careful to keep a clear break between the wet room and the bedroom, otherwise the energy present in the bedroom can be severely drained, with ill effects for the sleeper's feng shui and health.
- Bathrooms should not be energized, as this increases the quantity of *sha ch'i.*

Storerooms and garages

STOREROOMS AND GUEST BEDROOMS *are seldom visited,*
and therefore the ch'i does not have any serious impact upon the occupants
of the house. Where garages are an integral part of the house, they do have
an impact on the feng shui.

Obviously we spend little time in the garage, unless you are a Do-It-Yourself fan.
But they constitute a sort of ch'i hollow in the house. Bedrooms situated above
garages have a slight feeling of insecurity for this reason. Traditionally, bedrooms
above a hollow have been seen as rooms with not very good feng shui, so if you are
tempted to build above your garage think carefully about the function of the new
room. A master bedroom would certainly not be a good use of this space.

■ **There is no bedroom** *above this integral garage. Since a garage forms a ch'i hollow, those sleeping in*
a room above one may feel drained of energy in the morning.

Corridors and stairways

IF THE FRONT DOOR IS THE MOUTH of the house, then halls and stairways are the lungs or channels via which ch'i is circulated through the house. Stairs are, in fact, just sharply tilted corridors. However, because of the angle, stairs cause ch'i to move even more rapidly, so you should pay particular attention to the top and bottom of staircases. Check what they point at, and protect anything sensitive like a bedroom from their direct access. Ideally, the main hall should be well lit to encourage the entry of ch'i.

Hallways

A hall passing directly to the back door is bad feng shui, as ch'i will pass directly through without accumulating. In such a case, add decorative features like indoor plants or a hall table to deflect the ch'i from this direct path. Another remedy is to hang a wind chime from the ceiling of the hall to slow the passage of the ch'i.

Other rules about halls include:

- The front door should not directly face a staircase, particularly not one leading downwards. To open onto both descending and ascending stairs is the very worst configuration, and some type of screen or baffle must be introduced to screen the staircases from the door.
- Halls should not be dark and yin, but instead bright and yang, as they conduct ch'i from one part of the house to another.
- Doors facing each other across a corridor should be of the same size, and should not overlap or underlap each other. A vertical mirror strip can be added if necessary to even up the width of these doorways.
- Poorly lit or low-ceilinged stairs can oppress and restrict ch'i flow between floors. Use a bright light to enhance circulation.

Stairs

Like halls, which carry the ch'i from one room to another, so stairs distribute the ch'i from one floor to another. In many Western houses the staircase follows almost directly after a short stretch of hall. This allows ch'i to come in the front door and rush straight up the stairs, which is not advisable – the best ch'i flows slowly and not in direct straight lines.

A partial solution to this problem is the hanging of a wind chime between the door and the stairs to slow down the ch'i. Ideally, the staircase should turn away from the front door. In some commercial buildings this is a deliberate feature of the architecture.

■ **A stairway** *leading directly from the front door to the second floor encourages ch'i from the entrance to race up the stairs and into the home too quickly. One solution to this problem would be to hang a wind chime between the door and stairs to slow down the ch'i.*

Ways of generating ch'i

On staircases where the ch'i cannot be coaxed up in sufficient quantities to enliven the upstairs rooms, it is sometimes useful to place stronger lights on the staircase itself. In extreme cases a special feng shui item resembling a small barber's pole, which turns in a spiral fashion, can be placed on the landings to promote the movement of ch'i up the stairs. These are available in some feng shui shops in Hong Kong.

Paradoxically, although ch'i should be encouraged to move in a circular fashion, spiral staircases are not considered good feng shui and should be avoided where possible, as they encourage a destructive corkscrew acceleration of ch'i.

A simple summary

✔ Don't activate the wet rooms because this will only stimulate negative ch'i. A mirror placed on the outside of the door can be used to help a bathroom "disappear."

✔ Try not to have visible drainage exits.

✔ The kitchen is a special case, being the source of "food ch'i" (if I can be forgiven for coining such a phrase).

✔ Make sure that a wet room is not located above a kitchen.

✔ Oven mouth direction is most important.

✔ Storerooms should occupy negative locations in the home.

✔ In halls and staircases, try to slow down the flow of ch'i.

✔ Don't site a bedroom above a garage or void space.

Chapter 12

Business Feng Shui and Color

THE FENG SHUI of your workplace is quite important because you might spend upward of 8 hours there every working day. Obviously, if you own the business, it is most important that you get the feng shui right for it to prosper. You should also check the feng shui of your particular office, or if you don't have one to yourself, decide what else you can do to improve the area around your desk. Color has real feng shui significance, and it should be considered both in the office and the home.

In this chapter...

✓ Overall office layout

✓ Your own office

✓ Auspicious color schemes

✓ Mirror, mirror on the wall

IMPROVING THE FENG SHUI OF YOUR BUSINESS OR OFFICE WILL BENEFIT YOUR TURNOVER AND PROFITS

Overall office layout

LET'S LOOK AT THE OFFICE *from the outside in. If possible, there should be an open area, called a* ming tang *or "bright hall," for ch'i collection in front of the main doors. If, for example, your office has a wide pavement in front of its doors, or is across the road from a public park, this open area can function very nicely as your bright hall. Keep any fronting area as clear as possible, and, of course, make sure that garbage from neighboring businesses does not accumulate in front of your door. Even your own office rubbish should not be piled here for any longer than necessary.*

Try to ensure that the main doors do not open directly on to any lampposts or single trees, or other sizeable visual obstructions. This is most important. Quite often you do not have any choice in the matter if the city puts up a structure. To my knowledge, no

■ **An office building's main entrance** *serves to usher auspicious ch'i into the premises while keeping negative energy at bay. The entrance should be wide and well lit, with a bright hall area for ch'i collection in front of the main doors.*

appeal against this on the grounds of feng shui has ever succeeded anywhere in the world except Hong Kong (where the government used to pay villagers financial compensation for its rural feng shui infringements). The best you can do is consider using a different door as the main door.

If the option exists, it might be possible to protect the entrance of your office building with two stone or cement lions (sometimes called *fu* dogs) such as you sometimes see outside large Chinese banks or restaurants. These help to reduce the entry of bad ch'i into the building. However, positioning these often requires landlord and city council permission, which is not lightly granted.

Ensure that the entrance door to the office is wide, welcoming, and well lit, perhaps with up-lighters. Putting a moving water feature at, or just inside, the main door will welcome in good ch'i. A bubbling water column is useful here.

Internal layout

Make sure that the internal office layout is such that people (and therefore ch'i) can move smoothly through the office without bumping into badly placed furniture. If you can't conga comfortably around most of the office, then the layout needs to be seriously looked at!

Trivia...
I have seen at least one flourishing business brought to its knees in a matter of months after a local council decided to erect an unfortunate parking bollard (a post to prevent cars from parking) directly in line with its main door.
There was nothing the business owner could legally do, although he did think seriously about employing heavy lifting gear in the middle of the night!

Trivia...
In one of the main shopping streets of Kuala Lumpur (Bukit Bintang), 20-foot-high bubbling water columns have been carefully sited outside a major shopping center to bring in business. Adjacent shopping centers, using conventional non-feng shui attractions like large-format TV screens, were not attracting nearly as much business.

There should be no pockets or dead-ends that can trap ch'i. Check the layout of the overall office to make sure there are no long, straight corridors or furniture alignments. Avoid like the plague the rows of desks in an open-plan office, which were so popular in the 1950s.

Inside the office, get rid of, or cover up, as many sharp convex corners as practical. Don't worry about concave (non-protruding) corners.

Eight Mansion formula applied to the office

Although we will come to the Eight Mansion formula in chapter 17, I have here summarized those parts of this formula that are particularly appropriate to the office environment. There are several parts of the office that will benefit from these specific feng shui activations. These are the southeast, northwest, and perhaps the south. All directions are best plotted from the precise center of the office, using a scale plan and a good compass.

Activate the Prosperity sector in the southeast of the office by installing a Water feature, such as a fountain or fish tank supplied with air bubblers and bright goldfish. Activate the Fame sector (in the south), especially if your business depends on public recognition, by installing red furnishings or other representations of Fire, such as strong lighting, in it. Candles, understandably, won't usually be possible in an office environment! Activate the Networking sector in the northwest of your business with Metal (filing cabinets and electronic equipment will do nicely). Alternatively, use its producing Element Earth by introducing large crystals. See chapter 17 for more details of the application of the Eight Mansion formula.

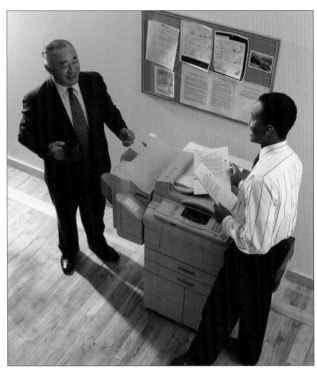

■ **Electronic equipment,** *such as a photocopier, represents the Element Metal and can be placed in the northwest area of your office to stimulate the networking sector.*

Some of the world's most financially savvy businesses have used fish tanks located in precise office locations. These include Bloomberg's London offices and Orange Telecom.

Incidentally, if you have a private office within the company offices, you might like to repeat these activations on a smaller scale, with one addition. You should also install a water feature in the north corner of your office to help promote your own career.

Your own office

IF YOU ARE THE BOSS, it is very important to improve your personal feng shui first, as the business is an extension of you and your decisions. It's a bit like the safety instructions on a plane: "Put your own mask on first before attending to the masks of those nearby you." But even if you are not the boss, your office environment is most important.

The most important consideration is to ensure that "secret arrows" do not hit your desk. In other words, try not to have it located at the end of a long corridor, or pointed at by the corners of walls or pillars or (to a lesser extent) other desks. If you can't get your desk moved, then try to blunt these secret arrows by placing softeners such as indoor plants or screens in front of them. In the case of a particularly strong secret arrow you may find that the potted plant you place in front of it to act as a screen keeps dying. Never mind, just persist, and be grateful that you are being screened, even if the plants keep suffering!

■ **If your desk** *is situated at the end of a long corridor, it will become a target for poison arrows, which will affect the quality of your work. You should also be able to clearly see the doorway of your own office.*

Support yourself

Make sure that you do not sit with your back to a door, a window, a corridor, or open area. Try to ensure that there is "support" behind your chair, in the form of a solid wall. A picture of something solid like a mountain is sometimes recommended for behind-chair support, but nothing beats an actual wall. Make sure you are facing a direction that enables you to easily see the door and anyone entering it.

Next, try to position your desk so that you are facing your best direction. If you are a staff member, and not the boss, it is not always possible to position your own desk in the optimal position. If you want to face your best, or *sheng ch'i* direction, it is frequently impossible to position your desk diagonally to the other desks in the office, or at an awkward angle.

Consequently when you have calculated your four best directions (see chapter 20), you may have to utilize your second, third, or even fourth best-facing direction. If there is a conflict between this and the Form School considerations of secret arrows and support orientation, then the latter considerations usually take precedence.

■ **Ideally, the desk** *should be positioned so its occupant has his or her back to the wall. This "anchors" the desk and gives it maximum exposure to auspicious ch'i in the room. At the same time, the wall is said to protect the person by figuratively "watching his or her back."*

Clutter clearing

A lot of stuff has been written about clutter. Clutter clearing is not part of traditional feng shui, but it is useful to eliminate clutter around your desk.

Throw away those non-essential piles of paper you have been keeping just in case, or at least put them out of sight in a filing cabinet.

Remember the old saying: "Out of sight, out of mind." This means that when clutter is tidied up, it can no longer act as a subconscious energy drainer. Out of sight means out of mind, and, more importantly, out of your feng shui environment.

If you are not the master of your own space in the office, then at least concentrate on the micro feng shui of your desk. Remove clutter, or at least organize it effectively with trays. As a matter of good work practice, you should eliminate clutter on your desk by improving the filing system and reducing unnecessarily full in-trays.

Remember that it does not hurt to have piles of paper that frequently change or turn over. It's only the piles that sit for weeks untouched that are really negative. Institute procedures to keep different projects separately in appropriately marked folders.

■ **Keep your desk** *clear of clutter and improve its micro feng shui by placing a desk lamp to the south, or the furthest edge of your desk, to help improve your "fame" and raise your profile within the organization.*

If you own the business, then it is very important where you place your own office within the office complex. As a general rule, it should be as far as possible from the main entrance but where you also have an overview of as many key staff as possible (if it's an open or semi-open plan office). The boss must be well supported with a solid wall behind him or her, and have a good view of their own inner office door.

Directions

Thought should be given to the positioning of the manager's or owner's office in the overall ground plan of the office. Using the *pa kua*, you might position this office in the Knowledge (northeast) sector of the overall office, if it is a knowledge-based business, or in the Mentor/Networking sector (northwest) if the business especially relies upon contacts with other outside businesses. A favorite, of course, is the southwest or Wealth position – but often this may be a more appropriate location for wealth producing or money handling staff such as cashiers.

Company logos

From a feng shui point of view, the company logo needs to be scrutinized. It should be easily recognizable, with predominantly yang colors, as it has to represent a business that should be yang in relation to other businesses that it deals with.

A good principle is to mix a metallic color (representing money) with a strong yang color, to energize it. Silver with purple, or red with gold are favorite combinations of a metallic and a yang color.

Avoid yin pastel colors for company logos. Try to think of one very successful company with a pastel logo. Difficult, isn't it? The logo itself should not be fussy in its detail, and should visually move in an upward direction if possible. Colors are important in ways other than just the logo of the company.

Auspicious color schemes

COLOR HAS BOTH PSYCHOLOGICAL *and feng shui significance. Feng shui changes can be simply brought about by appropriately changing the decor to either stress or reduce one or other of the five Elements. To do this we can introduce changes in color, shape, or material, or actually introduce the physical Element itself. The most potent change is the latter.*

Any and every trick of the interior decorator's trade can be brought to bear upon a feng shui problem or enhancement.

To amplify an Element using color, simply introduce more of its color, or the color of the Element that produces it, using the following table:

ELEMENT	COLOR OF ELEMENT	COLOR OF PRODUCING ELEMENT
Fire	Red	Green
Earth	Yellow	Red
Wood	Green	Black or dark blue
Metal	Metallic, silver, or gold	Yellow
Water	Black or dark blue	Metallic, silver, or gold

Colors follow the Elements

The basic Chinese palette is rather stark, and variations on this basic coloration can be substituted. For example, you might like to use a salmon color (derived from red and yellow, with a touch of white) to stimulate the Element Earth. This works because yellow is the color of Earth, and red is the color of Fire, which produces Earth.

Fire is attributed to the south where shades of red and orange are appropriate. Sometimes purple is attributed to *Li*, or Fire. In fact this color is more appropriate to the center where yellow and its opposite purple are attributed to Earth. Silver (Metal) and purple (Earth which produces Metal) together are a very prosperity-producing combination.

■ **In this office lobby area,** *the combination of silver and purple with a touch of black, which represents water (symbolic of wealth) is a color scheme that promotes prosperity.*

Earth is attributed to the center, southwest, and northeast, and here browns, from ocher to bright yellows, are appropriate. As with Fire, be careful not to mix too much white here for best results. A small quantity of red adds an interesting galvanizing effect. Never use black or blue in this area.

Wood (east and southeast) is growing vegetation and therefore green, through to azure, are appropriate colors to use in these areas. The black and dark blue of water are supportive and strengthening.

Metal (west and northwest) is an interesting Element, sometimes translated as gold. Hence colors include gold, silver, and white. Purple and silver make an excellent energizing combination in this area. Yellow, representative of the producing Element Earth, is also useful here.

Water (north) is traditionally symbolized by black, but blue has found its way onto the palette of Water colors. A touch of gold representing Water's producing Element Metal works wonders here. Water is symbolic of money, and so the combination of gold or silver on black has often been used to stimulate the flow of prosperity. Be careful not to use fiery red here, as Water is inimical to Fire.

A more subtle color approach

Obviously, the use of primary colors all the time in accordance with the Elements will not provide a completely tenable interior decoration palette. Mixed colors like beige might replace the glare of primary yellow (Earth). Salmon and peach may replace the intense drama of red (Fire).

The thing to really watch is to use a color that will not drain the Element you wish to enhance. For example, a Fire sector area will not respond well to being doused by blue, nor will a Wood area flourish if you decorate it in cutting metallic colors.

Using charge colors

A *charge* color often considerably strengthens the main color. The effect is both visual and psychological. Even a fleck of the charge color helps to strengthen the main color without draining it.

This chart shows the principal charge colors with their corresponding main colors.

MAIN COLOR	CHARGE COLOR	MAIN COLOR	CHARGE COLOR
Red	Green	White	Black
Blue	Orange	Purple	Yellow
Yellow	Purple	Orange	Blue
Black	White	Green	Red

Avoiding draining yin colors

Very yin or drab colors into which a lot of brown or black has been introduced are not a good idea. Muting colors with black or brown is depressing, both psychologically and from a feng shui perspective.

The Georgian period color palette of taupe, brown, bull's blood, and olive would have produced a draining atmosphere. Even the color eau-de-nil can have a similar yin effect.

One other color to be careful of is blue. Although blue has been recommended by many feng shui practitioners for bedrooms, because of its calming effect or some other psychological reason, Water in the bedroom, and, indeed, the boardroom, is also draining and so blue is best not used.

This is recommended for the same reason that you would not place an aquarium in the bedroom. Many blues are cold and unwelcoming. If you must use blue, make it a "live" blue and not a heavy, yin Prussian blue.

■ **Shades of brown** *are extremely yin. They should be avoided because they are depressing and produce a draining atmosphere.*

Mirror, mirror on the wall

ALONG WITH COLOR, MIRRORS *can produce startling feng shui and interior decor effects. Mirrors are very magical things, which is probably why so many stories have been written about passing through them to another world (such as Lewis Carroll's* Through the Looking Glass*).*

If you sit in front of a mirror, and really think about it, the explanations provided by the physics of reflected light beams do not really seem to explain why you see yourself reversed, or why you can suddenly see behind your own head. Yes, all you physicists out there, I know the theory. But the theory is about as convincing as the idea that diffraction in a million raindrops causes a rainbow. The logic works but intuitively it does not seem right.

There are two schools of thought regarding the use of mirrors in feng shui, and both are right. There are Masters who say that

Trivia...

Anyone who doubts that mirrors have a distinctly magical role to play in feng shui should remember that Tien Mu, a goddess in charge of lightning, and hence involved in manipulating the Weather ch'i, was traditionally known to have used mirrors to do her work. She is supposed to have worked in conjunction with the dragons of air and water, in other words she was heavily involved in feng shui.

■ **Placing a mirror** *so that it faces into a room can increase yang energy in a room that's too yin. Bear in mind, though, that a mirror should not hang so that it faces a room's door.*

mirrors have no influence on feng shui. It is debatable whether mirrors can change the flow of ch'i energy. But you will remember that alignments are another important aspect of feng shui. Now, mirrors can alter real or apparent alignments, and so can definitely have an effect on feng shui. Beside which there is something very watery about mirrors, water surfaces being naturally-occurring mirrors.

A simple summary

✓ In the business context, make sure that appropriate functions are located in the correct offices, with the bosses' office located far from the entrance, and income functions located in the wealth sector in the southeast.

✓ You can apply the Eight Mansion formula to your office as well as your home.

✓ Water features with air bubblers are particularly effective in the southeast Prosperity sector, and Metal activators are useful in the northwest Mentor/ Networking sector.

✓ Getting the feng shui right in the bosses' office is equally important to the business.

✓ Keep the business frontage clear and free of garbage.

✓ In your own office, make sure that you have a strong back support and a view of the inner door, and that you cannot be hit by any poison arrows.

✓ Endeavor to face one of your four best directions.

✓ Use colors to subtly enhance appropriate Elements. Charge colors can be used to considerably strengthen the main color.

✓ Avoid draining yin colors.

✓ Mirrors can have an effect on feng shui alignments, and possibly on ch'i.

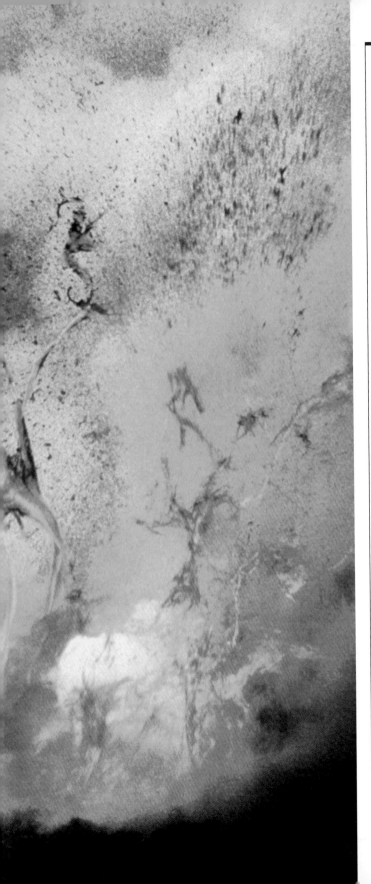

PART FOUR

FIRE IS A TRANSFORMATIONAL ENERGY

THE FENG SHUI OF EXTERIORS

NOW THAT YOU HAVE had a taste of what feng shui can do for you in your home or office, it's time to move outside again. Here you will get a *deeper appreciation* of Form School feng shui and how a classical Form School feng shui landscape is structured and the effect it has on our lives.

Exterior feng shui relates the knowledge we have gained about the interior of our homes to the outside. We will look at how you can *"feng shui your garden"* very effectively. In fact some feng shui Masters even refer to the garden as your "outside room," and as such it is one of the most important rooms "in" your house. Even if you are an apartment dweller, this chapter can give you advice on how your external surroundings can have a profound effect on your feng shui.

Chapter 13

The Four Celestial Animals

FORM SCHOOL FENG SHUI was originally concerned with the relationship between a building and the surrounding landscape. The ideal positioning of such a building was explained in terms of what was to be seen in each of the four Directions, looking out from the front of the building. These landforms should ideally be shaped like an armchair, with a high backrest, two side-protecting hill ranges, and an open expanse in front, beyond which is a small hillock, or footrest. These features were given poetic names: The Green Dragon, Red Bird, White Tiger, and Black Tortoise. I will look at each of these features in turn, and show you how to identify them in your landscape. Finally, we will look at how to identify an excellent site for an excellently sited house.

In this chapter...

✓ The four Directions

✓ How to use the Celestial Animals

THE WHITE TIGER, ONE OF THE FOUR CELESTIAL ANIMALS, IS A PROTECTIVE SYMBOL ON THE ALTAR

The four Directions

THE FOUR MAIN DIRECTIONS *are the cardinal points north, south, east, and west that we encountered in chapter 6. Each is traditionally associated with one of four so-called Celestial Animals: the Black Tortoise, Green Dragon, Red Bird, and White Tiger. These Celestial Animals also represent the four quarters of the sky. As such, each contains seven of the 28 constellations (hsiu) of Chinese astronomy, a quarter of the sky each. These four Directions are related to the four seasons, four of the eight Trigrams, colors, and the Elements.*

The colors give clear hints to which direction is associated with which Element.

ANIMAL	DIRECTION	COLOR	ELEMENT
Dragon	East	Green	Wood
Tiger	West	White	Metal
Tortoise	North	Black	Water
Bird	South	Red	Fire

As well as having astronomical associations, these four animals are also labels for specific landforms. For example, the Black Tortoise is always the range of hills or mountains behind a building, regardless of whether the back of the building faces north or not. The Green Dragon is the lower range of hills to the left (looking out from the front of the door), and so on.

The Celestial Animals started off as fixed animal symbols of specific compass quarters for an ideal south-facing house. For houses facing other directions, the landforms have the same relationship with the building: The Tortoise is behind, the Bird in front, the Dragon to the left, and the Tiger to the right of the building (looking outward). The trick is to see these features manifested in the surrounding landforms.

The yang Green Dragon of the east

The cycle begins in the east with perhaps the most important creature in Chinese culture and in feng shui, the dragon. This eastern quarter is connected with the Element Wood. The color of this Element is green, the color of vegetative growth, the color of spring. Therefore this quarter is the Green Dragon.

LUNG (DRAGON)

In the landscape, the Green Dragon should be identified as a low range of hills or, in an urban context, a wall or adjacent building. It must, however, be yang in comparison to the yin of the right side, or the White Tiger. In other words, it should be higher or stronger than whatever landform or feature occurs on the right side (looking out) of your site or home.

The Green Dragon is the ching lung. "Lung" is the Chinese word for "dragon." "Ching" is the Chinese word for "green." It's also the word for "blue." So is the dragon blue or green? Translators have got round this problem by calling it the Azure, or Cerulean, Dragon. But its color must describe the new green growth of spring, not the blue of the South China Sea, as one writer suggested.

■ **The Green Dragon,** *seen here carved in ivory and surrounded by clouds, refers to a range of hills to the left of a site.*

The yin White Tiger of the west

The White Tiger is a rare beast and not at all the same as an ordinary tiger. While the ordinary tiger is a strong, ferocious yang animal, the White Tiger is, surprisingly, a yin animal.

虎

HU (TIGER)

From a landform point of view, the White Tiger should be a low embracing range of hills in the west or, in an urban context, the wall or building to the right of the building under consideration.

■ **These houses nestling** *at the foot of the wall of rock are in the perfect urban White Tiger setting, as the residents are protected by the rock face situated to the west.*

The Black Tortoise of the north

Perhaps the most important feature of a good site is to have a high mountain behind it. This is symbolized by the Black Tortoise. The words "turtle" and "tortoise" are the same character in Chinese, and hence no distinction is made between them.

GUI (TORTOISE)

■ **Table Mountain** *in South Africa is a good example of a Black Tortoise, or Dark Warrior. From a feng shui point of view, any settlement located in front of such a high mountain is well protected. As the Dark Warrior, such a high mountain would protect what lies before it from strong northerly winds.*

Another name for the tortoise is "Dark Warrior," which implies protection, and that is exactly what the Black Tortoise provides, protecting the site from the cold harsh winds from the northern, or winter, quarter.

Traditionally, the tortoise shell has 24 plates on it. These correspond to the 24 Divisions of perhaps the most important ring on the feng shui compass (see chapter 23). The 24 plates also correspond to the 24 divisions of the agricultural year (in the Chinese solar calendar). In addition, the *lo shu*, a very important feng shui figure (see chapter 8), was originally discovered, so the story goes, marked on a tortoise shell. Thus, time is tied to the feng shui compass, the seasons, and the *lo shu* by the highly symbolic tortoise.

■ **The image of a tortoise** *or turtle is often seen crowning stone gravestones, thus symbolically extending longevity to immortality.*

A further mystery of this quarter is the ancient Chinese belief that turtles were always female (a very yin creature). These female tortoises therefore had to mate with snakes in order to reproduce. Hence the Celestial Creature of the yin north was often painted as a snake wrapped in sexual embrace around a tortoise.

A further suggestive mystery is that the tortoise was sometimes called *wang pa*, or literally "King Eight," or perhaps king of the eight Trigrams. Strangely, *wang pa* is also a very insulting and yin term, since it means "brothel keeper."

Trivia...

It's no coincidence that the book and film characters popular in the 1980s and 90s, the Teenage Mutant Ninja Turtles, reflected a strong tradition of turtles as heroes. The turtle has often been associated with heroes in Chinese mythology.

"Tortoise" has been used as a term of insult in Chinese culture and, in fact, is a taboo word in some contexts. Because of this, the Celestial Animal of the north was sometimes replaced with the figure of the "Dark Warrior."

The Red Bird of the south

Ideally, water should be located in front of the site. If water is absent, then there should be an open space and beyond that a low rise called the Red Bird. Most books in English call it the Red Phoenix, but this is very misleading, since it does not rise from the ashes or do any of the

鳳 凰

FENG HUANG (RED BIRD)

things associated with the phoenix in Western mythology. For this reason, I prefer to refer to it as the Red Bird, rather than by its more fanciful name of Red Phoenix.

■ **The Red Bird**, *also known as the Red Phoenix, can be represented in the landscape by a bump or gentle rise, a road, or a wall at the front of a site.*

In addition to Red Bird and Red Phoenix, there is also a case for calling this symbol the Red Raven, as feng shui author Eva Wong does. The south is associated with the sun, and the bird of the sun is the raven. Also, the raven has a couple of other special meanings in feng shui, which are too complex to go into in this book.

From a landform point of view, this bump, or gentle rise, is a kind of low feature or lip at the front of the site. It prevents, if you like, ch'i spilling out away from the flat area in front of the site.

If we apply this to an urban landscape, we can replace hills with buildings and rivers with roads as carriers of ch'i. In an urban context, the feature representing the Red Bird might be the front garden wall belonging to the neighbors opposite.

Finally, an empty space in front of the site accumulates ch'i and is called the *ming tang*, or "Bright Hall" space. If this area is crossed by a wall or other obstruction, it used to be the practice in China to open a hole in the wall, or make some of the wall in open brickwork. If your own garden wall or that of a neighbor obstructs your *ming tang*, then you could adapt this idea when seeking to clear the space in front of your home.

■ **At Po Lin Monastery** *in Hong Kong, a moon gate has been made in a wall that crossed the* ming tang, *thus removing the obstruction to the beneficial ch'i accumulating in this open space.*

■ **In the ideal rural landscape,** *a house should have a mountain to the rear, low-lying hills to the left and right, an open ming tang space in front, and some gently rising ground beyond.*

NORTH

Black Tortoise mountain

Green Dragon hills (yang)

White Tiger hills (yin)

WEST

EAST

Ming tang open area

Stream

Red Bird hillocks

SOUTH

■ **In an urban landscape,** *the mountain, low-lying hills, and hillocks are replaced by a tower block, houses, and bushes, respectively, while the ch'i is now carried past the house by a road rather than a stream.*

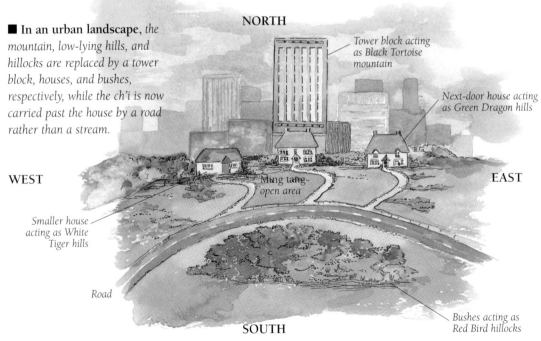

NORTH

Tower block acting as Black Tortoise mountain

Next-door house acting as Green Dragon hills

WEST

EAST

Ming tang open area

Smaller house acting as White Tiger hills

Road

Bushes acting as Red Bird hillocks

SOUTH

How to use the Celestial Animals

THE FIRST QUESTION *you should be asking yourself is, "Well, this is all very picturesque, but how does it affect my home?" Or perhaps, "What if my home doesn't face south, what then?"*

Most books show the ideal positioning of the four Celestial Animals located at the four Compass Directions, but, as noted already, regardless of which direction a house faces, the Black Tortoise landform is always at the back and the Red Bird landform is always in the front. Once you have appreciated that the four Celestial Animals are "house-relative," you are close to understanding Form School feng shui.

These "house-relative" features form what could be considered an armchair-like shape around the ideal site. Taken together, with a high hill or mountain at the back and two "armrests" of hills on either side, the ideal Form School landscape configuration does look a bit like an armchair. To complete the image, the Red Bird formation at the front is called a "footrest."

The point of this whole Form School armchair-shaped configuration is to trap ch'i in the most efficient way. Which sort of ch'i depends on which way the house faces, and for that calculation you need to use Compass School feng shui. Then, to see if the house is good for you personally, you need to use the East Life/West Life formula. Both of these calculations are taught in this book.

Putting it into practice

Can the four Celestial Animals be anywhere? No, the four Celestial Animals are always located in relation to the house or site that is being surveyed.

Does that mean that one person's Black Tortoise mountain could be someone else's White Tiger hill? Or that for some houses with flat land behind them, there may be no Black Tortoise at all? You are catching on fast: It is precisely the absence or presence of these landforms, and their relative strength to one another, that enables you to do a basic Form School feng shui diagnosis.

In locating the Dragon and Tiger sides, remember that the rule is to stand in front of the house, looking out. From that position, the Green Dragon side is on the left, and the White Tiger side is on the right, the Red Bird is in front of you, and the Black Tortoise is behind you and the house.

Let's try it out. In the figure below, you have an example of two houses (1 and 2) relating to the same landform in different ways. In this naturalistic setting, both houses face east but this does not matter for what we are about to consider.

For both houses, the four Celestial Animals are in the same position relative to the house being considered. But you will see that the hills at B, for example, are the Green Dragon for House 1, but the Black Tortoise for House 2. Obviously not all four Celestial Animals will be there every time. In fact, in this figure, House 2 is missing its Red Bird feature.

■ **Two neighboring houses** *will share the four Celestial Animals, but each Animal may be represented by a different landform, relative to the position of each house. Try working it out before you look at the bottom of the page.*

HOUSE 1
Black Tortoise: mountain C
White Tiger: neighbor's house A
Green Dragon: hills at B
Red Bird: bushes near crossroad F

HOUSE 2
Black Tortoise: hills at B
White Tiger: wall at E
Green Dragon: tree at D
Red Bird: missing

Support from behind

If a house is missing the Black Tortoise landform, then such a house is said to lack support from behind. Strangely, you will often find this mirrored in the lives of the occupants. If the breadwinner of such a household runs their own company, their partner and staff will tend not to be supportive. If working in a big company, he or she will frequently be the victim of office politics, getting "stabbed in the back."

Knowing the colors of the Celestial Animals can also help in choosing color schemes. If, for example, there is some doubt as to which color to apply to a garden wall on the left-hand side of the house (looking out), then verification that the wall is in the position of the Green Dragon leaves you in no doubt of the most appropriate color: green.

Corral that ch'i: the fronting ming tang

The space in front of the house is most important. It should be open and clear of rubbish, the idea being to accumulate ch'i here that can easily be utilized by the house. Originally, a water feature in front of the house was called the *ming tang*, but now the term also refers to the whole flat open area.

At the most basic level, you should look to keep your front garden neat. Make sure that there are no obstructions directly in front of the door. If a tree occupies this position, then it would be wise to have it cut down.

Trivia...

The old HSBC bank headquarters in Hong Kong made very sure that the land in front of the bank would never be built on. They bought it and gave it to the government on condition that it would always be used as a public park. This ensured that the bank entrance would always open onto a ming tang.

Ideally, the yang Green Dragon side should be stronger, larger, or brighter than the yin Tiger side. This is because of the rule that the houses of the living should be three-fifths yang to two-fifths yin. So the same applies to the surrounding landforms.

A typical result of imbalance between the four Celestial Animals occurs when the yin White Tiger side is stronger than the yang Green Dragon side. In such a situation, the woman in the house will predominate, while the man is likely to be henpecked and frequently come home late from work.

■ **Siting houses near highways and freeways** *would be most inauspicious in feng shui. The fast-moving traffic and long, straight stretches of road create aggressive sha ch'i.*

Roads

Roads carry ch'i in the urban environment, just as rivers carry it in nature. The color of Water is black, and so the typical black tarmac surface of a road is a suitable reminder of water. Roads are more than just symbolic rivers, as the movement of traffic actually does move ch'i. Obviously, rivers carry a slower-moving and more beneficial ch'i than roads. As you know, rivers tend to meander in a way that encourages beneficial ch'i, while roads, particularly long, straight stretches, often generate cutting ch'i, which moves too fast to be beneficial. However, there is a rough parallel between rivers and roads, which means that many of the old texts on river configuration can be updated and applied to road configurations.

One of the key formulas of feng shui relates to the direction of movement of any water passing the front door of a house. We will look at this in detail in chapter 15. In the case of a road, the important direction is the direction in which the traffic moves in the lanes closest to the house under consideration.

Finding the perfect home

So, in conclusion, if you are looking for a new house, try to get as many of the following Form School features as possible in your favor:

1 A high building or mountain behind the house (Black Tortoise).

2 Enfolding hills, trees, or a building to the left side (looking out), slightly larger than that on the right side (Green Dragon).

3 Enfolding hills, trees, or a building to the right side (looking out) (White Tiger).

4 A clear space in front of the door (sometimes this is just the sidewalk) (*ming tang*).

5 A moving source of ch'i, be it road or river, in front of the building and moving in the correct direction (preferably meandering, and not too fast).

6 Some kind of low rise in front of the road or river (Red Bird).

This, of course, is a counsel of perfection.

A simple summary

✔ The four directions are related to four Celestial Animals: the Black Tortoise, Red Bird, Green Dragon, and White Tiger.

✔ Together they form the armchair-shaped configuration of Form School feng shui.

✔ Behind the site should be the supportive Black Tortoise mountain or building.

✔ The left-hand side of the site (looking outward) is the Green Dragon, which should be a range of hills or a building slightly higher than the White Tiger.

✔ The White Tiger, on the right-hand side of the site (looking outward), should be a lower, protective range of hills or building.

✔ In the front should be the *ming tang*, or open space, probably containing a river or road.

✔ A small hillock or low wall in front of the *ming tang* represents the Red Bird feature.

✔ You need to identify the Celestial Animals in the surroundings of any site to help you judge the feng shui quality of that site.

Chapter 14

Feng Shui Outside Your Home

THE FENG SHUI OF THE SURROUNDINGS is stronger than anything you can do inside the home or office. The surroundings determine the type and quality of ch'i arriving at the site. It is therefore really important to understand Form School feng shui, which enables you to check and change the effect of feng shui influences coming from the surroundings. We see that ch'i is carried through "dragon veins" which are strongest in mountains. We look at the effects of mountains and large buildings on our surroundings. Finally, we see how roads take the place of rivers in cities.

In this chapter...

✓ Make the power of the landscape work for you

✓ Mountains and dragons

✓ How landscape works in cities

✓ Roads and rivers

ROADS ARE THE URBAN EQUIVALENT TO RIVERS AND CARRY FAST-FLOWING CH'I

Make the power of the landscape work for you

IN ANCIENT TIMES, wealthy Chinese families would have the landscape altered to improve their feng shui. Pointed mountains might be flattened, rivers diverted into "auspicious shapes," and cuts in the earth, like quarries or roads, filled in and grassed over.

The vast Summer Palace Gardens just northwest of Beijing were a piece of landscaping and practical feng shui carried out solely for the benefit of the Emperor and his courtiers. In the 21st century, greening expressway embankments or returning sand quarries to nature reserves are echoes of these landscaping activities. The difference is that the ancient Chinese families made these changes for their own material feng shui benefit rather than for the common good or some abstract green environmental concept.

In modern times, the kind of money required to change the landscape massively is mostly public money. Some is still spent on elaborate private feng shui gardens, but these are seldom seen by anyone outside the owners' immediate family circle.

For those of you who have your own garden, the opportunity exists for you as well to get your exterior feng shui into shape, like the ancient Emperors, and to reap the benefits.

On large-scale maps of southern China, or indeed on the ground itself, you can see villages and houses partly surrounded by moats and waterways shaped by man into feng shui patterns. Even in pre-takeover Hong Kong, legal cases were fought and won by villagers whose good feng shui had been compromised by government roadworks nearby. The government often conceded and paid up.

On a smaller scale, Chinese gardens, or your own garden, can echo the features of the bigger landscape. Special stones can take the place of mountains, ponds and streams replace lakes and rivers, and bushes or bonsais replace clumps of trees. The rules of feng shui can be applied on any scale, so your garden can be sculptured to improve the exterior feng shui of your home.

BONSAI TREE

Despite the claims of some authors, you cannot do Form School feng shui in a window box. It just isn't practical.

It's all a question of balance. Single large stones can bring an element of yang to an otherwise yin lawn, while shady paths can bring an element of yin to an otherwise too bright yang garden.

Dragons of various types

Chinese dragons, or *lung*, are primarily air and water creatures (and therefore "feng" and "shui" creatures). They are portrayed with a serpentine body, scaly skin, feet and claws, with small horns like a deer, and ears like an ox. They are not at all related to the fire-breathing dragon of Western legend.

You might expect to find dragons at those places where air and water intersect: typically in clouds, in rivers, or in the sea. In fact, the *I Ching* says, "clouds emanate from dragons." High mountain tops are also favorite lurking places for dragons. Dragons are found in deep pools in rivers, especially where vortexes suck air down into the water.

DRAGONS

Almost all English feng shui books confuse the different types of dragons, so it is worth taking a moment to meet the five kinds of Chinese dragons, or *lung*. These are all concerned with water:

LUNG (DRAGON)

1. *T'ien lung* – Heaven dragon. The most important of all. The Emperor portrayed himself as a dragon, and son of Heaven.

2. *Shen lung* – Spirit dragon. These are the dragons that play in the clouds and cause rain to fall.

3. *Ti lung* – Earth dragon. These live in and rule over water on the surface of the Earth, such as springs and watercourses.

4. *Fu tz'ang lung* – Treasure-guarding dragon. These are concerned with water (and treasure) deep in the veins and caverns of the Earth.

5. *Lung wang* – Dragon king. These rule the four oceans and are salt water dragons, if you like.

The five Elements as mountain or building types

Not only are the five Elements associated with Directions, Trigrams, and colors, they are also associated with natural landforms. It was Kuo P'o (AD 276–324) and later Yang Yun Sung (AD 840–c. 888) who first really codified mountain shapes in a logical manner. Let us look at their typical shapes.

Mountains (or buildings) taking Element shapes are a serious feng shui consideration and, where they appear, must be taken into account in any feng shui analysis. For example, a front door opening directly on to a view of sharply conical mountains will introduce a strong Fire Element into the home. Where a Wood mountain is adjoined to a Fire mountain, the possibility of conflagration is considerably increased.

■ **The Transamerica Pyramid** in San Francisco, with its sharply pointed form, is a perfect example of a Fire building.

One of the consequences of being able to identify the Element nature of a structure is that it immediately becomes apparent what shape not to build near it. For example, if you were considering building on a site overlooked by a Wood-shaped skyscraper, it would not be advantageous to build a low, flat-roofed Earth structure.

The reason? In the Destructive Cycle of the Elements, Wood destroys Earth. Much better to erect a structure with a pointed Fire-like roof, so that it will overcome the neighboring Wood building. In fact, Wood creates Fire, so the original Wood building will strengthen the new Fire building. I don't mean that it will literally set it on fire – just that the Fire building will then have a feng shui advantage over the larger Wood building. The Productive and Destructive Cycles (see chapter 6) give useful guidance in choosing basic shapes.

THE ELEMENTAL FORMS OF MOUNTAINS

Fire mountains tend to be sharply pointed or conical. A volcano is, of course, an extreme example of a Fire mountain. Buildings in cities can also be considered in the same way. In London, the pyramidal top of the Canary Wharf building qualifies as a Fire feature. A number of US skyscrapers built in the 1920s and 1930s featured ziggurat-shaped Fire Element tops. Examples of these include New York's Empire State and Chrysler buildings, Chicago's Tribune Tower, the Los Angeles Central Library, and, particularly, the 1972 Transamerica Pyramid in San Francisco.

FIRE

Wood mountains tend to be tall and upright or columnar in structure, with flat tops and steep or straight sides. In cities, most contemporary skyscrapers emulate the Wood mountain shape.

Earth mountains tend to be lower and broader than Wood mountains. They can even be mesa shaped. Sometimes flat-topped hills qualify. In the city, low, flat-roofed buildings such as warehouses qualify as Earth structures.

WOOD

EARTH

Metal mountains are rarer, as they are arched or domed. Uluru (Ayers Rock) in central Australia is Metal shaped. Hills with domed summits qualify as belonging to the Element Metal. In cities, the Millennium Dome in London is an example of an ill-fated Metal building; the Houston Astrodome is a rather more successful one.

METAL

Water mountains are alive, crooked, moving, or "wiggly." Harder to recognize immediately, a range of low, irregular hills can often qualify as a Water feature. Man-made structures are seldom Water shaped, but the new rail terminal for the Eurostar train in London winds in a way that makes it an excellent example of a Water building. Its glass structure gives it an even more pronounced Water quality.

WATER

Mountains and dragons

LOOK AT ANY CHINESE LANDSCAPE *for long enough and you will probably see the hidden form of a dragon. Dragons are primarily wind and water creatures, but the mountains and their energy are also spoken about as dragons.*

Dragon veins

The Chinese word for veins, *mei*, is used for the channels in the body through which ch'i flows, and which connect the acupuncture points. Indeed, *mei* is also used to refer to actual blood vessels. This means that, from the traditional Chinese point of view, the channels through which ch'i flows in the earth, or the body, are just as real as the body's blood vessels. Traditionally, there are 360 standard acupuncture points in the body, just as there are 360 degrees in a circle and on the feng shui compass. (Some authorities sometimes add another 48 or 49 acupuncture points.)

In feng shui, *mei* refers to the channels in the earth through which ch'i flows. We know that *lung* is the Chinese word for dragon. Put together, *lung mei* means dragon veins, the channels through which Earth ch'i flows.

Finding "dragon veins," or channels of ch'i, is one of the most important goals of feng shui practitioners working on new building sites or in the country. Why? Because the place where these veins meet, or where the ch'i accumulates, is the most powerful spot to locate a new building or grave.

The importance of ch'i cycles

The quality of the ch'i flowing through these veins fluctuates. Just as the tides ebb and flow, so the tides of ch'i also ebb and flow, not only through the day but also through the seasons. Ch'i also changes from year to year: in a very long cycle of 180 year periods, ch'i changes substantially every 20 years. We can all appreciate the daily and seasonal fluctuations, but the longer-range fluctuations need a particular form of feng shui, Flying Star, which is too complicated for this book. A good feng shui practitioner can harness these ch'i cycles so that his or her client buys, rents, or builds an office or home as the ch'i is waxing rather than waning. So, determining the state of ch'i requires a clock and a calendar, which is why I have gone into this in some detail in chapter 21.

One of the great Chinese feng shui classics, the *Site Classic*, expresses this in a way that could not be clearer:

"Every year has 12 months, and each month has positions in time and space of vital and torpid ch'i. Whenever one builds on a vital ch'i position of a month, wealth will come his way and accumulate. To violate a monthly position of torpid ch'i will bring bad luck and calamity."

The big clock that governs these fluctuations, and which is therefore crucial for feng shui, is the interaction between the 12 Earthly Branches and the ten Heavenly Stems (explained in chapter 22) – making the full cycle of 60 character pairs.

Finding your lair, or hsueh

The **hsueh** is the place where the Green Dragon and the White Tiger meet (see chapter 13) and where yin and yang ch'i are mixed in the right proportion. This spot is sometimes expressed as the place where the Dragon and Tiger couple – making it a place of maximum fertility in every sense of that word. Such sites are good for building a home. Unfortunately, with today's strong zoning laws, it is no longer easy to build a home exactly where you want.

DEFINITION

The point of strongest accumulation of well-balanced ch'i in any landscape, the "it" place if you like, the absolutely best place to build or bury, is called the **hsueh**, *or dragon's lair.*

In the United States, many such good feng shui sites still exist, but their potential is often unrecognized by their current owners.

■ The **hsueh**, *or dragon's lair, can still be found in the city, but a little imagination is required to recognize the vital Dragon and Tiger structures among the skyscrapers of Manhattan.*

How landscape works in cities

OF COURSE, THIS LANDSCAPE *feng shui is all very well if you live in the deep country or in a small rural community. However, most of us live in big cities and our families have done so since the Industrial Revolution. Feng shui also works in the city. There the roads, as well as rivers, carry ch'i, and alignments become much more important. Long, straight roads carry fast-moving, destructive ch'i, just as curved roads carry more moderate ch'i. There are also many more poison arrows that have to be protected against in a city.*

Building shape

Buildings should be treated as if they were mountains. Tall buildings are really tall man-made mountains and are often made of the same material as mountains: stone, brick (clay), steel (iron ore), or cement (limestone). They therefore act on the local feng shui of a town in much the same way. Their shape is in most cases oblong, and so most city buildings are Wood-type mountains.

This is one of the main reasons why the few buildings with a different Element shape really get noticed in any city environment. Indeed, any architect wishing to make his or her mark might decide to plan a non-Wood-type building. For example, the pyramid at

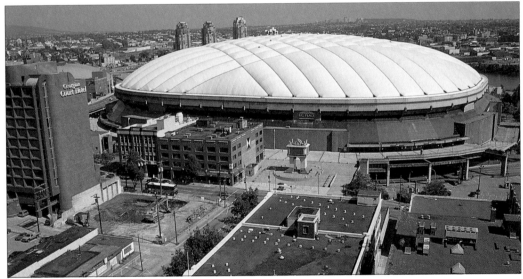

■ **BC Place Station** *in Vancouver, Canada, often described as a large white mushroom, is a perfect example of a Metal building. It stands out dramatically against all the surrounding Wood city blocks.*

the Louvre in Paris, the top of the Canary Wharf building in London, or the pyramids of ancient Egypt are all Fire-shaped buildings. The Dome built for the millennium celebrations in London is a domed Metal shape. All these buildings have attracted more than their fair share of controversy. Mind you, the Millennium Dome's feng shui is really not very good, especially because its entrance turns away from the surrounding river – a mistake so elementary that anyone with even a passing knowledge of feng shui could have spotted it. In fact, it has been a disaster in both feng shui and financial terms. It cost over £700 million (over $1 billion) and, after only a year of operation and a lot of controversy, it was closed and its contents sold off.

Building plot shapes

Another important part of Form School feng shui is the shape of the building plot. Basically, the ideal shape is square or rectangular. L-shaped plots are seen as having a missing corner, which will affect the feng shui qualities of the whole plot. Plots that get narrower as you move from the street, or entrance, toward the back of the plot are seen as restricting your luck. Likewise, plots that widen toward the back are seen as having restricted mouths and are therefore not ideal from a feng shui point of view.

The backrest of the armchair configuration

After considering the plot shape, it is important to consider the setting. Using the typical Form School armchair configuration we looked at in chapter 13, try to ensure you have support from tall buildings behind the site you are considering, protection from lower buildings at the side, and an open space in front.

Everybody requires a backrest – or they get tired. A building is no different. No, I don't mean the building needs literally to be propped up – at least I hope not! – it's just that every building needs some kind of back protection.

Perhaps the single most important feature in a city is to have adequate support behind your building. The best is a mountain, but a substantial skyscraper will do the same for you, as long as it is not so close that it overwhelms your building. In an ideal world, and as a rough rule, it is best to have the backing building laterally no further away than its height. It is no use having a 14-story building 5 miles away, nor is it beneficial to have the same building just across a narrow alley, where it can totally dominate your smaller building. As with so many things in feng shui, it is a question of balance.

Trivia...

I know of a Los Angeles restaurant that was "killed" by its success. When its popularity had reached a point where patrons complained they could no longer get parking, the owner decided to bulldoze the classic supporting high wall and shed behind his fashionable restaurant. He changed nothing else. No sooner had this rear area been turned into a flat, featureless, and unsupported parking lot, than the takings started to decline. Today, sadly, there are not enough patrons even to begin to fill the parking lot.

■ **The city of Seoul** *in South Korea has the perfect natural backrest, in the form of a mountain range, and the lower buildings also gain protection from their man-made backrest, the skyscrapers.*

Failing this, a wall or row of trees can provide the backing your building needs. If the backing feels protective rather than daunting, then you have probably got the proportions right. Using symbolic feng shui to provide a backrest is another possibility, but again it's a matter of scale and balance. A picture of a mountain is fine as a symbolic backrest behind your office chair, but it is not really good enough to provide backing to a whole building. It's a question of scale: Big support requires a big mountain.

Mountains and water

Two of the major factors in Form School feng shui are mountains and rivers (or water). Indeed, in geography, most landforms have been created by an interaction between mountains and water. If you think about it, even flat silt plains are made of silt washed down from the mountains or hills by water. These two factors arise again and again in all the schools of feng shui. On the *pa kua*, and in Eight Mansion feng shui, the Trigrams *Ken* and *K'an* are Mountain and Water, respectively. In Compass School feng shui, different rings of the feng shui compass apply to either mountains or water.

I have looked briefly at mountains and their urban equivalent, tall buildings, so it is now time to turn our attention to rivers and their urban equivalent, roads.

Roads and rivers

AFTER CHECKING THE MOUNTAIN shapes surrounding a building, the next thing you should look at are the river shapes. We can split these into three formations: bad, mixed, and good.

Bad formations

The basic rule is easy: fast-flowing ch'i aimed directly at your building or rushing past it is bad news. So check those alignments. The classic bad feng shui position (as mentioned in chapter 5) is to live in a house located at the top of a T-junction. Even to be opposite the entrance or exit of a narrow alleyway is bad, because the lane funnels a constant source of fast-moving ch'i, or poison arrows, at your building – day in, day out. Where a road comes straight toward your site, and then turns abruptly to the left or right, your site will also have poison arrows aimed at it.

The curve of a road should be wrapped around your site, not aimed at it like a cutting knife.

Siting a building on the outer edge of a curved road, particularly a busy one, is bad positioning, since this is seen as your building being "cut" by the blade-shaped road. The outer edge of an elevated expressway is even worse. A site at a square four-way junction is usually bad, as the ch'i is disturbed (not to say confused) by all the stop–start traffic activity outside. On the other hand, a skillful feng shui practitioner can take advantage of some of this energy (but those techniques are too complex to include here).

■ **This autobahn** *in Frankfurt, Germany, carries fast-flowing ch'i past the houses and office blocks alongside it. A Fire building and a Wood building dominate the horizon.*

■ **In the city of Seoul, South Korea,** *the old building in the foreground is overwhelmed by the modern building opposite, which occupies what should have been the "footrest" position for the old building.*

Mixed formations

Any urban site is really going to be a mixed formation because of the enormous number of influences acting on any inner city or town site. A site located on a rotary or traffic circle just about sums up the problem. Here you have the energy of all those cars going by, but you are also on the outer edge of a curved blade. But the movement is circular, and therefore much more beneficial that an ordinary four-way intersection. A clever feng shui practitioner can make use of the ch'i on a rotary, as long as no street on the other side of the road is aimed directly toward your site. The ch'i can then flow around the circle, without being allowed to overcome the buildings located on it.

Good formations

One ideal situation is a site partially enclosed in a loop of road or river. This formation is referred to as "the belly of the carp," and is especially favorable if the point where the road disappears is "invisible" from the house. In this way, energetic ch'i is seen to arrive but not to depart. Hence, conceptually, it accumulates. Where the road is two-way, you would tend to take most notice of the traffic flow direction of the lane(s) nearest the building.

Another good positioning with regard to roads is on the inner bend of a gentle curve, where there is a light but steady flow of traffic.

A simple summary

✔ Form School feng shui, which was once the province of Emperors, can be put to use by you, albeit on a smaller scale, in your garden.

✔ Dragons come in different varieties, and are wind and water creatures.

✔ Mountains can be classified according to the five Elements, and so can city buildings.

✔ Plot shape also needs to be considered: It should be square or rectangular, not tapered.

✔ Armchair-style support, particularly the backrest, is important for any site.

✔ Roads can be treated as if they were rivers for the purposes of feng shui diagnosis.

✔ There are good (inside the curve) and bad (at the end of a T-junction) places for buildings to be located in relation to roads.

Chapter 15

Water Dragon Feng Shui

I N THIS CHAPTER we will be concentrating on water, and the shape of watercourses, and the detailed feng shui rules that relate to them. We will look at classical feng shui Water Dragon patterns, and then apply this knowledge to creating a Water Dragon in your garden.

In this chapter...

✔ *A world of the weirdest river shapes*

✔ *Practical Water Dragons*

✔ *Creating a Water Dragon feature in your garden*

A JAPANESE SHISHI ODOSHI PRODUCES A CONTINUOUS FLOW OF WATER, PROMOTING GOOD FENG SHUI

A world of the weirdest river shapes

ANYONE WHO HAS LOOKED at the drawings of river formations from early Chinese feng shui texts might assume that there is no way that most of these formations could occur naturally in the world, unless the underlying strata were incredibly convoluted. However, Dr. Michael Paton, an expert on early Chinese Water Dragon feng shui texts, knows these formations well and has assured me that he has flown over such natural river patterns – even in Germany.

I believe that either as natural water formations or as elaborate feats of hydraulic engineering, "Water Dragons" must have certainly existed in the T'ang dynasty (AD 618–906), if not earlier. For a rice-growing culture, water was very important and such engineering may not have been as difficult as it looks.

Water Dragons

I had always assumed that Water Dragons would have to be artificially created. At least nature would have to be given a bit of a helping hand in making them, especially those shaped, for example, like a menorah or with intricate branch-like fingers. In fact, even single right-angled river junctions are very rare in nature, unless the underlying rock structure has been fractured at right angles to the folds of an eroded structure.

These water formations have names that are sheer poetry. The use of extremely lyrical descriptions of some ordinary things is a feature of Chinese life and literature, which is even evident in descriptions of food on Chinese menus. However, the extraordinary names of these water configurations give us useful clues to the theory behind these elaborate works of feng shui water engineering. Let us look at some examples.

Trivia...

If I were to tell you that water has perhaps the greatest impact on our wealth, or lack of it, would you perhaps pay more attention to this chapter? Well, "water dragon" formulas in feng shui are credited with making some of the richest moguls in Asia as rich as they are today . . . and that is very rich!

INTERNET

www.fengshui.net

Fengshui.net offers unique email addresses and access to classical feng shui. Check this site for the availability of key Chinese classical feng shui texts in English, such as the Shui Lung Ching.

■ **Water Dragons** *are designed to allow water to flow slowly around houses. Here a village is surrounded by paddy fields, which have been terraced so that rainwater flows down slowly from the top of the hillside.*

Practical Water Dragons

EACH SEPARATE ACTIVE STRETCH OF WATER in the following diagrams, redrawn from the classical feng shui text Shui Lung Ching, *is called a dragon. The tail of the dragon is always oriented toward the mountain (or the source of the water), the head toward the sea (or mouth of the watercourse).*

Water Dragon patterns

In the illustration below, the different dragons are quite clearly divided by sex: The upper one is the yang Water Dragon (with five fingers – a yang number), and the lower is a yin dragon (with two fingers – a yin number). This is a useful lesson in identifying the sex of the other Water Dragons illustrated here. You will notice a small dot, or circle, in the Water Dragon maps featured in this chapter. This is the *hseuh*, which, as I've mentioned, is where there is the most balanced and greatest concentration of favorable ch'i. It is an ideal place to build or bury. Arrows are marked to show the direction of the water flow.

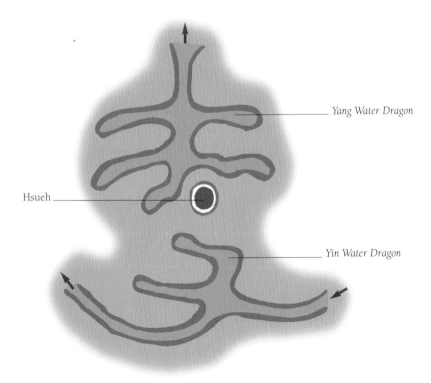

Yang Water Dragon

Hsueh

Yin Water Dragon

MALE AND FEMALE DRAGON PLAYING

Folding water patterns

The more folds in a Water Dragon, and preferably a yang number of folds, that is, 1, 3, 5, 7, or 9, the better. The reason for this is that folding the river concentrates the ch'i.

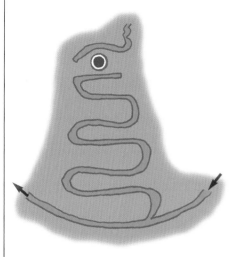

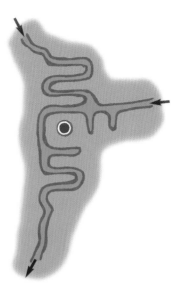

In China, Mandarin ducks are noted for their constancy and faithfulness between partners and, hence, are symbolic of true love. It is possible that this configuration is designed to promote marital happiness. This water formation folds no less than seven times in front of the *hsueh*.

The Winding Waters is a classic formation, using folding water from two sides, with the *hsueh* almost entirely surrounded. It is a very powerful pattern.

MANDARIN DUCKS IN EMBRACE

WINDING WATERS GATHER IN FRONT OF THE PALACE

Knot or junction patterns

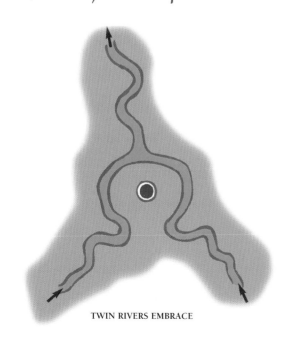

TWIN RIVERS EMBRACE

The main concern with this configuration is that, although two streams of water enter from behind, the channel leading away from the *hsueh* must meander and not show its exit point. The junction of two watercourses is considered a key dragon point. The position of this knot or junction must be carefully plotted in relation to the line of sight from the house or site under consideration.

In the Twin Rivers Embrace, the site is enfolded, and the exiting stream is meandering, thereby causing the ch'i to be retained. A variant of this classic shape appears in the junction of two rivers in Kuala Lumpur, Malaysia.

Annular patterns

Annular patterns are another device for allowing water to pass and re-pass the site. Circles within circles, like moats within moats, also strengthen the dragon.

Here, the moon is the island in the center, and the reference to clouds also relates to ch'i, which is sometimes actually seen as mist or clouds.

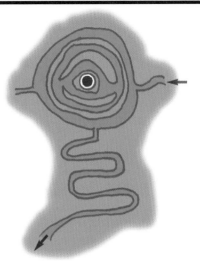

CLOUDS CIRCLE AROUND THE MOON

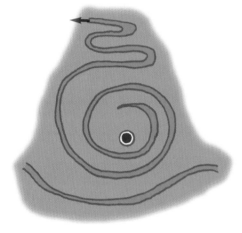

COILED DRAGON STIRRING WATER

Spiral patterns

The Coiled Dragon pattern is literally a spiral with a folded tail. The spiral acts in a similar way to the annular pattern, by embracing the *hsueh*. Like the folding pattern, it is another way to contrive to pass the river past the *hsueh* a number of times, thereby concentrating the ch'i.

Multiple feeder channel patterns

The more channels that can bring in the ch'i the better.

With the simple multiple channel feeder, it is an interesting problem deciding where water enters and where it leaves. There are three entry channels and one exit channel. Can you spot which is which? The exit channel should, of course, be a wiggly one, which will slow down the exit of ch'i. The example illustrated here, however, is a bad configuration because of the opposition of one pair of channels to the other pair.

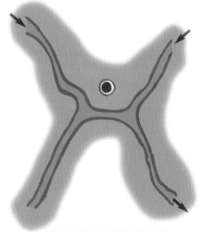

WATER LEAPS OVER PALACE

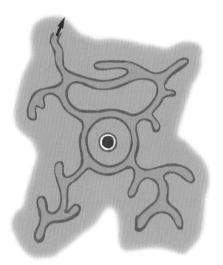

FOUR DRAGONS PLAYING WITH A PEARL

By now you should be able immediately to identify the *hsueh* in the center of the island, plus four feeder channels. Did I hear you say, "It's a yin formation because four is a yin number?" Well, nearly right. The top two feeder channels are linked, making it technically a three channel feeder structure. Sounds like cheating? No, it's just a bit more complicated.

Hand and finger patterns

Many patterns are structured like multifingered hands holding or embracing the *hsueh*.

Here the theme of hands holding the *hsueh* is quite explicit, and is even included in the title. Obviously, the "lute" is the double island structure shown bottom left.

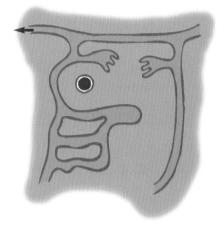

IMMORTAL HANDS PLAYING ON A LUTE

Here, two arms of the river encircle each side of the *hsueh*. Note that the longest finger comes from the Green Dragon side, ensuring that it remains stronger than the yin White Tiger (left) side. This is necessary because there are four fingers, rendering this a potentially yin configuration.

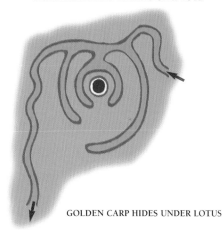

GOLDEN CARP HIDES UNDER LOTUS

Testing your Water Dragon skills

There are a number of other classical patterns, or themes, but the main ones have appeared above. If you have followed the logic of each one, you should now be able to place the *hsueh* spot correctly on the blank Water Dragon patterns on the opposite page. See page 352 for the correct answers.

Now go back and see if you can mark the head (source) and tail (exit) of each dragon. This is not always as easy as it looks, but it is a key part of this type of feng shui. Hint: Watch for the wiggly exit channels.

Then, if you are feeling brave (and assuming south is always at the top of the page), go back and mark down which of the eight Directions (N, S, E, W, NE, NW, SE, SW) is the exit direction for each of the patterns. There, that was not too bad!

You have gone a long way to being able to understand Water Dragons. The identification of the tail and mouth of the dragon (or its exit direction) is important because a number of Water Dragon formulas depend upon these directions.

An example of this, using the *pa kua*, is to relate the entry and exit directions to particular members of the family and see how the Water Dragon will specifically affect each of them, bringing wealth and honor to one but not to another. In ancient times this was a potent source of family feuds.

BASIC WATER DRAGON RULES

To summarize the basic rules, a good watercourse is one that:

a Flows in the correct direction in relation to the house, and especially the front door.

b Crosses and re-crosses the area in front of a site.

c Has no very sharp turns.

d Does not come in a straight line directly towards the home, unless it then makes a meandering exit.

e Has an exit that is invisible from the home.

PINPOINTING THE HSUEH

1
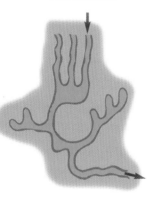
GOLDEN HOOK

2
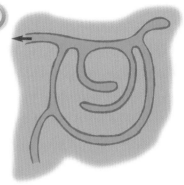
CROSSED SWORDS

3
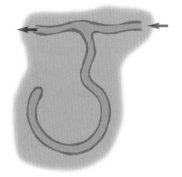
PHOENIX IN FLIGHT

4
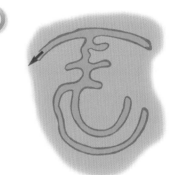
RAINBOW SWALLOWING AZURE CLOUDS

5
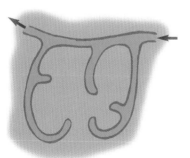
DOUBLE HOOK
(THIS NEEDS TWO *HSUEH*, AND IS A BIT TRICKY)

6

DRAGON TURNING BACK
(ONLY ONE *HSUEH* PLEASE!)

Creating a Water Dragon feature in your garden

HOW CAN YOU UTILIZE WATER FENG SHUI? Even if you have only a small garden, you can do on a small scale what a lot of ancient, and not so ancient, Chinese have done on a larger scale. You can build a miniature feng shui watercourse of your own.

Even with the tiniest garden, you can manage a small pond. You can improve on this by using an electric pump to circulate the water. The circulation is important because, as you know by now, stagnant water is going to have a very different and very negative effect on your feng shui. Where should the water circulate? Well, you can cheat a bit and install a fountain, which is simply fed from the bottom of the pond. Or you can organize an overflow at one end of the pond where the water is then pumped back to the fountain. In this way you get an actual and visible direction of flow. If this is the plan, then make sure that the visible current goes in the correct direction, and that the return water (moving in the wrong direction) is hidden in a buried pipe.

Although you may be tempted to use rubber or plastic liners, it is better to work with natural and semi-permeable channel liners so that the water can seep into the earth from the channels. This may not always be practical, however, especially on small water features where such leakage could drain away too rapidly.

When making your own garden Water Dragon feature, there are five things to watch out for: the tail of the dragon; the *ming tang*, or fronting pool; the fingers of the dragon; the direction of the dragon in relation to the front door; and the mouth of the dragon.

Tail of the dragon

The tail of the dragon is the source of the water and the incoming direction. Ideally, you should feed your Water Dragon from a small local stream. If this is not possible, try re-routing the direction of flow of surface drainage runoff or directing roof-collected rain through a downspout into the water feature.

■ **Water circulates continuously** *in these three linked pools in a Chinese public park. This design creates good feng shui, and can be recreated on a much smaller scale in the domestic garden.*

It is best to use rainwater, rather than fill the water feature with tap water. Tap water has been treated rather roughly by the city water and sewerage department and is less likely to be as strong in good ch'i as natural surface runoff or rainwater.

Any water flowing parallel with the rear wall and behind the building may indicate lost opportunities. If you can divert this water round to the front of the house, and contrive to have it pass by the front door in the correct direction, then you will have successfully done your first bit of Water Dragon engineering.

Ming tang, or fronting pool

Originally, even at grave-sites, it was customary to have some kind of a pool in front of the structure. It was part of the *ming tang*, or open area, in front of the site. (Originally, the word *ming tang* applied primarily to this pool.)

The pool serves three functions: accumulating both water and ch'i in front of the site, reflecting Heaven, specifically the moon, and bringing these influences into the site. Although this third function is seldom spoken about, it is just as important.

These pools can be square, rectangular, or sometimes circular. It is most common for them to be almost rectangular, with the side furthest from the building curved away from the building in a crescent shape. If this pool is fed solely from runoff and natural rainwater, it will not have a specific entry direction, and this may be the case with your homemade Water Dragon.

In large mansions or temples, these pools were sometimes painted red, reflecting the influence of the south (where they should ideally be located) and of the Fire Trigram *Li*.

Such ponds date back at least to the 5th century BC, when they were regularly installed by wealthy families.

The use of red paint is an interesting piece of symbolism that neatly ties together the north (Water, site of the Black Tortoise) and the south (Fire, site of the pool).

■ **Fronting pools,** *such as this ornate fountain, also play a part in European culture, gracing the entrances to many grand buildings.*

■ **During a drought**, *these fingers of the dragon are dry, but for the rest of the year water flows from the top of the hill, at the back of the house, and is directed along the channels to the front of the house.*

Fingers of the dragon

In the last section we looked in some detail at the structure of classical Water Dragons. You can also equip your garden Water Dragon with a yang number (1, 3, 5, 7, or 9) of folds. It will probably not be practicable to enfold your home in a number of fingers, as this entails building large channels on either side of your house.

However, if you plan to use natural roof rainwater runoff as your source of water, and your down-pipe is at the back of your house, this gives you an excellent reason to channel that water round the side of your house to the front. In which case, use what you know about classical patterns to make it an effective finger. The left side of the house (facing out), the Dragon (yang) side, is the best side to use for this channel.

233

Water Dragon formula

At some point, the water should flow past the front door. The simple rule to follow here concerns the direction of flow past the front door, which is always specified as if looking out from the front door. The general rule is that water should either flow:

1 **From right to left** – for houses whose front door faces the corner points of NW, SW, NE, SE, or more specifically: 307.5–352.5°, 217.5–262.5°, 37.5–82.5°, 127.5–172.5°.

2 **From left to right** – for houses whose front door faces the cardinal points of N, S, W, E, or more specifically: 352.5–360°, 1–37.5°, 172.5–217.5°, 262.5–307.5°, 82.5–127.5°.

Do not, if you can possibly help it, run the water past the back door. In addition, you need to bridge the water at some point with your front path. Do not put that bridge directly in front of the front door.

■ **To obscure the exit point** *of water from this garden pond, so that it is not visible from the house, the pipe has been covered by stone slabs and water plants.*

Mouth of the dragon

The mouth of the dragon, or the direction of exit flow, is particularly important because this is the direction in which ch'i may be lost, as ch'i always partly escapes with water. This is why the feng shui treatment of the wet rooms inside the house, such as the bathroom, is so essential.

The first rule, as we have mentioned, is that the actual exit point should not be visible from the house. So, if it is a small stream, it should turn a corner, perhaps behind some trees or a bush before exiting the site. If it is a home garden water feature, it could drain away invisibly down a pipe or into a rubble drain.

Obviously, if the pool is man-made, then the exact size and positioning of this exiting channel is the overflow that leads to the return pipe to the pump or fountain.

Formulas to calculate the exact exit point for wealth are too complex for this book, but I have covered them in my forthcoming book on water feng shui, *Classical Water Dragon Feng Shui.*

A simple summary

✔ Water Dragons are found in nature as well as being contrived by feng shui Masters.

✔ Water Dragons fall into basic types: folding, annular, spiral, multiple feeder channel, and hand and finger layouts.

✔ The basic rules for building your own Water Dragon in your garden include hiding the water exit, folding the watercourse, preventing sharp turns, and passing the front door in the correct direction.

✔ When building your own Water Dragon, you must work out the correct positioning for the tail (source), *ming tang*, finger layout, flow direction, and mouth (exit).

Chapter 16

The Feng Shui Garden

A FLOURISHING GARDEN is one of the best indicators of healthy feng shui in a home. Never leave dead or dying plants in your garden or allow weeds to flourish because they all accentuate the yin energies of nature. It is also important to root out old and moldering tree stumps. A lot of nonsense has been written about feng shui gardening. The usual assumption is that it is enough to divide the garden up into eight *pa kua* sectors. This is a huge oversimplification propounded by those who have no idea of the subtle symbolism and landscaping employed in Chinese gardens designed with feng shui in mind.

In this chapter...

✓ The four Celestial Animals in the garden

✓ Zen garden design

✓ The long and winding road

✓ Auspicious trees, fruits, and flowers

CREATE THE PERFECT FENG SHUI GARDEN USING THE PRINCIPLES OF THE FOUR CELESTIAL ANIMALS

The four Celestial Animals in the garden

REMEMBER THE FOUR CELESTIAL ANIMALS *in chapter 13? These should surround and protect any site or building. Try to organize the garden so that they are actually or symbolically present. For example, when siting a rockery, which is really a miniature mountain, think about the symbolic Black Tortoise, which, like a mountain, supports the back of the house.*

BLACK TORTOISE

It then becomes obvious that it would not be good feng shui to place a rockery at the front, or even at the sides, of a home or office building. If you already have a supportive mountain, high wall, or building behind your garden, then the supportive Black Tortoise is already in place. If not, then this position is where you might think about placing a rockery or wall, or planting a line of tall trees.

Conversely, in the front of the house, if possible, there should be an open area to allow beneficial ch'i to settle and accumulate. This is referred to as the *ming tang*, or "Bright Hall."

Balancing yin and yang

Any water feature, especially if it is a flowing one, is well sited in front of the house in this open area, according to the Form School model. Remember that water in feng shui is a special case, and although in general terms it should go in the front garden (in front of the building), its positioning has to be planned a bit more carefully. Beyond the open area there should be a small hillock or a low wall, like a curled lip, to retain the ch'i. This is symbolically the frontage Celestial Animal, called the Red Bird.

On either side of your house there should be a wall, or the vegetative equivalent, or enfolding hills. Remember that to the right, as you look out of the front door, is the yin White Tiger. This should be lower than the left side, which is the yang Green Dragon. A hedge or other strongly growing green feature, like bamboo, is good on that side. Remember, if the yin side is naturally more prominent, try to strengthen the yang Dragon side with garden lights or other structures to compensate.

Many books on feng shui have written about the garden as if it were an outside room. This is a legitimate view, but you should remember that the pa kua, the location of the eight Trigrams, and hence the location of the five Elements, is different outside the house than inside it.

Inside the home/office, always use the Later Heaven Sequence of the Trigrams, but outside, in the garden, you should use the Former Heaven Sequence of the Trigrams (see p. 124 for the arrangement of both).

Think also about lines of sight and visual framing. It is sometimes said that in such a garden you should not take more than three steps before, at a turning, another view presents itself. I think that perhaps five to eight steps is a more reasonable amount.

Most importantly, the balance of yin and yang should be maintained dynamically. Yin features include shade, hollows, darkness, and moisture, while yang features include sunlight, hillocks, stones, and dryness. This doesn't mean that yin features should be arbitrarily mixed with yang features just for the sake of it. It means that the garden should be laid out so that you pass from yin to yang vistas, and back again, with each part of the garden contrasting with its adjoining part. The object is to balance the yin and yang forces of nature in miniature, and deliver the ch'i energy to the *ming tang* area, where it can be absorbed by the house.

■ **Ponds accumulate beneficial ch'i,** *especially if they have gently curving sides like this one. Retain the gathering ch'i with a wall or hillock sited beyond the pond.*

Zen garden design

THE GARDEN IN THE CHINESE and Japanese tradition was very *carefully designed to imitate natural landscapes, but in a stylish and whimsical or exaggerated way. The Imperial Palace Summer Gardens near Beijing came complete with their own lakes and miniature mountains, which provided specially crafted views. The microcosm of the garden was meant to reflect the macrocosm of the natural world. The Chinese view is that the garden should be nature made perfect. The Japanese cultivate these same principles even more extremely and in a very stylized way.*

Feng shui features are common in these gardens. For example, bridges will often turn at right angles in the middle of a lake or stream. This avoids creating fast-moving *sha ch'i*, which would otherwise be created by a long, straight bridge.

Trees are often cut back in a stylish way. The ultimate expression of this is bonsai, where miniature landscapes are created with real, but artificially stunted, trees. It has sometimes been argued that bonsai is bad feng shui, because the natural growth energy has been restricted, but the careful planning that goes into these perfect miniatures belies that.

Bonsai are like the energy of a whole tree packed into a small space, and make very good Wood Element feng shui energizers when used indoors.

AN INTRICATELY STYLED BONSAI TREE PROMOTING GOOD FENG SHUI

The long and winding road

IF YOU ARE LUCKY ENOUGH to have your own garden, then you have an excellent opportunity to practice traditional Form School feng shui and so significantly improve the feng shui of your home. In your garden, there should be none of the rigid formality of French château gardens, where everything is squared off. Nor should there be the long, straight walks favored by English country houses. Instead, the lines of the garden should be curved and flowing, so that the ch'i energy is conducted smoothly through the garden and is contained rather than being allowed to escape to the street.

Make especially sure that no paths cut straight through your garden from one side and out the other side. Straight paths are anathema in a feng shui garden. This is especially true of the traditional straight path, which is often found linking the front door directly to the front gate. If there is an opportunity to curve this, without destroying an original feature, like a tessellated pavement, then by all means move the gate so that it is not directly in front of the door, and the path is forced to curve. Often this is not a practical thing to do if the space between door and gate is very short.

■ **Avoid formal patterns** *if you want to enhance the harmony of your garden. A natural-looking garden with curved paths and informal planting encourages ch'i to flow slowly and accumulate.*

If paths are made of large stepping stones, then gauge their positioning so that it is easy to take successive left then right footsteps. Walk the alignment first, taking comfortable steps, and marking where your feet fall. The gapping between the stones will definitely affect the speed of the walker and hence the speed of the ch'i following the path. Long gaps will promote a brisk stride, but short ones will force the walker to move more slowly. From this you can see that shorter gapping is preferable in stepping stone paths.

DEFINITION

*The **Tao** is the basic concept of Taoism, which is behind everything in the manifested universe. It is perhaps best visualized as the matrix behind everything, constantly changing, never repeating itself. The swirling mist was seen as just one image symbolic of the Tao.*

Stones with character

Stones are a very important part of feng shui garden design. This is particularly evident in Japanese Zen gardens. It can also be seen in the grounds of some Chinese temples and even in the grounds of Thai *wats*, or pagodas, where you can often find a collection of amazingly contorted "feng shui stones." These are sometimes fenced off from the rest of the compound. The stones are of natural origin, but they often have amazingly intricate and complex shapes, full of holes, and deeply eroded by water. These contortions are thought to mirror in nature the sinuous path of the *Tao* itself.

These stones can act as a yang piece within a yin setting. Quite often they are placed irregularly in an area of raked gravel, which represents water, so that they become the yang features in an otherwise flat yin area.

Stones can also represent Earth, being appropriate in those sectors of the garden where the Earth Element needs stimulating. Be careful, however: Form School feng shui has much to say about rocks that imitate fierce animals or that are rough and jagged. Such rocks will actually cause feng shui problems, and so should be excluded from your garden. Make sure that any rocks or stones you import into your garden both feel and look benevolent.

There is a famous lake in Anhui province in China that is the source of the best *lingbi* stones – highly eroded, smooth, hard pieces of limestone with great character. Taoist scholars sometimes pay huge prices to acquire small versions of these stones (often called philosophers' stones) to place in their gardens or their study, for contemplation. *Lingbi* stones can also be used as feng shui remedies when Earth needs to be strengthened.

■ **This miniature feng** *shui mountain, built up from sacred rocks, can be seen in the grounds of a Buddhist temple in Thailand.*

Water is a key feng shui feature. The austere lines of the Zen garden went even further and often symbolized real streams with raked swirls of gravel. Where real water was not practical, gravel acted as an imitation, and this principle could be echoed in the design of a domestic Western garden. The raking is often regular and wave-like, with an encircling wave around rocks, imitating the water ripples lapping around an island.

INTERNET

www.china-window.com

http://spirit-stones.com.

These two sites specialize in lingbi *stones.*

If you plan to use actual water, then see chapter 15 for some of the simple formulas that govern its placement in a garden. These depend on the exact degrees of the orientation of the front door, or ch'i mouth, of the house. Unless you make a special study of these methods, it's best to leave the siting of a significant body of water to a traditionally trained feng shui professional.

Garden lighting

It is not always possible, or even desirable, to redesign a garden totally. Garden lighting is, however, one thing that can make a huge difference and something over which you can have full control. Remember that light is yang, so to balance an excess of yin, simply increase the yang by adding garden lights.

LANTERN STYLES

In Japanese gardens, low stone lights, called *yukimi-gata*, or taller *tachi-gata* lanterns are used. Smaller *oki-gata* lanterns can be used low down beside a pond to throw reflected light across the water in the evenings. *Ikekomi-gata* lanterns, which are inserted straight into the ground, look good almost anywhere.

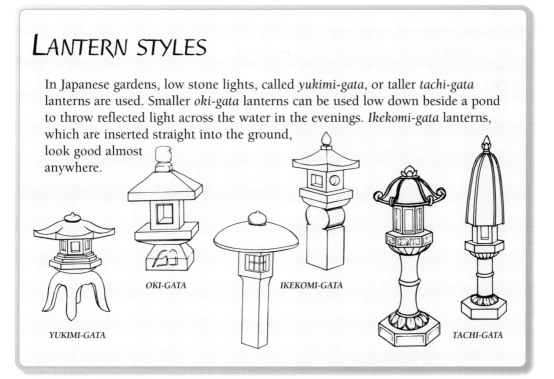

YUKIMI-GATA

OKI-GATA

IKEKOMI-GATA

TACHI-GATA

Lighting has been suggested as a cure for "missing corners" in a house shape, marking out where the house would have extended to if it had been built in a perfect rectangular shape. Such lighting then becomes an integral part of the feng shui features of the garden.

■ **Locate garden lighting** *in spots where you wish to increase the yang. Decorative pagoda-shaped lanterns, known as* tachi-gata, *will harmonize with tall shrubs and flowers.*

Where a corner of your garden is too yin – you know, dank, dark, or dismal – you should endeavor to "lift the ch'i." This can be done most easily with light, although sometimes a good clean-out can also do the trick. If you are using light in this way, you should ensure you preserve the balance of yin and yang, and do not over-compensate.

Plants are a key part of any garden. Try to plant shrubs and trees in such a way that the visitor to the garden cannot see everything at once. He or she should be surprised by new vistas at each turning.

There should be, if space permits, secret bowers and hidden views. Mix yin and yang, shade and sun, in interesting combinations – don't allow either shade or sun to predominate. Any good gardener will recognize the benefits of this immediately.

■ **Brightening a dark corner of the garden** *by introducing lively, variegated plants works in the same way as using lighting to "lift the ch'i."*

Auspicious trees, fruits, and flowers

BAMBOO

PLANT SYMBOLISM *has long been a part of Chinese culture and, consequently, feng shui symbolism. Specific trees and flowers have specific feng shui symbolic meanings. For example, the pine is seen as a symbol of longevity and should be planted where that quality is desirable, or where older relatives live in the home. The bamboo has a similar meaning, but is also celebrated for its tenacity and rapid growth. It makes an excellent Green Dragon plant to grow to the left of your front door (looking outward), and will soon outpace all but the largest White Tiger formations. Its stem is used for making flutes and also wind chimes, hinting at its ability to conduct ch'i.*

■ **Shou, the god of longevity,** *is a popular Chinese deity, shown here holding a ripe peach.*

Symbolic fruits

The "three fortunate fruits" are plants that also have a place in the feng shui garden. These are the pomegranate, the peach, and the finger-lemon. The pomegranate symbolizes fertility, as it is bursting with seeds. *Tzu*, which means "seeds" in Chinese, also means "children" when said with a different tone. This, incidentally, also appears as the north-pointing character *tzu* on the feng shui compass. This all ties together because the north is the yin darkness out of which the seed of spring forms. Because of its symbolism, the half-opened pomegranate is also a popular wedding present, and the tree will symbolically help to activate marital fertility.

The peach has a sexual symbolism, the soft down and shape being suggestive of the female vulva. It therefore represents the essence of yin. The basis of Chinese Taoist alchemy was to stimulate and accumulate the essence of yin in order to promote longevity, and so the peach is also seen as a symbol of longevity. The god Shou, who holds a peach in his hands, is the prototype of longevity and male success.

Peach wood is considered effective in driving away evil spirits, and is therefore used extensively to make pens and writing materials for Taoist talismans. It is also the best wood for constructing feng shui deflectors, including *pa kua* mirrors. Door guardians and household gods were often carved from peach wood. The peach is also considered the fruit of immortality, an interesting idea when put alongside the alleged cancer-curing effect of laetrile, which is extracted from peach stones. Interestingly, "peach blossom cave" is an old Chinese metaphor for a coffin, which ties it in with some of the doctrines of yin feng shui.

The third fortunate fruit, the finger-lemon, is a bizarre fruit not often seen in the West. In Chinese, it is called *fu-shou*, or "Buddha-hand," reflecting its finger-shaped excrescences. As such, it also symbolizes yang and the male genitals. You can see why it completes the trilogy of three fortunate fruits and may symbolically be applied to the cure of male impotence and similar problems.

PEACH BLOSSOM

Another fruit, which comes into its own during Chinese New Year celebrations when it is given as a present, is the orange. Its color reflects the color of gold and therefore it symbolizes the giving and receiving of wealth. Many other fruits have specific meanings, such as the red apricot, which stands for a married woman who is having an affair.

I am not for a moment suggesting that the planting of specific trees or flowers can incline the occupants toward such conduct, but it is possible to use the rich language of Chinese symbolism to reinforce your feng shui intentions.

Flowers of spring and fall

The plum is supposed to be the first tree to blossom in spring, and so is seen as special. The plum is described as "ice-skinned and jade-boned" and is compared (like spring) to an innocent girl emerging from the virginity of winter. "Plum-blossom" is a common Chinese metaphor for wench and so, by extension, sexual pleasure. Its feng shui symbolism, relating to marriage, derives from the same root. Shao Yung (1011–1077) even devised a system of fortune-telling related to the plum blossom, whose five petals reflect the five Elements.

■ **The chrysanthemum** *was adopted in China as the symbol for long life.*

The chrysanthemum is the seasonal opposite of the plum and is the flower of fall. Together, the chrysanthemum and the plum represent man and woman. The chrysanthemum's Chinese name sounds similar to the word for "nine," also giving it an association with the nine-chambered *lo shu.*

Beneficial plants

A plant rich with feng shui symbolism is the narcissus, or *shui hsien*, which means literally "water immortal." It is heavily symbolic of luck and its connections with the Element Water. Complementing this is the plant whose Chinese name sounds like wind, or *feng* – the maple – which is symbolic of appointment or career luck.

A water plant whose symbolism owes much to Buddhism is the lotus, which is a symbol of purity and spiritual attainment. At a more mundane level, when combined with other symbols, the lotus can represent many other things, in particular the opening of new opportunities or social advancement. Flowering as it does from the mud floor of ponds, it is an allegory of the perfect and the pure springing from the yin darkness.

■ **Lotus grows naturally** *in pond water but can be introduced into a garden in a man-made container.*

For associations with scholarship and the passing of examinations, you should look to the cinnamon (or cassia) tree. The expression "to break off a cinnamon twig" means "to pass the state examinations." The cinnamon could well be applied symbolically to enhance the Examination sector of a student's room.

■ **The jade, or money, plant** *has fleshy leaves, symbolizing the presence of wealth and the full enjoyment of life.*

A more specifically feng shui tree is the *wu-tung*, or tung tree. This is reputed to be the resting place of the Red Bird, and is therefore often planted in courtyards or in front of a site to represent this Celestial Animal. It is not auspicious to plant it directly in front of the main door.

In contrast to fleshy-leaved plants, those that are spiky, prickly, or have sharp-pointed flowers are considered negative, from a feng shui point of view, and should not be introduced into the garden.

The jade plant, which is also known as the money plant, has often been extolled as a feng shui plant that is ideal to keep indoors for activating the growth energies of Wood in the east or southeast.

■ **The seven-story pagoda** *is a traditional feng shui landscape addition. The roof points are turned upward to avoid creating* sha ch'i *for neighbors.*

Finally, the peony, or "queen of flowers," is the emblem of wealth and distinction. Of all its colors, red is the most auspicious. The peony also represents the female genitals, with dewdrops on its petals bearing an obvious sexual symbolism. Strangely, it is also considered a yang flower, probably because of its coloring, and is considered useful to families looking for a good marriage for one of their daughters. Planted with the hibiscus, it represents flourishing riches and reputation. Planted with the wild apple, the peony symbolizes riches and credit for the whole household.

Magical mushrooms

Although it is not a deliberately planted addition to any garden, the mushroom was valued by Taoists, and special varieties were sought after for their magical and hallucinogenic powers. Many Taoist adepts lived just on mushrooms, and many claims were made for the life-lengthening properties of specific varieties.

In 109 BC, a strange mushroom with nine stalks (symbolic of the *lo shu*) coming from one root spontaneously appeared in the Summer Palace in Beijing. Because of this, the Emperor declared a general amnesty on mushroom eating throughout the Empire, such was the importance of the mushroom.

The feng shui setting

Feng shui is at the heart of traditional Chinese gardens. These gardens were made to encourage contemplation and a feeling of stillness related to the mental disciplines of Zen (or Chan in the Chinese tradition). They were also there to provide a feng shui setting for the house, temple, or palace around which they were sited. The steady source of *sheng ch'i* generated by them is an asset to any house, ancient or modern.

A simple summary

✔ Yin–yang balance is the key to feng shui gardening, so that ch'i is generated and accumulated for the benefit of the house.

✔ Just splitting the garden into the eight sectors of the *pa kua*, and color planting accordingly, is not feng shui gardening.

✔ The garden should be structured to reflect the four Celestial Animals, which should enfold the house.

✔ The rear-supporting Black Tortoise is most important.

✔ Garden vistas should have a balanced mix of yin and yang.

✔ Water, which is sometimes replicated by gravel, is highly significant in the feng shui garden, and free-standing stones can form islands around which the "water" laps.

✔ Plants that are chosen on the basis of their symbolic meaning can be introduced into the garden to enrich your feng shui intentions. Examples include the "three fortunate fruits," the pine, the peony, and the lotus.

PART
FIVE

EARTH BALANCES THE FOUR OTHER ELEMENTS

REMEDIES AND FORMULAS

DON'T LET WORDS LIKE "FORMULAS" or "techniques" scare you off. This is where specific feng shui practices will be explained. The first formula is the Eight Mansion formula. It uses much of what you have learned in earlier chapters, especially the eight Directions and their eight Trigrams, the five Elements, and how they work with each other.

We will learn about "remedies," such as windchimes, colors, flutes, fountains, and mirrors. We will see how making one or two minimal changes to the Element balance of your decor will cause significant *changes to your life*. The East Life/West Life formula explains how to relate your personal feng shui to that of your house – an essential tool to use if you're buying a new home.

Chapter 17

The Eight Mansion Formula

ONE OF THE SIMPLEST but most effective Compass School feng shui techniques is the Eight House, or Eight Mansion, Formula. In Chinese it is called *pa chai* (also spelled *ba zhai*). This simple formula uses the four cardinal points of the compass (N, S, E, and W) plus the four intercardinal points (NE, SE, NW, and SW), in short the eight Directions. For this reason, you can even use an ordinary hiking compass to practice it. At its simplest, this formula makes you divide up the house or office being analyzed into the nine squares of the *lo shu* square (see chapter 8). This is then used to diagnose which parts of the house or office correspond to the relevant facets of your life, allowing you to target specific feng shui changes and pinpoint the areas in which they need to be made.

In this chapter...

✓ The Eight Mansion method

✓ Applying feng shui remedies

ACCURATE CALCULATIONS ARE VITAL FOR GOOD FENG SHUI, ESPECIALLY IN THE EARLY STAGES OF BUILDING

The Eight Mansion method

THIS TECHNIQUE IS USUALLY APPLIED *to a home, but can also be used for an office. In practice it's best to examine the whole house first, then apply a smaller* lo shu *square individually to the main rooms in turn, particularly the living room.*

The Eight Mansion formula

To use the Eight Mansion formula, there are eight simple steps to follow:

1 Draw an accurate scale plan of your house/office/apartment/room.

2 Mark the eight Directions of the compass, N, S, E, W, SE, SW, NE, NW, on the plan, using a compass.

3 Place the *lo shu* over the house plan and divide up the area into nine squares.

4 Identify the location of the Eight Life Aspirations (more of this soon).

5 Mark in the associated Element in each cell (and perhaps also its producing Element).

6 Select in turn each of the Aspirations and decide if it is OK, or if it needs enhancement or remedying.

7 Using your knowledge of the Elements, select an enhancement or remedy for that Aspiration(s).

8 Position the remedies in the correct places.

Next we'll look at these steps in detail.

■ **The Eight Mansion formula** *can be used for a whole apartment, house, or office, or it can be applied to just one room.*

Drawing an accurate scale plan

If you get the proportions wrong then you may finish up putting feng shui remedies in the wrong sectors, making it wrong shui rather than feng shui. If you are doing an important job (and let's face it, what job isn't?), then it can be quite useful to have a plan-drawing service quickly run you up an accurate plan to scale.

Marking in the eight Directions of the compass

Use a compass to make sure these are correctly marked. But how do you check where these directions are?

If you are working in a single room with a simple hiking compass:

1 Simply lay the compass on the floor in the center of the room. Turn it till the north pointer and the painted end of the needle line up.

2 Read off all the directions, without moving the compass again.

> ### Trivia...
> It is both a Chinese and a feng shui convention to draw maps and plans with south at the top of the page. Putting north at the top is just a European mapmakers' convention.

If you are working with a whole building:

1 Take your ordinary hiking compass and stand with your back to your front door, facing outward. Turn the compass till the marked line, or north point lines up with the painted end of the needle.

2 Looking outward from the house, check what direction is shown at the point of the compass dial furthest from you. Record this on your plan as the front door direction. From this you can work out the other three cardinal points.

3 If you feel safer, repeat the procedure looking outward from all the major exterior walls of your home. It is obvious, but make sure that north is marked opposite south on your plan, and that east is directly opposite west. Then fill in the intercardinal points, SW between S and W and so on.

Note that the procedure for compass alignment for the lo p'an, the professional feng shui compass, is slightly different and is described in detail in chapter 23.

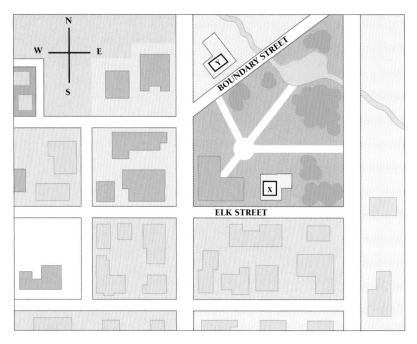

■ **This sample street map** *shows how you can easily use a map rather than a compass to determine in which direction your house faces.*

If you don't have a compass at hand, but are eager to get on with feng shui, then help can be found in your local city map or atlas:

1 Orientate the map so that north is at the top (well, this is a Western map, isn't it?). Find your street. If your street runs from the top down, then it runs north to south. If it runs left to right, then it's an east–west street.

2 Next figure out which side of the street your house is on. Let us assume you live on Elk Street, which runs across the middle of the map from left to right. So, from the compass directions we can see that Elk Street runs east–west. Now using a magnifying glass, find your house (marked at X). If it's on the north side of Elk Street, then it must face south. So we have identified that your house is south-facing, by using a map rather than a compass.

3 Fill in the other three cardinal points on your plan, then the inter-cardinal points.

Let's try another example. In which direction does your house face if it is located at Y on Boundary Street? The answer is southeast.

Remember, however, that a compass is the most accurate. At this point all we need are the eight Directions. But later, with more precise work, we must have a good compass to pick out the 24 Directions (three times more precise).

Placing the lo shu over the house plan

The way to do this is to measure the longest side and mark it off into three parts. Do the same with the shorter side, then draw in the dividing lines, which will break the area up into nine rectangles.

For a square house or office, facing neatly to one of the cardinal points of the compass, this is a simple job. If the house shape is square, then the lo shu will fit perfectly. If your house is rectangular, then the lo shu stretches to accommodate.

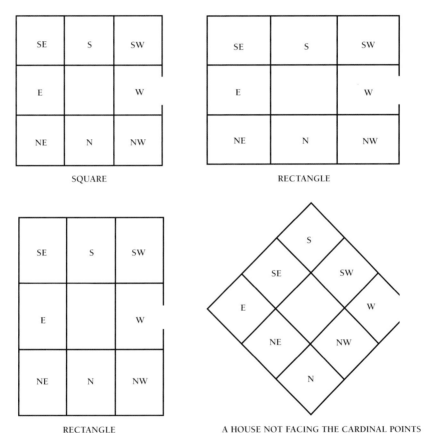

SQUARE

RECTANGLE

RECTANGLE

A HOUSE NOT FACING THE CARDINAL POINTS

When dividing up a house, it's tempting to talk of, for example, the southwest corner, but when the whole house has its corners pointing to the cardinal points, then the southwest becomes a side not a corner, and it becomes confusing.

So rather than say "southwest corner," I prefer to talk of the "southwest sector." The southwest can then be a corner in one house, but a side in another differently oriented house, without it becoming a problem.

Please note that the cardinal points do not move. It's just that different houses point in different directions. And, Chinese style, south is always drawn at the top.

It gets a bit more complicated, however, when there is an L-shaped or irregularly shaped house. Here feng shui Masters agree, but Western writers start to diverge. The rule is, if it's a temporary structure like a lean-to, it can be disregarded.

SE	S	
E		
NE	N	NW

L-SHAPED HOUSE

Otherwise, you should try to embrace the whole structure within the *lo shu*, as in the diagram (shown left), which plainly has a missing west and SW sector and a limited south sector. We will discover later the result of these "missing sectors." An important point to remember is that only if there are two quite distinct living areas should an L-shaped house be treated as two separate areas, each with its own *lo shu*.

Identifying the location of the eight Life Aspirations

Now that the building/apartment or room has been divided up into the nine sectors of the *lo shu*, the fun begins. Each of these areas is associated with one of life's eight main Aspirations, at least as feng shui sees them. Write these Aspirations into each of the cells of the *lo shu*.

The concept of the formula is that appropriate changes in specific parts of the building/room change the ch'i in such a way that it affects differing aspects of the life of the occupants of the building. The eight Life Aspirations are supposed to cover most things of key importance to us.

Fame (south) and Career (north) are represented at opposite sides of the building or room. In a way, these are complementary. Fame for most of us means to be well known amongst our friends and fellow workers. Few of us achieve real fame or notoriety. Fame in this sense is often the key to advancement in a job. Enhancing both is the way to go to secure advancement in your chosen career.

The east–west axis shows our place in the long line that stretches from our distant ancestors (in the east) to our immediate children and their

SE WEALTH	S FAME	SW ROMANCE
E FAMILY	CENTER HEALTH	W CHILDREN
NE KNOWLEDGE	N CAREER	NW MENTORS

THE EIGHT LIFE ASPIRATIONS

MODES OF DIVISION

Some schools of feng shui and some Masters (particularly in Hong Kong) prefer to find the exact center of gravity of the area, then divide it up into eight pie-wedge shapes. This is geometrically more accurate from a compass point of view, but inevitably these divisions will cut across many walls and make the division of rooms very messy. In addition, the pie-wedge way of doing things does not, to my knowledge, appear in pre-20th century feng shui texts.

By using the *lo shu* "tic-tac-toe" form, single rooms will often fall neatly into one cell or another, which is very useful for our analysis. The pie-wedge system of division can produce remarkably accurate results, but it is more difficult.

Yet another school uses unevenly proportioned pie wedges, following the Japanese system of Nine Star Ki. This is totally at odds with the intentions of traditional feng shui, and I would advise readers not to use it.

descendants (in the west), with us in the middle. More popularly, the east is associated with our parents and our family in that sense, while the west is associated with our children. At the end of the day, you don't always need to work on every aspect of your feng shui, and the west is a case in point if you do not have children, or want them.

The NW–SE axis is concerned with our prosperity and business. The SE is concerned with wealth, particularly that generated through our own efforts or business. What is most essential to such undertakings? Good connections, and if possible a powerful mentor (who is represented by the NW end of this axis). It makes sense to enhance both ends of this axis if you are in business.

The NE–SW axis is less obvious. The SW area is attributed to the getting of a good marriage, traditionally a serious concern in ancient China. In these more flippant days, romance and a good relationship can be enflamed by warming up the SW sector. But what has this to do with the NE corner, knowledge? Well, first you need to know that in China, prior to the 20th century, admission to the civil service, to the mandarin class, was via a system of examinations. The system was a true meritocracy, where even the poorest could rise through the ranks if they were able to learn enough to compete successfully in the exams. Your place in society was assured if you made a good marriage and passed the right exams. Not much has changed!

INTERNET

www.wofs.com

Go to the World of Feng Shui web site to see Lillian Too on Eight Mansion feng shui.

Applying feng shui remedies

LET'S STAND BACK and find out what might need remedying. Let's look at a few examples.

If, for example, we found that our children were having difficulty with their school, we would look in two places, the west sector (Children) and the NE sector (Examinations and Knowledge). Have a good look. Maybe the west sector corresponds to a storeroom filled with junk. Solution: Clear it out. Maybe the NE sector corresponds to a toilet. Oh dear, our children's examination luck might well be "flushed away." Solution: Close off the toilet as much as possible, even make it "disappear" by mirroring its whole door.

With more space we could go into other examples, but you will be surprised time and again when blockages in certain departments of your life turn out also to be physical blockages, like clutter in a corresponding part of your environment. The cure may simply be down to a bit of lateral thinking and ingenuity.

Marking in the associated Elements

OK, so we have now written these aspirations in on our plan, so we know which rooms or parts of a room correspond to which life aspiration. Now we have to put in the Elements, so we can start to work the feng shui. The diagram below will enable you to label your plan with the relevant Elements. You can immediately see that five Elements are not going to fit neatly into nine sectors. This is how it is done.

Opposites tend to be opposite each other, so that Fire (south) is opposite Water (north), and Wood (east and SE) is opposite Metal (west and NW). Earth, being the central Element, traces a diagonal from NE to SW via the Center.

So, what is the use of that? Simply put, this formula says that to enhance an Aspiration, simply add more of its Element to the appropriate sector.

THE EIGHT ASPIRATIONS, THEIR LOCATIONS, AND ELEMENTS

We can, of course, get more sophisticated and add the Element that produces the Element we want to the appropriate sector.

Remember that the remedies are ideally real Element remedies, which are more effective than symbolic remedies, like pictures representing the Element.

Selecting each of the Aspirations for enhancement

Some people try to enhance all the areas of their life, with the result that their life becomes a whirl.

I suggest strongly that you keep a diary. Plan to enhance one sector: Remedy one part of your life where you can identify specific problems that correlate to conditions in that room or sector of your house. Write down what you hope to achieve, what remedy you put in place, and when you did so.

Keeping a feng shui diary is the only way to objectively track feng shui changes so that as each kicks in, you have a clear idea of what has happened. Sometimes we all make mistakes, and such a diary will help you where you have inadvertently used the wrong remedy in the wrong sector. Having selected one Aspiration, set about designing an enhancement or remedy.

Using the Elements

A *feng shui remedy* (cure for a perceived problem) or enhancement (change designed to increase the amount of ch'i energy going into that particular aspect of our life) can be achieved by first identifying the appropriate sector and then by:

> **DEFINITION**
>
> A **feng shui remedy** or cure is a deliberate change in the ch'i flow or Element balance, designed to correct or enhance a particular area of the occupant's luck or life.

1 Adding more of the Element of that sector.

2 Adding more of the Producing Element.

3 Clearing out clutter, or clearing out items that "destroy" the Element we are trying to foster.

4 Changing the decor to make it sympathetic to one of the above Elements.

5 Placing specific remedies in that sector (more about this in the next chapter).

To do this we need a few more correspondences. The table below sets out the eight Aspirations, their Locations, Elements, and Colors:

ASPIRATIONS AND THE ELEMENTS

"HOME" LOCATION	"HOME" ASPIRATION	ELEMENT	COLOR OF ELEMENT	PRODUCING ELEMENT
N	Career	Water	Black, dark blue	Metal
NE	Knowledge, exam success	Earth	Yellow, earthy colors	Fire
E	Family, ancestors	Wood	Green	Water
SE	Wealth, prosperity	Wood	Green	Water
S	Fame, peer acceptance	Fire	Red	Wood
SW	Romance, love, good marriage	Earth	Yellow, earthy colors	Fire
W	Children, descendants	Metal	Gold, silver, white	Earth
NW	Mentors, networking	Metal	Gold, silver, white	Earth
Center	Health	Earth	Yellow, earthy colors	Fire

Don't be tempted to paint the four walls of your living room bright green, red, black, yellow, and gold. Feng shui is about balance and subtlety. Use one elementary color to energize just one Element.

Placing the remedies

Now you are in a position to actually make a feng shui change. Do it carefully, with attention and care. Then sit back and watch for results. Some changes come remarkably quickly within days, sometimes a trend takes root at the moment of change and things begin to improve steadily. Whatever happens, you will notice it.

■ **Yellow helps to energize**
Earth, but there are more subtle ways of doing this than painting every wall. Color can be introduced in more creative ways, such as by using flowers or pictures.

A simple summary

✔ In this chapter you have learned a completely self-contained and effective feng shui technique, the Eight Mansion formula.

✔ Many problems can be resolved using this technique, and it is probably the simplest to use and most widely known feng shui technique.

✔ It is most important to accurately ascertain the eight Directions and mark them on a *lo shu* grid placed over the house plan.

✔ Use this to identify the eight Life Aspirations on the plan.

✔ Enhance the correct Elements to derive the appropriate remedies.

Chapter 18

Feng Shui Remedies

Now that we understand which Element needs enhancing or diminishing, and where in the home or office this needs to be done, it only remains for us to discover what to use to make these changes. In other words, we need to know exactly what to prescribe. The idea of "prescribing" has caused many modern feng shui enthusiasts to think of this as selecting a remedy. So although it sounds medical, it has become accepted to talk about feng shui cures or remedies.

In this chapter...

✓ Remedies for each Element

✓ Light remedies

✓ Wind enhancers and flutes

✓ Movement remedies

✓ Blocking, deflecting, and absorbing remedies

CARVED DRAGON PILLARS AND BONSAI TREES ENHANCE THE FENG SHUI OF A CHINESE TEMPLE

Remedies for each Element

WE WILL DEAL FIRST *with the manipulation of the five Elements in order to bring about balance or to activate one or more of the Aspirations of the Eight Mansion formula. The theory behind these is contained in the Production, Destruction, and Reduction Cycles of the Elements, and I suggest you review these sections in chapter 6 before getting deeper into this chapter.*

There are two simple ways of activating an Element. First, add some more of that Element (or, less effectively, something symbolic of it). Remember that although you may be adding physical water, what you are really doing is stimulating Water energy.

Second, you could stimulate the Element that produces the Element you are trying to activate. For example, if you were trying to activate Wood energy, you could apply Water, since in the Production Cycle of the Elements Water produces (more) Wood.

The five Elements are considered to be a family, so that if you take a particular Element, then:

- The Element that produces it is its Parent (logically enough).
- The Element it produces is its Child.
- The Element that controls it is its Grandparent (isn't that often the way in an integrated family?).
- The same Element helps and supports it and is called its Sibling (or brother/sister).

Let's take Wood as a concrete example:

- The Element that produces it is its Parent – Water.
- The Element it produces is its Child – Fire.
- The Element that controls it is its Grandparent – Metal.
- The same Element is called its Sibling – Wood, of course.

Get the idea? The Chinese are very family minded, and family structure often features in their metaphors.

What we are really doing here is assisting the inner processes of growth and decay of the universe. Feng shui thus adjusts the energy and "luck" environment behind the scenes by changing the interaction of the five Elements. Simple, yes?

Let's say you have a situation where you want to strengthen a particular Element, or where you need to tame one that is too strong. First, you need to refer to the table below, which lists the remedies to strengthen, control, or destroy each Element (and the appropriate sector of the building or room in which this might suitably be applied). From this table you can easily choose which Element cure you need to introduce.

SECTOR	ELEMENT	SIBLING	PARENT	GRANDPARENT	CHILD
		(Add to reinforce Element)	(Add to produce more of Element)	(Add to control Element)	(Add to drain or weaken Element)
E, SE	WOOD	Wood	Water	Metal	Fire
S	FIRE	Fire	Wood	Water	Earth
SW, NE	EARTH	Earth	Fire	Wood	Metal
W, NW	METAL	Metal	Earth	Fire	Water
N	WATER	Water	Metal	Earth	Wood

Now you know which Elements to introduce, let's look at the sort of cures you might use.

Water

Water is located in the north sector. To activate it, you could add actual water, or things symbolic of Water, like the color black, or pictures of waterfalls. Water is also the producing Element for Wood, so adding Water in the east or southeast would also be appropriate.

水

SHUI (WATER)

Typical Water enhancers are an aquarium or a small interior fountain. It is critical that the water is moving (or yang) water and definitely not stagnant (or yin), since a stagnant fish tank will produce stagnant ch'i, and may be much worse than no remedy at all. Fish help to keep the water moving, too. Fish also perform a symbolic function – the golden scales of goldfish introduce a touch of Metal, and so the symbolism of wealth.

The addition of fish has three effects. First, their swimming helps to maintain movement. Second, in the case of goldfish or koi carp, their gold color is also symbolic of wealth (these fish were often placed in temple ponds). Third, make sure the tank is not out of proportion to the room: You don't want to "drown" the room with too much Water. Such an outsized tank in a business environment might increase turnover to the point where staff were "drowning" in work, with no time to ensure profitability.

■ **A small aquarium** *containing goldfish can affect the feng shui of a room, but make sure the aquarium has an air bubbler to disturb the surface, so that the water does not become stagnant.*

There is a lot of nonsense talked regarding the ideal number of fish. Enough for the tank is the right answer. But if you want to keep your symbolism correct, an odd number is best, because it is then a yang number.

If you are adding fish to the tank, nine would be a good odd number of fish, because it symbolizes the *lo shu* square. Some practitioners suggest a single black fish, "to absorb the negative energies." The Chinese attitude to such fish, which might seem kind of heartless, is that if they die this represents negative ch'i that has been absorbed by the fish rather than by you, which is therefore a good thing!

A small fountain is also ideal, as it recycles the water and really stimulates the Element. If used in the southeast or east, healthy aquatic weed can also symbolize the Wood Element of these sectors. This, incidentally, is a traditional remedy.

The traditional color for Water is black. Despite the desire by many Western decorators to avoid this color and go instead for blue, only the darkest blue will do. From a decorative point of view, it is far better to use dramatic black and then enhance it with silver or gold in filigree or detailing, producing a stunning result, than merely to depress an area by painting it dark blue.

Incidentally, both these metallic colors generate Water, so they are useful. Feng shui teacher Jes Lim, among others, puts up an argument for blue being the correct attribution, but I think any cursory study of Chinese architecture and interior decorating will dispel this idea in favor of the traditional ascription.

Fire

Fire is located in the south sector. To activate it, add fire or things symbolic of Fire. Fire is the producing Element for Earth, so adding Fire in the center, southwest, or northeast would also be appropriate.

HUO (FIRE)

Live flame, like a fire in a grate, or candles, is an excellent activator of Fire. Unfortunately, most houses or rooms equipped with fire grates will not necessarily have them in the right sector of the room, and candles can be a fire hazard. Fortunately, there are many other Fire enhancers, such as lights and red-colored items. Among the products now supplied by lighting specialists is a very interesting *faux* living flame light. The effect of this is created by illuminating twisting material, which blows upward, and for all the world looks like a live flame, but without the dangers of the real thing. Other Fire enhancers will be mentioned later, when we consider lighting.

■ **Glowing red candles** *can bring the Element of Fire to any room, though care should be taken to place them where no accidents can happen.*

The color to use for Fire is bright red. Maybe you can get away with dilutions of this color, particularly by adding yellow to create orange. Salmon is also possible, but that color has strayed a long way from the archetypal red. Purple is also sometimes suggested as a Fire color, but it is more appropriately used for Imperial purposes, and under certain circumstances in the central Earth cell of the *lo shu*.

Earth

Earth is located in the center and the southwest and northeast sectors. To activate it, you could add things symbolic of Earth. Earth is the producing Element for Metal, so adding Earth in the west or northwest would also be appropriate.

TI (EARTH)

Earth is a very interesting Element because it occupies three of the nine cells of the *lo shu*. Enhancers can be literally Earth in the sense of crystals, or stones like *lingbi* rocks – these are smooth but very interestingly shaped rocks that used to be collected by Taoist scholars. (Some of these have been sold recently at auction in New York by the William Doyle Galleries at prices around the $6,000 mark, showing that there are collectors who still take these lovely Taoist stones seriously.) Such an enhancer can also act as an anchor, and this is a very obvious use when larger rocks are featured in Chinese or Zen gardens.

Of course, crystals have a distinct part to play here. Not only do they come from the Earth, but they also refract yang light. Many feng shui shops in the Far East now sell crystal geodes, often amethyst, for feng shui purposes.

AMETHYST GEODE

Some are beautifully enhanced with rolling crystal balls supported and rotated on a constantly flowing pad of water. These are elaborate and sometimes expensive combination feng shui enhancers but they go a long way past simply stimulating Earth. I predict that they will gradually become more available in North America and Europe over the next few years.

Colors for Earth include yellow, buff, fawn, and, under very special conditions, purple.

Wood

Wood is located in the east and southeast sectors. To activate it, you could add growing plants or things symbolic of Wood. Wood is the producing Element for Fire, so adding Wood in the south would also be appropriate.

MU (WOOD)

Wood is, of course, growing vegetation, not just dead wood furniture. Virulent growers like bamboo have a place as Wood enhancers, just as do indoor plants of the non-spiky kind. Bundles of vigorously shooting bamboo canes constitute an excellent Wood enhancer, and they will flourish in water, with no need for earth. Remember that, like a stagnant aquarium, a moribund plant is worse than useless. Living plants also help to soften otherwise hard lines and sharp *sha*-producing corners.

It is said that artificial plants will do just as well as the real thing, but I feel that plastic, cloth, and silk cannot embody the true nature of Wood, which is vegetative growth.

■ **Healthy plants** *that do not have spiky leaves play an important part in bringing Wood into a room.*

Dead or less-than-fresh cut flowers are definitely out, as their potential for generating yin ch'i is much greater than any visual benefit they could confer. Anyone who has put their nose anywhere near the water from flowers well past their sell-by date will have no difficulty in understanding the meaning of *ssu ch'i*, or torpid ch'i!

Prickly plants like cacti or holly should also be avoided. Apart from any thought of tiny poison arrows, they are not comfortable plants to have around. Traditionally, a certain type of pond plant was also thought to be a Wood enhancer and was, in fact, listed as one of the 12 Imperial treasures.

The color for Wood is fresh light green, the color of new spring vegetation.

Metal

CHIN (METAL)

Metal is located in the west and northwest sectors. To activate it, you could add things symbolic of Metal. Metal is the producing Element for Water, so adding Metal in the north would also be appropriate.

Metal means several different things. It is literally the metal extracted from its "mother," the Earth. It is also symbolic of man-made things, particularly electronic items. Accordingly, good Metal enhancers include the TV and the PC, with the added bonus that movement and electrical charge yield a yang bonus. Metal sculptures will also do, but watch out for poison arrows projected from sharp and spiky sculptures.

The color of Metal is a bit of a tricky one. White is acceptable, since it is the opposing color to the black of Water, which is generated from Metal.

For some Chinese, white is seen culturally as the color that is representative of death. However, this is more like the faded-looking color of unbleached calico, rather than the crisp white that is symbolic of Metal.

■ **The family television** *is a good enhancer of Metal, and so plays a valuable role in the decor.*

You can avoid white if you like, however, because there are all the metallic shades to choose from. The Chinese root character for metal – *chin* – is the same as gold (perhaps reflecting the idea that all metals were just a corrupted form of gold), so the color of metallic gold makes a most appropriate and appealing decorative color in the west and northwest.

Light remedies

STAUNCH TRADITIONALISTS MIGHT SAY that only Element-related remedies are real feng shui remedies. But light, sound, and movement can certainly help to correct or enhance feng shui. All these are yang cures and the exact opposite of darkness, silence, and stillness, which are all yin qualities.

Lighting to lift ch'i

Light is yang and lifts ch'i. Light includes: natural sunlight, electric lights, naked flames such as candles, or prisms and chandelier lusters that catch and refract light. Light is not specifically any Element (except perhaps Fire), but it can be effectively used to expel excessive yin from dark corners. Remember that feng shui is about balance, and that ideally three-fifths of the mix in a home (possibly higher in an office) should be yang.

Light can also be used to help balance an L-shaped building. An outdoor lamp placed at the point that would have been the "other corner" if it had been a rectangle symbolically converts the L-shape into a rectangle. Uplighters can also help lift overhead beams.

Feng shui-inspired lighting is an art that can also make great psychological improvements to any building.

■ **Spotlights have been used here** *to supplement the natural light and try, ineffectively, to correct the bad feng shui of so many exposed beams.*

Wind enhancers and flutes

WIND AND SOUND are intimately linked. Sound is yang and a ch'i stimulator, and, of course, wind is half of the meaning of the characters "feng shui." Note that the word is "wind," not "air," indicating that ch'i needs movement, not stagnancy.

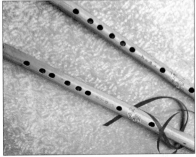

When you think of wind instruments, flutes come to mind. Tubes have been traditionally used as ch'i conductors. One such use of flutes is to reduce the downward "pressure" caused by overhead beams. To do this, they need to be hung on the side of the beam, in pairs and at a 45-degree angle pointing downward. They will then help to conduct downward part of the otherwise disturbed ch'i flow.

■ **Wind flutes** *are tubular and are used as ch'i conductors. They are also able to produce sound.*

Beams create disturbed ch'i, because they interrupt the flow of ch'i across the ceiling and are therefore inadvisable to sit or sleep under. If someone sits or sleeps regularly beneath one, the disturbed ch'i can cause headaches or even (in the case of sleeping under a beam) more serious medical conditions.

Trivia...

A 1st-century BC Chinese scientific experiment used tubes of different lengths (derived from the musical scale) filled with fine ash to measure the changing ch'i of the seasons. As each type of ch'i reached maturity during the course of the year, so the ash was expelled by it from the pipes. Hence tubes (of specific lengths) have been known to conduct ch'i for some considerable time, and so it is no surprise that they are used as remedies.

The other commonly used tubular feng shui remedy is the wind chime. These have the same qualities as the flute, but since they are made of multiple tubes of varying but specific length, they are more effective. Wind chimes are often used to regulate and slow down ch'i in positions like hallways. In more poetic feng shui texts, ch'i is personified as if it were seduced into stopping long enough to play with the wind chimes before passing on its way, rather than rushing straight through. Either way, wind chimes slow down ch'i.

Long hallways or areas where two (or worse, three) doorways face each other become sites of rapid ch'i flow. It is particularly important to slow down ch'i flow in a hall that runs direct from front to back door. Wind chimes can usefully perform that function.

Much has been written about how many tubes a wind chime should have, what they should be made of, and whether they should be solid or hollow. The archetypal wind chime should have five hollow metallic tubes, of specifically cut lengths, tuned to the Chinese pentatonic musical scale. It can be made of metal or wood.

In situations where metal would be a disadvantage (for example, where you want to accumulate Wood energy), a wood wind chime is a better choice. The question of five or six tubes comes down to symbolism. Solid metal wind chimes are often prescribed to press down on a negative energy, such as that generated by toilets. These will, of course, not be able to perform their ch'i-conducting purpose in the same way as hollow tubes, but they will provide extra moving, or yang, Metal.

INTERNET

www.bestcrystals.com/
geodes.html

www.surpluzz.com/cryst
alarium/index_about.htm

*There are a number of
sites featuring geodes,
but these are two of the
most interesting.*

Electronic equipment

Electronic equipment was not around when feng shui was first discovered and codified, but it is accepted that such equipment relates to the Element Metal and is yang in the sense that it provides movement and sound. Metal is most appropriately located in the west and northwest, also in the north where Metal creates Water. Try not to put too much Metal in the Wood sectors of east and southeast.

More about crystals

In Southeast Asia there are feng shui shops that sell crystals, from the very small to 6-foot-high geodes, crammed with many smaller crystals, often quartz or amethyst. Geodes are naturally occurring underground hollow tubes or cavities in which minerals have crystallized. They could almost be imagined as (Dragon) veins in the earth. Hence, they are archetypal Earth enhancers. Although not used in classical feng shui, they are popular today.

Combination enhancers are now being manufactured consisting of a stone ball mounted inside a geode and supported on a thin film of water so that it spins. This provides a combination of movement, Earth, and Water, and is sometimes even supplemented by the emission of ch'i-like water vapor.

COMBINATION ENHANCER

As feng shui revives in the East, ingenuity is being applied to many old remedies that are being dusted down and re-engineered. The few that have appeared in Western textbooks are only the tip of the iceberg.

Movement remedies

IN HONG KONG, *especially in some of the older rabbit-warren offices and apartment blocks, apartments can be a long way from the main street door. To encourage the ch'i to reach deep into these buildings, several intriguing devices, like a small rotating barber's pole, are stationed on landings and at the bends in staircases. These have the effect of coaxing the ch'i deeper into the building. These are also sometimes used at the entrances to restaurants and other commercial premises to similarly coax the ch'i of wealth and customers to enter.*

Flags have traditionally been a movement remedy, and long pennant-shaped ones can be seen in both Chinese and Japanese environments. Carp and dragon shapes are particularly appropriate.

Although the Chinese consider clocks dubious presents because they imply mortality, a grandfather clock with chimes and a long pendulum is sometimes prescribed where yang movement is needed to enliven an area. (Note that I didn't say "grandmother" clock because of the yin connotation.)

■ **Fluttering prayer flags** *provide movement to encourage ch'i to enter this formidable Nepalese temple.*

Blocking, deflecting, and absorbing remedies

TRADITIONALLY, ONE OF THE MOST important feng shui improvements is to block off sha ch'i alignments. These can include long straight streets aimed at your front door, or the edges of huge buildings, or the uncomfortable effects of lamp posts, spires, or poles located just outside, and pointing toward, your door or window.

Often you can't change the offending object, so the best bet is to block it off. What you can't see (or maybe what can't see you) can't affect you.

The most permanent form of blocking is, of course, a wall or a screen. In China, many entrances are blocked by a short piece of free-standing wall, so that it is not possible to directly approach and enter a doorway. This works on the principle that sha ch'i travels only in straight lines. I can tell you from experience that it also makes the direct approach of large furniture very difficult!

Deflecting is another thing you can do if blocking is not practical. For this a mirror, or in particular the special mirror surrounded by the eight Trigrams, or pa kua, is useful. When placing a mirror, make sure the offending object is fully reflected in it. Such deflectors have one downside – they may redirect the energy at another house.

Lastly, a retaliatory "destructor" is sometimes employed. An example of this is the use of an actual cannon to point at an opposing sha ch'i. An often quoted example of this is the cannon standing outside the Boustead building in Kuala Lumpur, which is pointed at the sha ch'i generated by the building on the opposite side of the road – not comfortable for the office directly opposite! There is a basis in tradition for this, where tubular structures were used to conduct ch'i.

■ **A mirror** surrounded by the eight Trigrams, or pa kua, is used to deflect any sha ch'i. Such mirrors should only be hung outdoors.

Resisting stones, or shih kan tang

A number of other traditional *sha ch'i* blockers are not even mentioned by modern Western feng shui writers (with the honorable exception of Derek Walters), but they are every bit as, if not more, effective. One example is the *shih kan tang*, a special stone that looks a little like a gravestone, deliberately planted in the path of a *sha ch'i* alignment. The Chinese calligraphy on the stone usually says something like, "this mountain dares defy" or "this stone dares to resist." They sometimes also have a carved *t'ai chi* (the tadpole-shaped yin/yang symbol) or a *pa kua* (eight Trigrams) on them for added strength. They are designed to stop the *sha ch'i* in its tracks, and are sometimes ornamented with a ferocious (yin) tiger's head. They are considered miniature versions of one of the eight sacred Taoist mountains of China, particularly Mount T'ai Shan.

Trivia...
The use of the shih kan tang to deflect evil is ancient, maybe dating back to 35 BC. In the time of the Chou dynasty (1027–221 BC), there was a family called Shih who adopted the motto "kan tang," or "dare-all." These stones were mentioned at length during the golden age of feng shui at the end of the T'ang dynasty, in about AD 770–888.

Another form of *sha*-resisting inscription, or *feng shi ye*, is the Master Lion of the Wind. These are massive stones with carved lion heads, which are erected to resist "bad winds," or sha ch'i. They were also thought to effectively deflect windblown disease.

You will sometimes see *shih kan tang* at the end of bridges, as bridges are thought to give a strong dose of *sha ch'i* to each river bank, more so than a straight road, because in crossing moving water, they pick up on this potent source of ch'i. If you are thinking of using one of these, they should be set up in the early morning, 12 days after the winter solstice for maximum effect. As the winter solstice fluctuates between December 20–22 each year, this means around January 1–3.

A milder version of the same device is sometimes found inscribed on peach-wood slips or slabs, and used for the same purpose. If peach-wood is not available at a pinch, they can be written on paper that is subsequently pasted to an appropriate wall.

Mirrors

There always has been something mysterious about mirrors. Not only do they reflect light and images, but they also reverse these images. Since Sarah Rossbach first wrote about using mirrors in feng shui design, they have in the West formed a significant feng shui implement.

Despite the fact that some practitioners believe they are not part of classical feng shui, there are a large number of competent feng shui Masters who believe that mirrors can create both bad and good feng shui.

Mirrors are of two types: the ordinary flat reflecting wall mirror, and the special octagonal or circular mirror (sometimes concave, sometime convex, and sometimes flat) inserted into the Former Heaven Sequence *pa kua* arrangement. Of course, the mirrors used in the *pa kua* design are one of the most common reflectors of *sha ch'i* and can be seen from the street in quantity in any Chinese-occupied areas across the world.

Mirrors are most commonly used as part of a *pa kua* mirror, but they can also be combined with the images of ferocious animals, particularly the lion or tiger, or the images of door guardians carrying weapons. A less common version of this is the eight-sided *pa kua* of Trigrams surrounding a circular mirror above a fierce figure of the god called the Purple Planet (yes, I know that sounds weird, but that is literally his name) riding a white tiger. The Chinese inscription is something like "the Purple

Planet shines directly," meaning its light protects this house. Even the furrows on the tiger's brow have been contorted into the Chinese character *wang*, meaning "king", to assert the power of rulership over evil. This plaque therefore has many elements of defense, more than just a simple *pa kua* mirror.

There is another special form of mirror, which has not been seen much in the West, called a White Tiger Mirror. This is effectively an inverting, or concave, mirror that is used because it is thought capable of overturning any antagonistic feature reflected in it. The use of this kind of mirror goes back quite a few centuries, and is an interesting remedy to apply to a deliberate feng shui attack.

Even ordinary mirrors are pressed into feng shui service in Chinese areas, and are not, as several authors suggest, just a recent (and *faux*) feature of Western feng shui.

■ A *pa kua* mirror *combined with the ferocious Purple Planet god riding a White Tiger is an extremely powerful form of protection.*

Menshen, or Door Guardians

Menshen are crudely or intricately painted paper figures of fierce-looking warriors or gods, which are usually pasted up every year at the New Year. They are a type of unpaid symbolic guard, and date back to at least the 4th century BC. Their duties include deflecting *kuei*, or ghosts, and *sha ch'i*. Maybe they even frighten off the more timid burglars; certainly they are credited with reducing the incidence of robbery.

Modernization even catches up with feng shui. In Tsang Tai, in what used to be called the New Territories of Hong Kong, a pair of traditional doors has the character *fu* meaning "luck" supported by two door guardians in the form of Mickey and Minnie Mouse! I'm sure Walt Disney would have approved.

■ **In this engraving,** *Menshen, or Door Guardians, on each door protect the residence and deflect* kuei *and* sha ch'i.

A simple summary

✔Using the five Elements is the most traditional feng shui remedy.

✔You can use either the Element itself or its Parent, the Element that produces it.

✔There are occasions when you might need to weaken an Element by using its Grandparent or Child Element.

✔Light can be used as a yang remedy to a yin situation, to "lift" an overhead weight or to mark a missing corner.

✔Flutes and wind chimes rely upon being able to conduct ch'i.

✔Ch'i responds to moving remedies, such as flags.

✔Mirrors, either plain or as part of a *pa kua* mirror, help deflect ch'i or adjust alignments.

✔Door guardians and resisting stones have a long history of use.

Chapter 19

Symbolic Feng Shui

BECAUSE FENG SHUI has such deep roots in Chinese culture, a lot of myth and folklore is incorporated into feng shui. Derek Walters in *The Feng Shui Handbook* even jokingly refers to this as almost a third school of feng shui, after Form and Compass. He describes it rather well as "really a large corpus of do's and don'ts – a heterogeneous assembly of adages drawn from many different sources. Some are half-learned truths . . . some have a kind of logicality behind them." I prefer to think of these "half-learned truths" as Symbolic feng shui. Along with these do's and don'ts comes a range of symbols and remedies, which we will also look at.

In this chapter...
✓ Animal luck protectors
✓ Feng shui symbols
✓ The gods
✓ Taoist talismans

TRADITIONAL SYMBOLS OF PROTECTION, GUARDIAN LIONS ARE PLACED AT THE ENTRANCES TO BANKS AND TEMPLES

Animal luck protectors

FOLKLORE SYMBOLS *have been used in China for a very long time and, because feng shui itself is highly symbolic, I have included some of them here. In the next chapter, I'll proceed with classical feng shui.*

But before you dismiss this chapter entirely as Chinese superstition, please remember that even the palaces in the Forbidden City, the Emperor's palace in Beijing, are adorned with these very symbolic animals, strategically placed according to feng shui principles.

Here we meet some of the most colorful aspects of Chinese culture. We should keep an eye out for interesting puns, which are very revealing about the Chinese attitude to luck and wealth generally.

Trivia...

In Chinese the word for bat, "fu," sounds the same as "fu," the word for "luck," as well as the word for "talisman." Accordingly, luck is associated with bats. Some of the images of the gods, and many pieces of Chinese porcelain, are adorned with bats. This is an example of punning symbolism.

Guardian lions

Perhaps the best known symbol of protection, pairs of guardian lions (sometimes confusingly called "*fu* dogs"), are seen flanking the entrance of many important Chinese institutions. The lion has long been extinct in China, so the animal that guards the entrance owes more to symbology than to natural history. Traditionally they come in pairs, a male and a female.

How can you tell the difference, without getting too personal? Look at their front paws. The male rests one paw on an elaborate ball, maybe even a symbolic pearl. The female rests her free paw on a curled-up cub. Next time you see a pair of these guardians, check to see which side the female is on. I think you can probably guess, if you remember that the yin side is on the right as you face outward. Also have a look at their manes – in theory, the number of clumps indicates the rank of the official responsible for the building they guard.

■ **This elaborate carving** *shows a female guardian lion protectively holding her cub.*

Three-legged toads

One of the most popular symbolic feng shui creatures is the three-legged toad, which is found in Chinese supermarkets and included in many mail-order feng shui catalogs. These statues, now often cast in resin or plaster, show a toad missing one of its legs, sitting upon a pile of traditional curved gold ingots, often wearing a crown. Bearing a Chinese coin in its mouth, the toad is claimed to bring prosperity to its owner.

■ **The three-legged toad** *watches over a pile of Chinese coins. These coins, which are no longer legal tender, are circular (symbolic of Heaven) with a square hole in the middle representing Earth.*

The legend behind the three-legged toad is an interesting one. Liu-hai, the Immortal, discovered a toad in the well in his garden, but as the toad had been wounded and had lost one of its back legs, it was unable to get out of the well. A water well is a very yin image – the toad within it is thus a very strong yin symbol. Liu-hai helped the toad, and in return it brought wealth to him. The coin in its mouth is from the treasure that it found and retrieved for Liu-hai. The theory is that by placing the toad comfortably in an inconspicuous place it should also bring treasure for you.

Two of the recurrent questions asked about this toad are, "Should I put its image in my house facing inward or outward? Is it bringing wealth into the home, as in the story, or should it face the door to receive the wealth?" Facing inward most closely conforms to the legend.

Trivia...

The Chinese refer to "10,000-year-old" (meaning very old) toads as "flesh-mushrooms." The mushroom is a very yin symbol. The yin value of the toad is reinforced by the slang Chinese name for the bridal bed, which used to be the "Toad Palace." Both allusions are demonstrations of the yin nature of the toad.

The three-legged toad (*ha ma* in Chinese) is a symbol of the moon, just as the raven is a symbol of the sun. Because the toad is reputed to live for a long time, and appears to reincarnate from its muddy tomb every spring, it also carries the meaning of longevity and reincarnation. Sometimes the toad is identified with Chang-E, who stole the elixir of immortality from her husband and fled to the moon, where she became a toad for her pains.

From a feng shui point of view, the most interesting thing about toads is that, according to legend, if you scratch the earth with a toad's leg, a spring of water will gush forth from this spot. This belief is a poetic way of connecting the toad with secret underground water, and perhaps wealth.

Kirins

"*Kirin*" is usually translated as "unicorn", but these mythical beasts are nothing like the horned horse of Western mythology. The *kirin* (or *qirin* or *qi-lin*) has the body of a deer, and has either one, two, or three horns. It has the tail of an ox and cloven feet, sometimes with five toes. It's often white. Along with the dragon, the phoenix, and the tortoise it makes up the "four supernatural creatures" and is considered chief of the "hairy creatures," just as the dragon is chief of the "scaly creatures."

Do not, as recommended in some books, set up images of the four Celestial Animals inside the home. These animals are landscape, not interior, symbols. This particularly applies to the yin White Tiger.

■ **This splendid statue** *of the mythical animal known as the* kirin *can be seen in the Royal Palace in Bangkok, Thailand, where it keeps inauspicious influences at bay.*

From the number and the horn symbolism, and because it's thought to help bring sons to a family, you can assume that the *kirin* is a yang beast. It can be used as a defensive guard against the entry of bad influences at the front door. I have even seen *kirins* gracing the reception desks of some grand hotels like the Hong Kong Mandarin Oriental, where they used to face the main door.

A more recent adaptation by modern feng shui practitioners is to use them in high-rise apartments to deflect the *sha ch'i* arriving from an adjacent building. They have the advantage of being deployable inside rather than outside the window, as in the case of *pa kua* mirrors. Climbing out of the 50th-floor window to place a *pa kua* mirror has the potential to cause more bad luck than it will ever deflect! By the way, one of the best places to find a good picture of a *kirin* is on a bottle of Kirin beer.

Feng shui symbols

SYMBOLS ARE MUCH MORE POTENT things than we in the West usually believe. As the psychologist Carl Jung would have put it, not only do they work at a deep, personal psychological level but they also act with the weight of millions of past applications, which have made a significant dent on the collective unconscious. Whether they affect our luck at an Earth luck level is still an open question, but they certainly do affect our Man luck.

Coins and coin swords

In almost every culture, coins have been signs of wealth. In Chinese culture, the redundant "cash" coins of earlier eras, with their square holes, are even more symbolic. Having been introduced into the West in the early 1960s as a divinatory adjunct to the *I Ching*, they are now readily available. The convention is that they should be "activated" by tying them with red thread or ribbon. Once activated, they may be tied in strips reflecting a yang, or odd number, for example three, seven, or nine coins. The coins can be purchased from various feng shui suppliers.

More traditionally, these coins come assembled into the form of a sword. These have been used in the past to repel or expel evil spirits. They can sometimes be seen hanging on walls.

INTERNET

www.fengshui warehouse.com

This is one of many sites selling feng shui-related items. Other sites you might want to visit are www.dragon-gate.com and www.houseoffengshui.com.

■ **In China, a sword made** *entirely of coins was hung over the bed of a sick person to dispel the demons that might be causing the illness.*

285

Other symbols of good fortune

Other symbols of good fortune include the calligraphic "double happiness" character for marital bliss, the peach or pine for longevity, and the carp or goldfish for success in business or studies.

■ **The favorite tree of Chinese painters,** *the pine symbolizes longevity and steadfastness because it withstands the cold and does not lose its needles in winter. It also epitomizes self-discipline.*

The word for fish is "yu," which sounds like one of the Chinese words for abundance, and hence by punning is associated with just that. In academic terms, graduation or exam success is traditionally referred to as turning the carp or goldfish, leaping upstream, into a dragon, which here is a symbol of achievement. Pictures of this event are popular pre-exam presents in China.

Symbols of defense and attack

As well as the more familiar forms of feng shui defense, there are a number of more aggressive images that are used in cases where opposing neighbors have escalated their feng shui activities to the point where *sha ch'i* is being batted backward and forward between opposing buildings. Such a case has been remarked upon in one of the main streets in Kuala Lumpur, where two otherwise sober-sided companies put up

■ **In a business context**, *energy often has to be managed on a large scale. In this vast modern office building, the curving structure of the roof allows for good energy flow and avoids negative* sha ch'i.

increasingly heavyweight feng shui symbols to counter each other. The original spat was caused by the construction of a massive pair of X-shaped escalators effectively aimed across the street at the building opposite. In retaliation, the other building even installed a full-scale cannon pointed directly at its neighbor. In the end, as a result of mutual weakening, both companies were subject to takeover advances.

However, the use of such military devices is echoed in traditional feng shui symbolism, where swords, axes, arrows, and ferocious animals (particularly the tiger and lion) have often been employed. A particularly strong image is that of a lion holding an unsheathed sword in its mouth. The installation of such symbols should be done on a yin day and in a yin hour, such as between 3 am and 5 am.

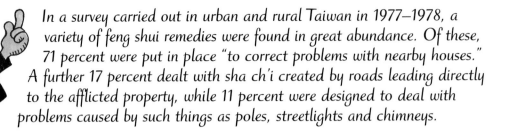

In a survey carried out in urban and rural Taiwan in 1977–1978, a variety of feng shui remedies were found in great abundance. Of these, 71 percent were put in place "to correct problems with nearby houses." A further 17 percent dealt with sha ch'i created by roads leading directly to the afflicted property, while 11 percent were designed to deal with problems caused by such things as poles, streetlights and chimneys.

The gods

CHINESE GODS *can come from any of the three main religions: Confucianism, Buddhism, or Taoism. As many of the gods are thought to have been originally human, they are prayed to not as if they were the supreme creators of the Universe but more as a Catholic Christian might pray to a saint, with a particular purpose in mind.*

Fu, Lu, and Shou

You can find these three Chinese gods in almost any Chinese home. They are sometimes spelled F'uk, Luk, and Sau, and represent the three traditional forms of happiness: Longevity, High Rank, and Luck. They are often called star gods, but are really more household gods, as they are to be found in millions of homes but in very few temples.

Fu, the god of Luck (which includes wealth, family fertility, and abundance), is taller than the other two and is always put at the center when they are displayed on a table or shelf. Fu is literally the word for "luck."

Lu, the god of High Rank, holds the scepter of authority.

Shou, the god of Longevity, has a high, domed head.

FU

LU

SHOU

An interesting Chinese practice that has become partially intertwined with feng shui is the "Reception of the God of Wealth" – a little ceremony that is carried out in many Chinese homes around the globe at the lunar New Year (between mid-January and mid-February) every year. This involves pails of water and further confirms the symbolic identification between water and wealth.

The fiercest money preservers

Associated with Fu, Lu, and Shou are several gods of wealth. Strangely, some of the most popular of these gods are also very warlike (although they do have a civil side as well).

Perhaps the most popular is Ts'ai Shen (sometimes spelled Cai Shen), depicted with a ring of cash coins (round Chinese coins with square holes in the middle) sewn around the hem of his gown. On his breast is a lotus, symbolic of fertility (rather than spirituality), in one hand is a golden mushroom (symbolic of longevity), and in the other a bowl of cash, growing like golden grass. You can see that wealth includes wealth of years and children as well as cash. He is often referred to affectionately as "grandfather Ts'ai Shen" and is associated with Lu, the god of High Rank. Ts'ai Shen, or the sage who became the god, is supposed to date from around 1121 BC. His particular day is the 20th day of the 7th lunar month.

Another warlike god of Wealth is Kuan Kung (or Kuan Ti or Kuan Yu), who looks very fierce and brandishes a long halberd. He is not just a patron of pawnshops, but is also the god of sudden windfalls. As a military god, Kuan Kung is very concerned with correct conduct, although such sentiments sit uneasily with the windfalls that came with the sacking of cities during war. I suspect that these gods were not originally concerned with acquiring wealth so much as protecting it when it had been acquired.

■ **Kuan Kung**, *the military god of Riches, is sometimes depicted as a dual being. Here he is shown seated with his civilian counterpart.*

KUAN KUNG

The individual who was later deified as Kuan Kung lived in AD 162–220. Isn't it fascinating to know the exact birthdate of a god – a by-product of age and the careful record keeping of Chinese civilization? Kuan Kung has over 1,600 state temples and thousands of smaller ones erected in China in his honor. He was hence one of the most popular gods in China. The Emperor Hsien Feng (1851–1862) even raised him to the same rank as Confucius.

Interestingly, Kuan Kung is also the "patron saint" of the Chinese police as well as that of their opposite numbers, the Triads. That must have made for some interesting temple meetings!

Even fiercer is Ch'ao Kung-ming, who rides upon a black tiger, uses pearls as hand grenades (you thought they were a modern invention, didn't you?), wields a steel whip, and is often depicted with a black face. In his capacity as god of Wealth, he also carries golden ingots. He sometimes has at his feet the magic bowl, the *chu-pao p'en*, from which sprouts new golden ingots in proportion to the speed they are taken out – very useful indeed. He appears in Ming dynasty (1368–1644) legends as the president of the celestial Ministry of Riches and Prosperity. However, the real god of Wealth, Ch'ao Kung-ming, has been overshadowed by Ts'ai Shen.

If you wish to have a figure of one or other of these gods in your home or office, give it the respect it deserves and place it on a high shelf or table, with its back metaphorically and actually supported by a wall.

■ **An endless supply** *of gold ingots is produced from the* chu-pao p'en, *or magic money bowl.*

Symbols of wealth

It is the by-products of the images of these gods of wealth that have become parts of the gadgetry of feng shui. These come in various forms:

1. Trees whose branches are made of strings of cash coins.

2. Trees with ingots of gold as fruits, which are supposed to re-grow when shaken onto the ground. This money-shedding tree is called a *yao chien shu*.

3. The magic money bowl, or *chu-pao p'en*.

4. A magic and inexhaustible casket full of gold and silver.

5. A ship bearing traditional curved gold ingots and numerous other wealth symbols, used by merchants and traders.

It is from these images that wealth vases and similar items have been popularized as part of feng shui. The tradition of the wealth vase can probably trace its origins back to a story about Chen Wan-san, who lived about 1400. He was an animal lover and was always doing kindly acts like letting fish off the

■ **The fabulous tree** *that sheds money is a frequent motif in Chinese pictures.*

hook. As a reward, the gods gave him a bowl that was instantly filled to the brim with money whenever he threw a single coin into it.

Taoist talismans

HERE WE GET INTO THE REALMS of spirits and Taoist magic. It is a long way from the purity of classical feng shui, but because some schools of feng shui deal in such things, it is as well that we look at them here.

A talisman is a painted or drawn piece of paper or other material that claims to be able to repel various sorts of evil, from ghosts, through spirits (*shen*), to demons. On it will be calligraphy, often in one of the strange Taoist script versions of Chinese, stylized shapes derived from calligraphy, or "knotted string" drawings, representing particular star constellations, plus the seals and drawings of the heads of gods, emperors, or animals (the fearsome tiger is a favorite).

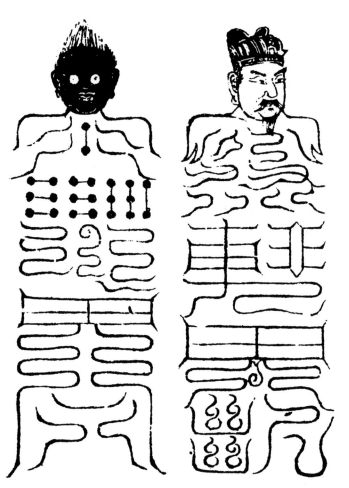

Taoist priests will make these for you at a price depending upon the reputation of the spiritual powers of the priest. They are often drawn with a peach-wood pen. They can also be bought ready-made from any Chinese religious shop, or found printed in the Almanac, or *Tung Shu*. A typical talisman, with feng shui implications, is a scroll or strip of paper showing one of the four Masters of the Four Directions. His head appears at the top, with his body made of sometimes very beautifully drawn rectilinear Chinese characters.

■ **Part drawing, part calligraphy,** *these images show the Black Supreme Ruler of the north and the White Supreme Ruler of the west.*

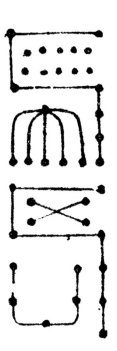

Knotted string diagrams

Even ordinary numbers – one to nine – were portrayed using "knotted string" diagrams. In fact, that is how these numbers are usually shown on the Chinese versions of the *lo shu* square. The knotted string figures were originally used as a way of noting down various constellations. The Big Dipper (or Ladle) constellation was considered the most magical, since it turned like a huge pointer around the northern Pole Star, and it often turns up on these talismans. Many feng shui Masters, in their capacity as Taoist priests, gave talismans to their clients as cures for feng shui problems. This is an area that has not been explored at all in most Western books on the subject.

■ **These two combined "knotted string" talismans** *represent specific constellations. In this example, they are supposed to bring good fortune if they are drawn or pasted on the wall.*

A simple summary

✔ Symbolic feng shui is almost seen as a third school after Form and Compass School feng shui.

✔ Animal guardians include lions and *kirins*. Three-legged toads are often considered to be feng shui wealth bringers.

✔ The gods of protection and wealth include warlike figures like Kuan Kung and Ch'ao Kung-ming.

✔ The household star gods – Fu, Lu, and Shou – are designed to promote longevity, career, and luck. Statues of them appear in almost every Chinese home, but they are hardly ever seen in temples.

✔ Products such as wealth vases, model ships, and money trees are Chinese cultural artifacts that are sometimes purveyed as feng shui equipment.

✔ Taoist talismans, on the other hand, are really part of traditional feng shui practice.

Chapter 20

The East Life/ West Life Formula

E AST LIFE/WEST LIFE FORMULA is the English name for two separate feng shui calculations. One formula calculates the *kua* (or Trigram) of any person, and the second calculates the *kua* of any house or building. The personal *kua* suggests the best, or most auspicious, way to face when doing important things. The house *kua* tells you which are the best and worst rooms to use for bedrooms, living rooms, kitchen, and bathrooms.

In this chapter...

✓ The East/West Life formula for people

✓ How to calculate your personal kua number

✓ Your best and worst directions

✓ Are you an East Life or West Life person?

✓ Is your house in the East or West Group?

FINDING A PARTNER WITH A COMPATIBLE PERSONAL *KUA* NUMBER IS HELPFUL FOR A LASTING RELATIONSHIP

The East/West Life formula for people

THE EAST/WEST LIFE FORMULA *is made up of two halves: the personal* kua *and the building's* kua. *Before we get down to calculating the personal* kua *number, we should just be clear as to the nature of the two halves of the formula:* ming kua *and* chai kua.

> **DEFINITION**
>
> **Ming kua** *is the calculation of your personal "destiny Trigram," and nothing to do with the Ming dynasty! This is the kua, or Trigram, corresponding to the Earthly Branch of your year of birth.* **Chai kua** *is the calculation of the kua, or Trigram, of your house or building.*

The ming kua

Using the *ming kua* formula you can determine:

1. Your best sitting, working, eating, and sleeping orientation, so that you know where to place the furniture in your home to maximize your personal feng shui.

2. Your compatibility with your partner, by discovering if your *kua* numbers fall into the same group.

The chai kua

Using the *chai kua* formula you can determine:

1. The best function for each room in your home to maximize the feng shui of the home, such as which room to use as a master bedroom.

2. Your compatibility with your house, by comparing your *ming kua* number with the house's *chai kua* number, to see if a new home will suit you, or how your present home affects you.

■ **Your personal *kua* numbers** *will reveal if you're destined to live happily ever after with your partner. If they're in the same group, your future may be rosy.*

Your "kua number"

The term "*kua* number" for an individual originally referred to the Hexagram generated for that individual.

Since kua in Chinese means both Trigram (with three lines) and Hexagram (with six lines), "kua number" has now come to mean just Trigram number. It has become customary to use "kua number" to refer just to the annual Trigram of the year in which the person was born, and I will continue to do so.

Your *kua* number is the number of the Trigram corresponding to the year in which you were born. This Trigram will in turn correspond with one of the eight Directions.

Discovering your good and bad directions

Once you know with which direction your Trigram corresponds, you can work out your four best directions and four worst directions. The very best direction is the *sheng ch'i* direction, and the very worst is the direction called *chueh ming*.

Don't worry about memorizing the Chinese names; you don't need to. We will come to what these terms mean precisely later on (see p. 305).

For example, if you are female and were born in 1971, then your *sheng ch'i*, or best direction, is north, and your worst directions are northwest, west, southwest, and southeast. There are times when a specific direction (not necessarily your *sheng ch'i*) is best: If you are ill for example, then your *t'ien yi* or "doctor from Heaven" direction is best for you to face to get the benefit of the right kind of ch'i, in this case healing ch'i. Don't worry if all this sounds confusing, as we have clearly laid it out in a table on pages 302–3.

It is interesting to note that a Japanese system called Nine Star Ki, which is derived from this Chinese system, omits to make a differentiation between the sexes. Since women are treated exactly like men when calculating their number with Nine Star Ki, the result will be different from that using traditional Chinese calculations.

It is better not to try and mix the Chinese and Japanese systems; stay with one or the other. My preference is for the original and traditional Chinese calculations.

How to calculate your personal kua number

SOME OF THE SHORTHAND METHODS of *calculating your kua number work only on 20th-century birth dates, and therefore need to be modified in the 21st century to make them work. Here, we will use a formula that works for either century.*

Watch out for those birth dates that fall between the beginning of the year and February 4th or 5th, because there is an added complication. If you were born before solar Chinese New Year on February 4th or 5th, then you must subtract 1 from the year number, as you were effectively born in the previous Chinese year.

Some books recommend that you use the date of the New Year from the Chinese lunar calendar to calculate your *kua* number. This date fluctuates between mid-January and mid-February every year. I believe that this makes no sense, and it is better to use the beginning of spring for the Chinese solar year, which is February 4th or 5th.

■ **The *Tung Shu**, or Chinese Almanac, contains the calendar details for the coming year, including the date of the New Year. More than 3 million copies are sold each year.*

Some feng shui schools go back even further and use the winter solstice of the previous December 20th, 21st, or 22nd as the change point between one year and the next. Having noted it, we will now proceed to ignore it.

The method

The method of finding your *kua* number is simply as follows:

1. Check if your birth date was before Chinese New Year on February 4th or 5th and, if so, subtract 1 from the year (as you were effectively born in the previous Chinese year).

2. Take the year in which you were born and add together all its digits.

3 If the result is greater than 9, add its digits together again.

4 If you are male, subtract the result from 11; if you are female, add the result to 4.

5 If the result is greater than 9, add its digits together again.

6 If the answer is 5, the *kua* number is 2 for a male, or 8 for a female; otherwise the result as noted in the previous step is your *kua* number.

FINDING THE KUA NUMBER FOR A MALE

Here's how to work out the *kua* number for Jack, born on January 5th, 1962:

1 Check if the birth date was before Chinese New Year on February 4th or 5th. If it is, subtract 1 from the year.

Since January 5th falls before the Chinese New Year, consider Jack to be born in 1961.

2 Take the year in which Jack was born – 1961 – and add together all its digits:

$1 + 9 + 6 + 1 = 17$

3 If the result is greater than 9, add its digits together:

17 needs this treatment, so $1 + 7 = 8$

4 Subtract this result from 11 (males only):

$11 - 8 = 3$

5 If the result is greater than 9, add its digits together:

No action required.

6 If the answer is 5, then change the *kua* number to 2 (as noted in step 6 above). In Jack's case, it isn't 5, so his *kua* number is, therefore, 3 (as calculated in step 4).

FINDING THE KUA NUMBER FOR A FEMALE

Now let's work out the kua number for Jill, born on June 6th, 1985.

1 Check if the birth date was before Chinese New Year on February 4th or 5th. If it is, subtract 1 from the year.

No action required.

2 Take the year in which Jill was born – 1985 – and add together all its digits:

$$1 + 9 + 8 + 5 = 23$$

3 If the result is greater than 9, add its digits together:

$$2 + 3 = 5$$

4 Add the result to 4 (females only):

$$5 + 4 = 9$$

5 If the result is greater than 9, add its digits together:

No action required.

6 If the answer is 5, change the kua number to 8 (see first step 6 on p. 299). In Jill's case, it isn't 5, so her kua number is 9 (see step 4 above).

It sounds fearsome, doesn't it? Well, it's not really, once you get the hang of it. And before you read another word, I want you to go back and calculate your *kua* number now, so you can see for yourself how easy it is. It is just like one of those mental arithmetic children's games where you have to "double it . . . and then add the number you first thought of."

There is a logical reason for these calculations, and they depend on the male and female *kua* numbers for the beginning of the last century. Believe me, the above method is quicker than counting from there on your fingers! The reason why the numbers are different is that yang (male) and yin (female) ch'i flow in opposite directions.

So, what does it all mean? Well, the *kua* number is the number of your personal Trigram. This Trigram governs two things:

1. The best way to face or orientate yourself (for important things like eating, working, sleeping, and studying). If you are facing the right way, the energy coming from that sector will help you get the most benefit out of what you are doing.

2. Your compatibility with your partner, by discovering if your *kua* numbers fall into the same group or not.

INTERNET

www.geomancy.net

Cecil Lee's very interesting site has versions of these calculations online that you can try out for yourself.

■ **Your personal Trigram** *dictates the best position to face when you're at work, so you can maximize the effect of the energy coming toward you.*

Your best and worst directions

THESE DIRECTIONS *have very graphic Chinese names. I have put them in for the sake of completeness, but they sound so extreme that many books leave them out. Just as Chinese menus describe dishes as "Five Precious Jade . . ." when they simply mean five stir-fried vegetables, so the Chinese names of the best and worst directions have considerable in-built drama. When you hear that a particular direction is that of "Five Ghosts" or "Six Curses," please accept that there is a tendency to overdramatize the results of facing that direction or sleeping in that sector of your house.*

Once you have calculated your personal *kua* number, you can then use it to find out your best and worst directions by checking in the table below. This table will give you your four best, and worst, directions, which you should endeavor to memorize.

THE FOUR BEST AND FOUR WORST DIRECTIONS

Sang's Easy Letter	CHINESE NAME (Literal meaning)	INFLUENCE
	Best four directions:	
A	*Sheng ch'i* (generating ch'i)	success and great prosperity
C	*Nien yen* (lengthening years)	longevity, good for relationships and family
B	*T'ien i/yi* (Heavenly Doctor*)	health and regeneration
D	*Fu wei* (direction faced by the main door)	mild good fortune/stability
	Worst four directions:	
E	*Hai huo** (accidents and mishaps)	mild bad luck/physical injury
G	*Wu kuei*** (five ghosts)	mischief and quarrels
F	*Liu sha**** (six curses/six imps)	six setbacks
H	*Chueh ming* (severed fate)	total loss/end of life, the worst

Notes: * Literally "Celestial monad". ** Sometimes shown as *Ho hai*.
*** Sometimes spelled *Wu kwei*. **** *Liu* = six. This is not *lui sha*, as some writers spell it.

Take a few minutes to check (in your head) where you habitually sit/sleep in relation to your best/worst directions.

If you find the Chinese names a nuisance to memorize, you could use the system devised by Master Larry Sang, which simply gives each direction an "easy letter." Thus the best directions are labeled A, B, C, D, while the worst directions are labeled E, F, G, H.

Note that these directions have been arbitrarily labeled A to H. Unfortunately, feng shui books have not used the same convention each time, even for this simplified alphabetic labeling. For example, Derek Walters labeled them alphabetically in 1991, but in a different order. As the letters are totally arbitrary, in this case I prefer the order used by Larry Sang, as he progresses logically from the best direction at A to the worst direction at H.

Now you know what your best directions are, how do you use this knowledge?

FOR EACH PERSONAL KUA NUMBER

				KUA NUMBERS						Walters' Easy Letter
1	2	3	4	5 (male)	5 (female)	6	7	8	9	*Letter*
SE	NE	S	N	NE	SW	W	NW	SW	E	*F*
S	NW	SE	E	NW	W	SW	NE	W	N	*D*
E	W	N	S	W	NW	NE	SW	NW	SE	*G*
N	SW	E	SE	SW	NE	NW	W	NE	S	*H*
W	E	SW	NW	E	S	SE	N	S	NE	*E*
NE	SE	NW	SW	SE	N	E	S	N	W	*B*
NW	S	NE	W	S	E	N	SE	E	SW	*A*
SW	N	W	NE	N	SE	S	E	SE	NW	*C*

Applying the best directions

The idea of best seating positions is not unlike the Victorian habit of allocating the head of table position to the senior male member of the household. In the case of feng shui positioning, "head of the table" means the breadwinner facing his or her *sheng ch'i*, or best direction. The *kua* number tells you the best directions to face at your desk, in your armchair, your bed, or anywhere you are sitting or sleeping for long periods. Not only will this be beneficial when placing furniture, but it may also give you the edge in crucial business meetings.

Taking a pocket compass and quickly checking your best seating direction in that important business meeting can often pay handsome dividends.

■ **Using your kua number** *to work out the best seat for yourself at a meeting may give you the upper hand and make all the difference to the final outcome.*

Which way should you sit?

If your *kua* number is 1, your *sheng ch'i*, or best direction, is southeast (see table on page 303). If there is a round table meeting and a choice of chairs, try to select the chair facing southeast, as this will give you a psychological advantage in the meeting, if not more. Be aware, however, that the physical alignments of the room take precedence over the best directions.

Don't, for example, sit in a chair with its back to the door or to the window, and therefore unsupported, if you can help it. Even a southeast-facing chair with its back to the door should be avoided. In such a case, choose from the east-, south-, or north-facing chairs, as your next best directions, in that descending order. On the other hand, try to avoid regularly doing anything important for long periods of time facing any of your four worst directions.

Two opposing views

There are two schools of thought about best directions. One says that you should sit facing your best direction, while the other suggests that you sit with your best direction supporting you from behind. Both schools of thought agree that the sleeping position should be with the head pointing toward one of the four best directions. I take the view that, like the ancient Chinese Emperors, who faced south (the direction of greatest yang), you should face your best direction for maximum benefit.

Don't confuse your personal kua number with the Eight Mansion formula. For example, someone looking to marry might face their nien yen direction, which must not be confused with the southwest Location of the Eight Mansion formula, which is where changes might be made with the furnishings to enhance the "romance luck" of the whole household.

Let's examine each of the four best directions in turn:

1. *Sheng ch'i*: As this is an energizer, a producer of new ch'i, face it when you are eating (ingesting ch'i) or when you are studying or working.

2. *T'ien i*: If you are ill or simply want to boost your health or regenerate your energies, face the Heavenly Doctor direction when eating or sleeping.

3. *Nien yen*: If romance or a good marriage is your objective, sleep with your head pointed in this direction.

4. *Fu wei*: If you want a good night's sleep, point your head in this direction. Instead of energizing with your *sheng ch'i*, simply use *fu wei* to ensure you sleep well.

Are you an East Life or West Life person?

IF YOU LOOK AGAIN CAREFULLY at the table on pages 302–3, you'll notice that the best directions are grouped either as SE/E/S/N or NE/W/NW/SW, although not necessarily in that order.

From this observation, it can be seen that people fall into one of two categories:

1. Those with a "West Life" *kua* number, whose best directions are NE/W/NW/SW, that is, west plus three inter-cardinal points.

2. Those with an "East Life" *kua* number, whose best directions are SE/E/S/N, that is, southeast plus three of the cardinal points.

If you look at the table on pages 302–3, you will see that *kua* numbers 1, 3, 4, and 9 are East Life, and *kua* numbers 2, 5, 6, 7, and 8 are West Life.

Your partner

You may find that if you are living with someone, you will be more compatible if both of you are West Life or both of you East Life, as you will then share the same set of good directions. One of the questions most often asked is, what if my partner's directions are quite contrary to mine? Well, this is good news if you are deciding upon study quarters. You can each easily face different directions. In terms of sitting around the dining room table, this is again a benefit because you can both choose your best direction.

The only conflict is in sleeping positions. However, if you are both West Life or both East Life, there is no real problem: One partner (usually the breadwinner) takes the *sheng ch'i* direction, while the other takes whichever of their other good directions coincides with their partner's *sheng ch'i*.

■ **There are no directional clashes** *in the bedroom if you are both East Life or both West Life.*

Is your house in the East or West Group?

AS WELL AS CALCULATING KUA NUMBERS for people, and then categorizing them as either East Life or West Life, houses can also be given a Trigram and categorized as an East Group house or West Group house. This calculation is called chai (house) kua (Trigram). Obviously East Life people suit East Group houses and West Life people do better in West Group houses.

So how do you tell the *kua* of a house? Simply by observing where the house sits. But what do I mean exactly? I hear you ask. Let me try and take you through the process with a quick question-and-answer session.

 What do you mean by a sitting position? How can a house sit?

First decide which way a house faces. Many times the facing side will be where it has its front door. But it can also be the side facing the road.

 Then what?

Then the sitting side is the opposite of the facing side.

 So a house that faced the street to the west, would actually be sitting in the east?

That's right. If it faces west, it must sit east. Or, if it faces southeast, it must sit northwest, and so on. Some books on feng shui simplify this procedure by saying the sitting direction is where the back door is, but from the above question and answer you can see that such an approach is rather oversimplified. Once you know the sitting position, you can find out what type of house it is.

■ **Although the back door** *usually defines the sitting direction of the house, there are exceptions to the rule.*

HOUSE GROUPS AND TRIGRAMS

SITTING POSITION	FACING POSITION	HOUSE TRIGRAM	ELEMENT	WEST/EAST GROUP
S	N	*Li*	Fire	East
SW	NE	*K'un*	Earth	West
W	E	*Tui*	Metal	West
NW	SE	*Ch'ien*	Metal	West
N	S	*K'an*	Water	East
NE	SW	*Ken*	Earth	West
E	W	*Chen*	Wood	East
SE	NW	*Hsun*	Wood	East

So, having studied House Groups and Trigrams (above), you now know that West Group houses have sitting positions of W/NW/SW/NE, which are associated with Metal and Earth, while East Group houses have sitting positions of S/N/E/SE, which are associated with Water, Wood, and Fire.

The right house for you

Now that we have worked out which Trigram you are, whether you are an East Life or a West Life person, and worked out the Trigram and East/West Grouping of your house, all that remains is to see if you are compatible with your house. By analyzing these results, you can see (at a basic level) whether the house is good for you or not.

If, for example, my *kua* number is 7, I am a West Life person and,

■ **This south-facing house** *is ideal for an East Life person. However, if your partner is West Life, they might use the back door as their main entrance.*

therefore, should really try to live in a West Group house, such as the *K'un*, *Tui*, *Ch'ien*, or *Ken* house. The very best for me would be the *Ch'ien* house which sits in my *sheng ch'i* direction of northwest. So there you have it.

Moving house may be a bit extreme if you find that you clash with your house. But it might be worth looking at the idea of using a different entrance – the back door, for example, might then become your front door. Some feng shui practitioners believe this can resolve the situation.

Where husband and wife are from opposite Life Groups, it may be beneficial for them to use different front doors.

A simple summary

✔ Everyone has his or her own personal *kua* number or annual Trigram. This is derived from their sex and year of birth, and conditions their best orientation.

✔ Each of the *kua* numbers is associated with four good directions and four not-so-good directions.

✔ It's always beneficial to be aligned with one of your four good directions (especially your *sheng ch'i* direction) when you are doing important things such as studying, eating, and sleeping. You will be amazed at what a difference it makes, especially with studying. For a start, it often stops procrastination.

✔ There are really two types of people, West Life (whose best directions are NE, NW, W, SW) and East Life (whose best directions are E, N, S, SE).

✔ Houses can be identified by a Trigram, or *kua* number, according to the house's sitting direction. People tend to flourish better in a house drawn from the same East/West Group as their personal *kua* number.

PART SIX

TIMING IS OF THE ESSENCE IN FENG SHUI

COMPASS SCHOOL FENG SHUI

Put the time element of feng shui into perspective. You know that sometimes things are easy to do, sometimes they couldn't be harder. Feng shui timing enables you to do things at the *right times* and for the *best advantage*. But first we must master the machinery of the calendar and the mysteries of the Heavenly Stems and Earthly Branches, for feng shui measures *time* as well as *space*.

In fact, I don't think there is another practice that so completely unifies the measurement of time and space. Everything you have learned so far is summarized on the face of the *lo p'an*. We will look at the use of just one of the basic rings of this compass.

Chapter 21

Time and the Calendar

BEFORE WE GET DOWN to maximizing your luck using the correct timing, we have to look at the nature of time itself. The Chinese have a longer history of astronomical observation and record keeping than any other civilization. As you would expect, their calendar is in some senses more complex than the Western calendar. The simple animal signs of popular Chinese astrology comprise only the trite tip of a very large and interesting iceberg. The Chinese view on history is so long term that they count in epochs of 3,600 years! Luck changes over time, and so feng shui has a time dimension: What is lucky for you today may not be so in 20 years' time. To understand time dimension feng shui you need to understand how the Chinese measure time.

In this chapter...

✓ Measuring time using God's clocks

✓ The 24 ch'i seasons

✓ Good and bad days

STONEHENGE IS BELIEVED TO HAVE BEEN USED TO STUDY THE MOVEMENTS OF THE SUN, MOON, AND PLANETS

Measuring time using God's clocks

PRECISION TIMEPIECE

THE MEASUREMENT OF DATE AND TIME
*has always been linked with the movement of the
heavenly bodies. Unfortunately, these bodies do not
move in a way that human (as distinct from divine)
arithmetic sees as simple. In all calendars, the day is
related to the apparent rising and setting of the sun. The
day (divided into 24 hours, or 12 following the Chinese
model) is the most obvious unit of time. Most, but not all, calendars also use the
time it takes for the Earth to go round the sun (365.242199 days) as a second
unit. Some calendars use the time from one new moon to the next as another
unit (29.53059 days). Unfortunately, none of these key numbers divides exactly
into each other, and that is where the problems begin.*

The solar calendar

In North America, Europe, and a multitude of other countries, there is only one
calendar. It is solar, meaning it is linked very closely with the rotation of the Earth
around the sun. In fact it was devised by Julius Caesar (in 46 BC) and modified by
Pope Gregory (in 1582). One of the problems with a solar calendar is that the period
of rotation of the Earth around the sun is not an even number of days. In other words,
there is no exact number of days in the year. How inconsiderate of God!

*In the West, in the calendar devised by Emperor Julius and Pope
Gregory, we accommodate the difficulty of the solar calendar year
by adding an extra day every leap year. A year that is divisible by
4 is a leap year. However, if it is evenly divisible by 100 but not by 400,
it is not a leap year, so 2000 is a leap year but not 1800 or 1900.*

Other calendars have used that other luminary, the moon, as their timekeeper. These
calendars are called lunar calendars, from the Latin *luna*, meaning "moon." Again, the
problem arises that there is not an even number of days in one moon cycle (29.53059
days), and there is not an even number of moon cycles in the year (12.36826).

Our Western solar calendar, however, still needs to look at lunar events for religious dating: Every year Easter falls on a different date determined by the phases of the moon. A little bit of lunar paganism leavening a core Christian festival, you might say! So what do we do? We compromise. The Chinese, however, having kept records of heavenly phenomena for longer and with more consistency than any other culture on Earth, were keen to have an all-embracing calendar. Accordingly, being very aware of the heavens, they have both a lunar and a solar calendar. But don't despair, we are going to use only the more logical of these two.

The Chinese lunar calendar

It is fairly commonly known that the Chinese have a lunar calendar. If we experimentally divide the number of days in the year (365.242199) by the number of days in one lunar cycle (29.53059) we get 12.36826 lunar cycles per year. Unfortunately, not a whole number! The Chinese solved this problem by using 12 lunar months of either 29 or 30 days per year, and then introducing a 13th (a so-called intercalary) month in seven out of every 19 years. This system works, but it is hardly elegant: sometimes there are 12 and sometimes 13 lunar months in a year. Where there are 13, the inserted month takes the name of the month before – very confusing to have two months with the same name.

The start of the Chinese lunar New Year (the day when everyone Chinese goes around saying "kung hey fat choy") therefore moves from year to year within the range of mid-January to mid-February. For example, in 2001 lunar New Year fell on January 24th, but in 2002 it fell on February 12th.

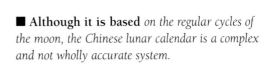

■ **Although it is based** on the regular cycles of the moon, the Chinese lunar calendar is a complex and not wholly accurate system.

■ **New Year celebrations** *are one of the most spectacular events that take place in Chinese communities. They fall not on a consistent date each year but on a day determined by the lunar calendar.*

THE BEGINNING OF TIME

Traditionally, the Chinese measure dates from 2637 BC when the Yellow Emperor, Huang Ti, introduced the cycle of 60 characters (see chapter 22) to measure cycles of 60 years. The big picture was organized like this:

- 1 Epoch = 60 Cycles
- 1 Cycle = 5 Great Years
- 1 Great Year = 12 years, therefore
- 1 Epoch = 3,600 years

Talk about long-range planning! Therefore, more than 4,637 years after the introduction of the origin point of the Chinese calendar, we are in the 78th cycle of 60 years. So if I wanted to use Chinese dating, I could say that I am writing this book in the year of the Metal Snake, in the 18th cycle of the 2nd Epoch (or in short 2001). In practice, most Chinese dates were written in the form, "the Xth year of the reign of Emperor Y, of the Z dynasty."

CHINESE LUNAR NEW YEAR

Year	Start date	Animal sign
2000	February 5th	dragon
2001	January 24th	snake
2002	February 12th	horse
2003	February 1st	sheep/goat
2004	January 22nd	monkey
2005	February 9th	chicken
2006	January 29th	dog
2007	February 18th	pig
2008	February 7th	rat
2009	January 26th	ox
2010	February 14th	tiger
2011	February 3rd	rabbit
2012	January 23rd	dragon
2013	February 10th	snake
2014	January 31st	horse
2015	February 19th	sheep/goat
2016	February 8th	monkey

CHINESE ASTROLOGICAL ANIMAL SIGNS

To find your animal sign, just keep adding 12 to your year of birth till you reach one of the years listed above. But if you were born before the Chinese lunar New Year, you'll need to subtract one year before you start.

Measuring seasons and tides of ch'i

You can clearly see that the lunar calendar is contrived to make the numbers fit, and it will be precisely right only once in 19 years. Not terrifically accurate! The setting of festivities and the timing of various gods' and humans' birthdays and feast days are, however, done according to the lunar calendar.

Although Chinese New Year festivities and popular Chinese astrology are governed by the lunar calendar, for feng shui and agricultural purposes we must use the Chinese solar calendar. Hence to measure the objective seasons and actual tides of ch'i, so important to feng shui, you need to use the Chinese solar calendar, which more closely reflects astronomical reality. Some books on feng shui in English get the two calendars rather mixed up.

Trivia...

In Imperial China, officials were paid every lunar month. You can imagine how much everybody liked those 13-month years: 13 pay packets instead of 12, it must have felt like an instant 8.5 percent salary rise! It wasn't of course – just a longer working year.

The Chinese solar calendar

The Chinese solar calendar is called the *Hsia* calendar (or the farmers' calendar) and it regulates agriculture because the sun is all-important in determining seasons.

The solar year starts with the beginning of spring. Fortunately, solar New Year always falls on either February 4th or 5th.

■ **More logical** *and of greater practical use than the lunar calendar, the Chinese solar calendar is based on the relationship between the sun and the seasons of the year.*

How can solar New Year fall on the same day every year when it falls on two possible dates? From 1981 till 2000 the date of the beginning of spring has been at varying times on February 4th but occasionally this time "wobbles" forward into February 5th (because of the leap year "defect" in our own Western calendar). In fact, objectively measured from the stars, this first date of spring does not move at all.

SOLAR CALENDAR YIN AND YANG

The solar calendar does not change, but there are some circumstances under which the beginning of the year's growth energies should be taken as the winter solstice, in other words, December 20th, 21st, or 22nd of the previous Western calendar year.

The reasoning behind this is that, according to yin/yang theory, the beginning of the yang growth cycle should date from the depth, or most extreme point, of the previous yin cycle.

The 24 ch'i seasons

OF COURSE, THE SEASONS are basic to the solar calendar, because the sun governs the progress of the seasons. Four seasons are enough for city-dwellers. But four seasons are really too simple for the average farmer who wants to know exactly when the last frost will occur and when he should plant his grain. It is not good enough simply saying "sometime in spring", when "sometime" is a 3-month period: far too imprecise. So the Chinese solar agricultural calendar divided the year into 24 divisions, which it called ch'i or chieh seasons.

I see a few hands waving! Yes, there are 24 divisions on the main ring of the feng shui compass and ch'i is of course central to feng shui. These divisions are not just important to farmers, but are important in terms of measuring the natural forces arriving at a particular site. The same goes for ch'i tides: we want to know precisely when to make a feng shui change.

DEFINITION

*The **equinoxes** occur around March 21st and September 21st (plus or minus a day or two) and are the points in the calendar where everywhere on Earth has equal daylight and night hours. The **solstices** are halfway between the equinoxes and fall on December 21st and June 21st (plus or minus a day or two) and mark the date of least daylight and most daylight hours respectively. If you are reading this in the southern hemisphere, please switch the words "least" and "most"!*

Fitting everything together

The 24 ch'i seasons also have to fit with the all-important days beginning each season, and those key dates, the solstices and equinoxes. One of the calendar mistakes that we make in the West is assuming that the *equinoxes* and *solstices* mark the beginning of seasons. In fact, they always mark the middle of each season. The key for us is to see where the five Elements and planets fit in. You'll see how all this works on the table overleaf.

The bright-eyed among you will notice that only four out of the five Elements are used. There have been various schemes devised to fit all five Elements in, but the truth is that the Element Earth remains in the centre and is not strictly part of the annual cycle. The table shows how everything fits together in the Chinese solar calendar. You will need to use it to determine the Element of the season and the precise dates of the seasons. The 24 "little seasons" are confusingly called ch'i seasons because they show the changes in the quality of ch'i from yang through to yin, from spring to deepest winter.

It is a point of some contention as to how to use feng shui in the southern hemisphere, especially as the seasons in the southern hemisphere are the reverse of those in the northern hemisphere.

CHINESE & WESTERN CALENDAR CONCORDANCE

DATE* OF START OF CH'I	CH'I NO.	CHINESE NAME FOR CH'I SEASON	ENGLISH NAME FOR CH'I SEASON	EARTHLY BRANCH***	RULING PLANET
Feb 4th	1	Li ch'un	Spring commences	III – Yin	Jupiter
Feb 19th	2	Yu shui	Rain water		
Mar 5th	3	Ching chih	Insects waken	IV – Mao	
Mar 20th	4	Ch'un fen	Spring equinox		
Apr 4th	5	Ch'ing ming	Clear brightness	V – Ch'en	
Apr 20th	6	Ku yu	Corn rain		
May 5th	7	Li hsia	Summer commences	VI – Ssu	Mars
May 21st	8	Hsiao man	Corn sprouting		
Jun 5th	9	Mang chung	Corn in ear	VII – Wu	
Jun 21st	10	Hsia chih	Summer solstice		
Jul 7th	11	Hsiao shu	Little heat	VIII – Wei	
Jul 22nd	12	Ta shu	Great heat		
Aug 7th	13	Li ch'iu	Fall commences	IX – Shen	Venus
Aug 23rd	14	Ch'u shu	Heat finishes		
Sep 7th	15	Pai lu	White dew	X – Yu	
Sep 23rd	16	Ch'iu fen	Fall equinox		
Oct 8th	17	Han lu	Cold dew	XI – Hsu	
Oct 23rd	18	Shuang chiang	Frost descends		
Nov 7th	19	Li tung	Winter commences	XII – Hai	Mercury
Nov 22nd	20	Hsiao hsueh	Little snow		
Dec 7th	21	Ta hsueh	Great snow	I – Tzu	
Dec 21st	22	Tung chih	Winter solstice		
Jan 5th	23	Hsiao han	Little cold	II – Ch'ou	
Jan 20th	24	Ta han	Great cold		

* plus 1 day in some years   ** plus or minus 2 days in some years   *** see chapter 22
Notes: The year 2000 was a leap year, but it makes little difference as Chinese calendar spring always starts on either February 4th or 5th.

YEAR 2000 TAKEN AS EXAMPLE

ELEMENT (excluding Earth)	BEGINNING SEASON	MID-SEASON	DATE BEGINS*	MID DATE**	SEASON LENGTH (in days)
Wood	Spring		Feb 4		
		Spring equinox		Mar 20	
					90
Fire	Summer		May 5		
		Summer solstice		Jun 21	
					94
Metal	Fall		Aug 7		
		Fall equinox		Sep 23	
					92
Water	Winter		Nov 7		
		Winter solstice		Dec 21	
					90

The solstice and the equinox are the mid-points of each season, as shown above, not the beginning of the season as is commonly thought in the West.

Feng shui in both hemispheres

Consider the northern and southern hemispheres. The traditional view is that the ch'i tides do not intrinsically change their behavior as you cross the equator. Nor does south suddenly change from Trigram *Li* to its opposite. Some practitioners, like Roger Green, have devised a special southern hemisphere version of feng shui, reversing some of the traditional ascriptions. My own view is that "the proof of the pudding is in the eating." I leave you, my reader, to experiment and draw your own conclusions. However, tradition should not be turned on its head till there is a very cogent body of experiment to support an alternative view.

I have to declare a personal bias here. Having been born in the southern hemisphere, I have found that the Four Pillars calculation (see chapter 22), done by the traditional rules seems to apply to me much more closely than the "reversed" southern hemisphere version.

INTERNET

www.astro-fengshui.com

Go to Joseph Yu's Chinese Astrology and Feng Shui site for more on the northern/southern hemisphere controversy.

Good and bad days

SO HOW CAN WE USE these cycles practically? One of the most popular pages in Feng Shui for Modern Living *magazine was the so-called "feng shui horoscope". In fact this wasn't a horoscope. It was two tables of good and bad days. The first gave general indications for each of the 12 animal signs as to which was a good, bad, or indifferent day for each sign.*

We all understand that there are days when everything just goes well, the sun shines, the members of both sexes smile at you in the street, the boss is reasonable, and nothing is really difficult.

We also understand that there are those days when everything, and I mean *everything*, goes wrong: You get up late, you nick yourself while shaving, you have nothing but bills in the mail, you miss the bus, the boss is on a real search-and-destroy mission, and your girl- or boyfriend decides he or she is still offended over something you did last Friday, which you can hardly remember. In other words, a day from hell.

It's nice to know in advance when these days are going to happen.

■ **On a bad day,** *nothing seems to go right and even your journey to work can be frustrating. You can get advance warning of the good and the bad days with the help of the Chinese Almanac.*

The two tables

The first table of good and bad days compares the Earthly Branch of the year in which you were born with the Branch and Stem of the specific day, giving you reasonable odds on which way the day will turn out for you.

The chien ch'u are the tables of good and bad days in the ancient Chinese Almanac called the Tung Shu. It is referred to by millions of Chinese daily, and is one of the bestselling books in the world, certainly outselling the Bible in the East.

In the *Tung Shu* the second table applies to everyone, and shows the best days to do certain things. Intuitively, we can all understand that there is a good and a bad day to get married. Nobody wants their life's odyssey with their chosen partner to begin on a traumatic and trying day. But it's more than this – there is a good and bad day on which to sign a contract, or even on which to wash your hair! Observing these dates improves your percentage of successful contracts . . . or dates. If you had already known this, then some of the business or personal relationships that went sour might not necessarily have turned out that way.

Timing it right

This second table relies not upon your year of birth but upon combinations of the Earthly Branch of the day and the Earthly Branch of the current month. The result determines the suitability for a particular action on this day. These actions can be as serious as marriage, or as trivial as digging a garden pond. Nobody, if they knew about this, would risk deliberately marrying on a bad day. There is even a type of day where the old Almanac says "Be joyous and drink wine: all else is of little use." We can all instinctively recognize the kind of day when it's better to stay in bed, but usually only after it has passed us by.

■ **Why not increase your chances** *of success by consulting the Chinese Almanac before deciding on a particular course of action? It might be your lucky day.*

Improving your luck

Some days really are better than other days, and by using your knowledge of feng shui and Chinese astrology you can improve your luck and opportunities. Although you can calculate these yourself, it gets a bit complex as there are at least 17 formulas for doing so. Much easier is to look it up in the Chinese Almanac, or *Tung Shu*, which is published each year in Hong Kong, Taiwan, and other Chinese-populated areas outside of China.

The print run for this extraordinary publication is 3 million in Hong Kong alone. Increasingly, however, English versions of the Almanac are appearing, translated by authorities such as Victor Dy, Kwok Man Ho, and Ricky Tan. So if you can't get a hold of the latest month's edition of *Feng Shui for Modern Living*, then look out for one of these translations, but you do need the current year!

INTERNET

www.aballantine.com

Go to the web site for Andrew Ballantine Technology where you can purchase Software for Feng Shui, which can calculate these dates for any month or year you choose. Also, check out www.amazon.com for English versions of the Chinese Almanac.

A simple summary

✓ Calendar-making is a complex art, because the number of days in the Earth's cycle does not mesh with the number of days in the moon's cycle.

✓ The Chinese count their Epochs in blocks of 3,600 years, and take their starting date as 2637 BC.

✓ The Chinese use both a solar and a lunar calendar. The start of the Chinese solar calendar is the beginning of spring on February 4th or 5th every year.

This is the calendar that is relevant for feng shui.

✓ The equinoxes and solstices mark the middle of each of the four seasons.

✓ The 12 animal signs of popular Chinese astrology are related to the Chinese lunar year.

✓ The Chinese Almanac, or *Tung Shu*, has calendar details, plus calculations of good and bad days for particular animal signs and for particular activities.

Chapter 22

Heavenly Stems and Earthly Branches

So NOW THAT WE HAVE the calendar year in perspective, let us look at the cyclical nature of Chinese time-keeping. This is expressed in words that use plant metaphors. Heaven is measured by the ten Celestial Stems, and Earth is measured by the 12 Earthly Branches. Taken together, they form the 60-fold basis of Chinese measurement of time and space, which is also measured by the rotation of Jupiter around the sun. But these combinations are useful for much more than that and are the basis of the Four Pillar Chinese horoscope.

In this chapter...

✓ **The ten Heavenly Stems**

✓ **The 12 Earthly Branches**

✓ **The Sexagenary combinations**

✓ **Your Four Pillars of Destiny**

THE CHINESE CALENDAR USES JUPITER'S ORBIT AROUND THE SUN TO MARK THE 12 SIGNS OF THE ZODIAC

The ten Heavenly Stems

THE TEN HEAVENLY STEMS *are simply the five Elements run through twice. Why run twice? Well, everything is either yin or yang, and the Elements are no exception, so the Stems are 5 x 2 = 10.*

The ten Heavenly Stems are a very old set of symbols, and apart from an oblique connection with the stars of the Milky Way, their names do not really mean much to the modern Chinese any more. The ten Heavenly Stems were at one point looked upon as literally the stems on which the stars were seated, although this may simply have been a poetic interpretation. They are described as lucky or unlucky according to the yin/yang balance of their associated Trigram.

THE T'IEN KAN (HEAVENLY STEMS)

NUMBER	NAME	ELEMENT	YIN/YANG	LUCKY/UNLUCKY
1	Chia	Wood	yang	U
2	I	Wood	yin	U
3	Ping	Fire	yang	L
4	Ting	Fire	yin	L
5	Wu	Earth	yang	–
6	Chi	Earth	yin	–
7	Keng	Metal	yang	L
8	Hsin	Metal	yin	L
9	Jen	Water	yang	U
10	Kuei	Water	yin	U

Note the alternation of yin and yang, and that each Element is therefore represented twice. Note also that the order of the Elements is that of the Productive Cycle of the Elements (see chapter 6).

The 12 Earthly Branches

THE 12 EARTHLY BRANCHES *are most commonly remembered as the 12 so-called "animal zodiacal signs" of popular Chinese astrology.*

The Branches are used to measure many things, but particularly the 12 solar months. These begin at Branch *Tzu* in mid-winter, at the point of maximum cold, or yin. Accordingly, by the time they reach the beginning of spring (February 4th or 5th), they have arrived at the 3rd Earthly Branch.

It does not at first sight seem logical, but the solar year starts with yin, Branch III. Remember that the first month of the solar calendar is the 3rd Branch. This is important because when you come to calculate your Four Pillars horoscope, one of the eight parts of this is the Branch of the month.

Note that the Branch yin is not the same as yin/yang.

Remember, as in feng shui, it is the solar calendar that matters. It's simple to use. When you want to check it, just look up the master Calendar Table on pages 320–21 and it will be immediately obvious which is the right Branch for which month.

It is traditional to number Branches with Roman numerals (I–XII), so as not to confuse them with the Stems that are numbered 1–10.

The Branches and compass directions

The Branches therefore also correlate with the seasons (4 seasons x 3 months each = 12 Branches), and the 12 hours of the day. Yes, there are 12 Chinese hours of 120 minutes duration in each day. Even today, the Chinese use these "double-hours." Most important, for our purposes, is the attribution of each of the 12 Earthly Branches to the compass directions. The main Branches marking the four cardinal points are highlighted, so you can see that the Branches tie time and years to compass directions.

The sharp-eyed among you will notice that not every degree of the compass is covered. As we will see in the next chapter, these "missing" degrees are covered by some of the Heavenly Stems and Trigrams.

Separately, the Stems and the Branches don't mean very much, but when combined they are used for all sorts of counting. Taken together they are referred to as the *Kan* (Stems) *Shih* (Branches) system. *Kan shih* is sometimes spelled *Ganzhi*.

THE TI'CHIH (EARTHLY BRANCHES)

BRANCH		DIRECTION		YEARS	SEASON	MONTH	HOUR
Branch number	Earthly Branch name	Compass Direction in degrees	Animal sign	Example corresponding years	Early/Mid-/Late	Solar number	Double hour
I	Tzu	352.5–7.5 (N)	Rat	1996, 2008	mid-winter	11	11pm–1am
II	Ch'ou	22.5–37.5	Ox	1997, 2009	late winter	12	1am–3am
III	Yin	52.5–67.5	Tiger	1998, 2010	early spring	1	3am–5am
IV	Mao	82.5–97.5 (E)	Rabbit	1999, 2011	mid-spring	2	5am–7am
V	Ch'en	112.5–127.5	Dragon	2000, 2012	late spring	3	7am–9am
VI	Ssu	142.5–157.5	Snake	1989, 2001	early summer	4	9am–11am
VII	Wu	172.5–187.5 (S)	Horse	1990, 2002	mid-summer	5	11am–1pm
VIII	Wei	202.5–217.5	Sheep	1991, 2003	late summer	6	1pm–3pm
IX	Shen	232.5–247.5	Monkey	1992, 2004	early fall	7	3pm–5pm
X	Yu	262.5–277.5 (W)	Rooster	1993, 2005	mid-fall	8	5pm–7pm
XI	Hsu	292.5–307.5	Dog	1994, 2006	late fall	9	7pm–9pm
XII	Hai	322.5–337.5	Pig	1995, 2007, etc	early winter	10	9pm–11pm

The 12 Earthly Branches integrate directions with various time periods. You can see, for example, that the Branch Tzu correlates with the sign of the Rat, the north, mid-winter, and midnight.

The Sexagenary combinations

OUR PARENTS OR MAYBE OUR GRANDPARENTS *were comfortable with counting things by the dozen. Dozens always "packed neater," as they would say, than tens. After all, a box containing three rows of four balls is closer to a square than anything you can do to pack ten balls. The day (in China) has 12 hours, and the year has 12 months.*

Counting by tens, or the decimal system, is much newer: Ten dimes to the dollar, 1,000 grams to the kilogram, etc. These two methods of counting are distinct and different. How can we fit them together? Well, the smallest number that can contain an even number of dozens and an even number of tens is the number 60.

Ah! Sixty, another number that is an essential part of our culture. There are 60 seconds in the minute, and 60 minutes in the hour. Maybe there is some rhyme or reason behind all these inconvenient non-decimal numbers. Hold on to that thought, and it will come into its own in chapter 23.

Let's look at a few more 60s now. The Mayans and the Babylonians counted in periods of 60 years (as, we already know, do the Chinese). Even the modern French, when they count, do so in the normal way by tens up to 60 . . . *dix, vingt, trente, quarante, cinquante, soixante.* But after 60 they count *soixante-dix* ("60 plus 10" for 70), *quatre-vingts* ("four 20s" for 80), and *quatre-vingt-dix* ("four 20s plus 10" for 90). How weird! Not really, it just harks back to the days when they too counted in 60s, not in 100s.

■ **The number 60** *is at the heart of our method of time-keeping.*

Pairing Stems and Branches

If there are ten Heavenly Stems and 12 Earthly Branches, how many combinations can you have? 120? Wrong: just 60 combinations. The reason is that essentially the ten Stems are made up of two sets, the yin and yang versions of the five Elements. Therefore, when it comes to combining them with the 12 Earthly Branches, the rule is that only yin Stems can go with yin Branches, and yang Stems with yang Branches, resulting in just 5 x 12 = 60 combinations.

In the older textbooks on feng shui and Chinese horoscopes, these 60 combinations are called the *Sexagenary* characters or combinations – what a mouthful!

> **DEFINITION**
>
> **Sexagenary** *is just another way of saying 60-fold.*

The Sexagenary combinations of Heavenly Stems and Earthly Branches

STEM (across) →				1	2	3	4	5	6	7	8	9	10
				Chia	I/Yi	Ping	Ting	Wu*	Chi	Keng	Hsin	Jen	Kuei
			yin/yang	yang	yin	yang	yin	yang	yin	yang	yin	yang	yin
BRANCH (down) ↓			Element	Wood	Wood	Fire	Fire	Earth	Earth	Metal	Metal	Water	Water
I	Tzu	Rat	yang / Water	1		13		25		37		49	
II	Ch'ou	Ox	yin / Earth		2		14		26		38		50
III	Yin	Tiger	yang / Wood	51		3		15		27		39	
IV	Mao	Rabbit	yin / Wood		52		4		16		28		40
V	Ch'en	Dragon	yang / Earth	41		53		5		17		29	
VI	Ssu	Snake	yin / Fire		42		54		6		18		30
VII	Wu*	Horse	yang / Fire	31		43		55		7		19	
VIII	Wei	Sheep	yin / Earth		32		44		56		8		20
IX	Shen	Monkey	yang / Metal	21		33		45		57		9	
X	Yu	Rooster	yin / Metal		22		34		46		58		10
XI	Hsu	Dog	yang / Earth	11		23		35		47		59	
XII	Hai	Pig	yin / Water		12		24		36		48		60

Read the table by selecting combinations of one Stem and one Branch. Where they intersect is the number of the Sexagenary combination. You can see clearly why there are only 60 and not 120 combinations. Half the combinations are disallowed because they mix yin and yang. Only yin Branches mate with yin Stems, and only yang Branches mate with yang Stems.

* Don't confuse the Stem Wu with the Branch Wu: They are different words in Chinese.

However, this simply means the 60-fold pairs of character combinations made of one Branch with one Stem. The 60 Sexagenary combinations are also sometimes called Binomials, literally the "two numbers."

The first Sexagenary combination, for example, is *Chia tzu* (i.e. the first Stem *Chia* plus the first Branch *Tzu*). Read the table to the left by selecting combinations of Branch with Stem. For example, read down the column headed by the Stem *Chia*, and across the line of the Branch *Tzu*. From this you can see that the combination *Chia tzu* is Sexagenary combination number 1. It is a yang combination made up of Stem 1 and Branch I.

Let's try something more complicated. Find Sexagenary combination 52. Yes, it's Branch IV and Stem number 2, or "*I mao.*"

What about the combination Ping ch'ou? The square is blank . . . it is not there because Ping is yang, but Ch'ou is yin, therefore the combination can never exist. The combinations are either one sex or the other!

Now let us look at the other information on the table. Look, for example, at the 53rd Sexagenary combination. It is *Ping ch'en*. What are its qualities? It is a yang Fire (*Ping*) Dragon (*Ch'en*). Ah, a yang Fire Dragon. Suddenly these otherwise inscrutable pairs of Chinese words have meaningful qualities. Look at another one, take *Chia shen*. Its qualities are yang Wood Monkey.

Looking at 60-year cycles

Earlier we saw that big-time cycles are 60 years long. Guess what? It's our friends the Sexagenary combinations that are used to label each of these years. So we can see that particular years have a character derived from the Stem and Branch used to label them.

At a popular Chinese astrology level people talk about a Dragon year (2000 for example) or a Snake year (2001). What they should really be saying is that the year 2000 is governed by the Branch *Ch'en*, whilst the year 2001 is governed by the Branch *Ssu*. "*Ssu*" just happens to sound like a snake hiss! Obviously the Elements also play a part – 2000 was the year of the Metal Dragon, and 2001 that of the Metal Snake.

We know the Sexagenary combinations measure years, so that the first Sexagenary combination, or *Chia tzu*, corresponds to 1984, the year of the yang Wood Rat. (Check the first line of the table.) This combination is therefore the beginning of every cycle of 60 years, which is why we will learn later that 1984 was an important cycle change year. The combination will repeat in 1984 + 60 years = 2044. This is how the Sexagenary combinations measure the cycles of 60 years.

There is also a Great Cycle of 180 years, which began in 1864. It is divided into three cycles of 60 years, the third of which began in 1984.

Sexagenary combinations are also used to measure months, days, and hours. So you can see that each of these time units has a yin/yang reading, an Element, and a Branch (animal sign) associated with it. This may sound complicated, but suddenly the calendar and the measurement of time becomes so much richer. You can tell, by checking the Sexagenary combination, what exactly the qualities are of any particular time or date. This has important implications for:

● Buildings (when were they built?)
● Humans (when were they born?)
● Feng shui (what ch'i tide is running now, and when will it change?)

Ch'i changes its quality according to the time of day, month, or year. Anyone who has watched the sunrise across the ocean on a clear day will understand that the ch'i tide running at that time is fundamentally different from that running at midnight or sundown. The Stems and Branches help us measure these tides.

The qualities of the time of birth are imprinted on people or buildings and continue to influence them all their lives. Put very simply, checking the Sexagenary combinations of a person against those of a building will help indicate if the building is going to be good for them to live in or not (see chapter 20).

■ **The flow of ch'i** *can be thought of as a tide that constantly changes. The type of ch'i flowing at a particular time can be pinpointed by using the Heavenly Stems and Earthly Branches.*

Sexagenary combinations and personality

The Sexagenary combinations define the type of ch'i flowing in that particular year, month, day, and hour. A person born at a particular moment will "inhale" a particular type of ch'i with their first breath, which will define their personality and the broad outline of their fate during the course of their life. This is the basis of Four Pillar astrology where everyone's destiny can be read from the Sexagenary combination for the hour, day, month, and year of their birth.

The same idea that the moment of birth defines your life and destiny is present in Western astrology. Scientific research by the French astrological statistician Michel Gauquelin (1928–1991) has proven statistically, and beyond any reasonable doubt, that people born during certain times of the year – during a certain ch'i tide, as it were – are much more likely to take up a particular profession.

These tides have a very real effect on people, and an analysis of the time of birth can really tell you statistically important things about a person. It was also no fluke that the same researcher, Gauquelin, conducted exhaustive statistical analysis on the planets and showed that Mars was rising at the birth of champion athletes, soldiers, and surgeons. Remember that surgeons also draw blood!

The same results appeared in an analysis of the United Kingdom 1971 census, where electricians were most likely to be born in the Metal part of the year, while farmers were much more likely to be born during the Wood season, representative of vegetative growth. Therefore, it's not unreasonable to assume that other facets of your career or destiny may be affected/predicted by your Four Pillars horoscope.

Lastly, our friends the Sexagenary combinations occupy many of the rings of the feng shui compass, and are an integral part of advanced feng shui.

■ **According to Four Pillar astrology,** *the character and destiny of this rice farmer may well have been decided at the time of his birth.*

Your Four Pillars of Destiny

MUCH HAS BEEN WRITTEN about the Four Pillars of Destiny, but in a nutshell they are simply the four Sexagenary combinations for the year, month, day, and hour of your birth.

Chinese astrology in the West has been seen primarily as connected with your animal zodiacal sign, one for each year. A whole industry has grown up based on books written about this apparently simple system and the "character" of each of these signs. In fact, these are not zodiacal signs in the strict sense at all, because they change yearly, not monthly.

As we have seen, these 12 Earthly Branches cycle round every 12 years. It is the Branches that are important, and no serious Chinese astrology book deals with the so-called animal signs except to mention them in passing in connection with the Branches. The animal signs, therefore, are just the popularization of a small piece of just one of several forms of Chinese astrology.

Four Pillar astrology

If we look a bit more closely at Four Pillar astrology, we find that there are two characters for the year, two for the month, two for the day, and two for the hour of birth. They are usually stacked on the page to form four "pillars" – one pillar for the year, one for the month, one for the day, and one for the hour. The Chinese name for this form of astrology is *Pa tzu*, or eight character, or Four Pillar astrology.

As you may have guessed, each Pillar is a Sexagenary combination and has one Branch character and one Stem character. The popular animal sign is only one of these eight characters of the horoscope, in fact the Branch character of the year.

As we have seen, each Stem and each Branch has one of the five Elements and a yin/yang reading assigned to it. It is this balance of Elements that is used to judge the basic character of the person being "read." Other, more complicated, indications map out the Destiny, or Heaven Luck, of the person concerned during their life.

Trivia...

There are a number of forms of Chinese astrology. Perhaps the two main Schools are the Pa tzu (or Four Pillars astrology, also spelled Ba zi) and the Tzu wei tou shu (or Purple Star System, also spelled Zi wei dou shu), which was invented by Chen Hsi I, an astrologer of the Sung dynasty (960–1279). We will be looking only briefly at the Four Pillar system in this book.

A matter of balance

Your full horoscope will have eight (4 + 4 = 8) characters, each with an associated Element. The balance of these Elements is what tells you if you have a balanced or unbalanced grouping of the Elements. For example, if you had an Element balance of three Fire, two Wood, one Earth, and two Metal, it would be obvious that you have an excess of Fire in your nature. This is, in fact, aggravated by the two Woods, which will contribute to producing more Fire (according to the Productive Cycle of the Elements). In addition, there is no Water, which might have acted as a control on the Fire.

The feng shui upshot of this is that when you furnish your home or office, you should, for example, use dark blues and blacks to strengthen the Water content of your environment, making for more balance. Obviously, it can become much more complicated than that, but you get the general idea.

Now because this book is about feng shui, I am not going into the complex process of calculating the complete horoscope. There are plenty of good books on this process, particularly those by Raymond Lo, Elizabeth Moran, and David Twicken.

INTERNET

www.aballantine.com

If you want to avoid altogether the tiresome process of calculating the Four Pillars, then just go to www.aballantine.com, where you can purchase Software for Feng Shui. This is a reliable Four Pillars program that will take the headache out of calculation and give you your Pillars, your Element balance, your fate periods, and what to do about them.

A simple summary

✔ The ten Heavenly Stems combine with the 12 Earthly Branches to form the 60 Sexagenary combinations.

✔ This is called the *Kan shih*, or *Ganzhi*, system.

✔ With Sexagenary combinations only yin Stems combine with yin Branches. Only yang Stems combine with yang Branches.

✔ These Sexagenary combinations measure cycles of 60 years – the current cycle started at the beginning of 1984.

✔ Every year, month, day, and hour has one of these Sexagenary combinations attributed to it, eight characters in all.

✔ These eight characters make up your Four Pillar horoscope.

Chapter 23

Compass School Feng Shui Tools

I N THIS CHAPTER we finally get to fit the pieces of the jigsaw puzzle together. Where do they fit? They all fit onto that wonderful encyclopedia of feng shui, the feng shui compass, or *lo p'an* (sometimes spelled *luopan*). We will look at the history of this complex instrument very briefly, and then move on to examine how it is made. The *lo p'an* has up to 39 different rings. We will particularly analyze the symbols that compose one ring of the *lo p'an*, the ring containing the 24 Directions. With only this ring, we learn how the *lo p'an* is used practically by taking the compass direction readings of a front door. We will also take a quick look at the six inner rings of a typical *lo p'an* and discover their importance in feng shui.

In this chapter...

✓ What is the Chinese compass?

✓ The 24 Directions, or Mountains

✓ How to use a Chinese compass

THE *LO P'AN* COMPASS IS THE KEY INSTRUMENT IN CALCULATING FENG SHUI ALIGNMENTS

What is the Chinese compass?

THE CHINESE COMPASS *is much more complicated than a maritime compass. In fact, it was the predecessor of the maritime compass. This we know because of one of the common Chinese sailor's prayers that was said out loud over the compass before long voyages. Alongside the usual list of gods and saints, some of the early Masters of feng shui, such as Ching Wu, are called upon to protect its function. This prayer shows that the compass was originally a feng shui device, which was later inherited and adapted by mariners. It would make no sense otherwise mentioning Masters from a land-based tradition.*

The first Chinese compass dates back to the 4th century BC, some 1,500 years before the adoption of the compass for navigation in Europe in around 1190. Even in China the use of the compass for navigation was probably delayed till AD 850. Before that it was used for land navigation and feng shui.

Kuei-ku Tzu, whose name intriguingly means "the Master of Ghost Valley," was a 4th-century BC "Master of the yin-yang school of thought" (which is another name for the philosophy behind feng shui). He wrote about the compass, and remarked that "when the people of Cheng go out to collect jade, they carry a south-pointer (or compass) with them so as not to lose their way." This suggests that the compass and yin-yang philosophy (feng shui) go back, hand in hand, a very long way.

The physical lo p'an

As we saw in chapter 4, Wang Chih (who lived during Northern Sung dynasty, 960–1127) established the *lo p'an* in its modern form, with about 17 rings, at least one of which had on it the 24 Directions, or Mountains.

By this time the compass came in two distinct parts, a square wooden base into which snugly fitted a wooden saucer-shaped disc, averaging 6 to 8 inches across. This disc, or "Heaven Plate," revolved freely in the square "Earth base." Across the compass from side to side were two sighting lines, like the crosshairs of a rifle sight, made of red thread. In the centre was a glassed-over "well" containing the needle, which was magnetized and finely suspended. This needle pointed north–south, but the Chinese always thought of it as pointing south.

what you usually have to determine is into which of these 24 Directions, or sectors, a particular house, water, or hill alignment falls.

How it all fits together

A Chinese *lo p'an* is a sort of round *lo shu*. You probably remember from chapter 8 that the *lo shu* is related to the eight Directions. The illustration below shows the eight Directions, which are divided again into three sub-sections, making a total of 8 x 3 = 24 Directions.

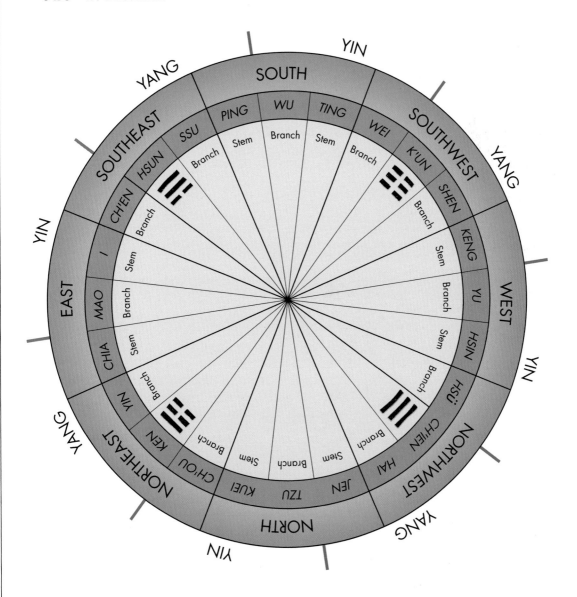

The 24 Directions, or Mountains

AT THIS POINT, WE ASSEMBLE what is possibly the most important ring on the face of the lo p'an, or feng shui compass. This ring has 24 segments, which are usually called (slightly confusingly) the 24 Directions, or Mountains. In fact, this ring is so important that it is repeated no less than three times on San Ho lo p'ans. (San Ho is one of the three major types of lo p'an.) These segments are sometimes referred to as the 24 Compass Directions, but we will call them the 24 Directions.

Each of the 24 Directions, or Mountains, consists of 15 degrees of the ring. Why 15 degrees? The whole circle has 360 degrees. So, if we take just one twenty-fourth of the circle (360/24), we get 15 degrees.

What is on this ring?

Rather confusingly, this ring is made up of three different sets of symbols that we have already encountered: The Trigrams (chapter 8), the Heavenly Stems (chapter 22), and the Earthly Branches. Did I hear you ask, "How can eight Trigrams, 10 Stems, and 12 Branches add up to 24 Directions?" Let me explain:

1. Firstly, the so-called "corner points" of SW, NW, NE, and SE are marked out by four of the eight Trigrams. These important Trigrams are, respectively, *K'un*, *Ch'ien*, *Ken*, and *Hsun*.

2. Next, we take the 12 Earthly Branches. We put one Branch at each of the cardinal points: N, S, E, and W. Then we put one Branch on either side of each of the four Trigrams, using up all 12 Branches. Since the lo p'an measures Earth energies, you would expect the Branches to be fully represented.

3. Finally, we take eight of the Heavenly Stems, and fill the remaining vacant places on the ring.

What we are left with is the full ring of 24 Directions, as shown in the table opposite.

LEARNING ABOUT THE 24 DIRECTIONS

	DIRECTION	COMPASS DEGREES	CHINESE NAME	STEM/BRANCH/ TRIGRAM	CHINESE CHARACTER
SOUTH	S1	157.5-172.5	Ping	Stem	
	S2	172.5-187.5	Wu	Branch	
	S3	187.5-202.5	Ting	Stem	
	SW1	202.5-217.5	Wei	Branch	
	SW2	217.5-232.5	K'un	Trigram	
	SW3	232.5-247.5	Shen	Branch	
WEST	W1	247.5-262.5	Keng	Stem	
	W2	262.5-277.5	Yu	Branch	
	W3	277.5-292.5	Hsin	Stem	
	NW1	292.5-307.5	Hsu	Branch	
	NW2	307.5-322.5	Ch'ien	Trigram	
	NW3	322.5-337.5	Hai	Branch	
NORTH	N1	337.5-352.5	Jen	Stem	
	N2	352.5-7.5	Tzu	Branch	
	N3	7.5-22.5	Kuei	Stem	
	NE1	22.5-37.5	Ch'ou	Branch	
	NE2	37.5-52.5	Ken	Trigram	
	NE3	52.5-67.5	Yin	Branch	
EAST	E1	67.5-82.5	Chia	Stem	
	E2	82.5-97.5	Mao	Branch	
	E3	97.5-112.5	I	Stem	
	SE1	112.5-127.5	Ch'en	Branch	
	SE2	127.5-142.5	Hsun	Trigram	
	SE3	142.5-157.5	Ssu	Branch	

Chinese characters (from top-right blocks):

丙 午 丁
未 坤 申
庚 酉 辛
戌 乾 亥
壬 子 癸
丑 艮 寅
甲 卯 乙
辰 巽 巳

How to use a Chinese compass

INTERNET

www.dragon-gate.com

To look at examples of lo p'an, or if you are thinking of buying one on the Internet, go to the Superstore page at this web site.

ASSUMING YOU HAVE BEEN LUCKY enough *to have acquired a good* lo p'an, *to get familiar with how it works, let's start by using it. If you don't have a* lo p'an, *try to lay your hands on a trekking compass and read off the degrees (for later conversion to their Chinese equivalent, use the table on page 345).*

■ **At the center of a *lo p'an*** *is the "Heaven Pool," or the compass needle and well. The two dots should be aligned with the needle end and with the circular mark.*

So, how do we find out, for example, which direction the front door of a house faces? First, stand outside, in front of the front door, and holding the *lo p'an* level with both hands, place one edge of the compass firmly against the door. Using your thumbs, turn the disc slowly till the needle lines up with the line on the bottom of the well. Make sure that the end with the circular mark lines up between the two dots on the bottom of the well.

Keep it level

Check again to see that you are holding the whole compass level. Now look at the crosshairs. One points at right angles out from the door. Where it crosses the inner ring containing the 24 Directions furthest from the door is the facing direction. When you have found this particular character, you have just done your first real Compass School feng shui reading.

Then look along the same crosshair to the part closest to the door. Where it crosses the inner ring of 24 Directions is the sitting direction. The sitting direction is *always* exactly opposite the facing direction.

Overcoming problems

There are a couple of things you should be aware of with this reading. One is magnetic interference with the needle, which is often shown by the needle swinging backwards and forwards a lot before settling down. It is usually caused by the presence of metal or electrical equipment. I will deal with this problem on page 348.

There's also the basic problem that most *lo p'ans* are inscribed in Chinese. A few have been produced with English inscriptions, but if you want to use them you might as well go back to using an ordinary trekking compass. You can overcome this difficulty with a little study. Having taken the reading, put your thumb on the facing character and take the compass to a table where you can sit down and carefully match this character with the table on page 345. From this table you can jot down the relevant one of the 24 Directions in its English form and, if you like, also its range of degrees.

Alternatively, if you use a trekking compass you can use the same table to convert a numerical reading in degrees to one of the Chinese 24 Directions. If you use both, you will soon discover that the *lo p'an* is much easier to align, even if it takes a few minutes to decipher the character.

Using the "Earth Plate" ring

Another problem is that there are usually three rings containing the 24 Directions on most compasses. For the purposes of this book we will need to use only the inner ring of 24 Directions.

For those of you who want to know a bit more, you might notice that the three rings of 24 Directions all carry the same characters, in the same order, but the two outer rings are turned slightly (7.5 degrees) to the left or right of the innermost ring.

The inner ring is the "Earth Plate" ring, and this is the one we will use for basic feng shui. The second similar 24 Direction ring (moving outward from the center) is the "Man Plate" ring, and it is turned 7.5 degrees west of north. The outer ring of 24 Directions is the "Heaven Plate" ring, and it is turned 7.5 degrees east of north. To keep it simple, you can, if you like, now forget the contents of this whole paragraph and just keep on looking at the inner ring of 24 Directions!

The reason for these three similar rings is not that magnetic declination has changed over a period of time, an incorrect reason put forward even by Chinese books on feng shui. The reason is that each of these rings has a very different purpose and relates to other things such as water entry points, but we won't go into these here.

Why not use a trekking compass instead?

Many feng shui books recommend you use a trekking or military compass instead of a *lo p'an*. There is nothing wrong with this if all you really want is a rough idea of which of the eight compass points the house, office, or building faces. However, if you want to practice the more complicated Compass School formulas, then there is one big drawback: Most of these Western compasses are round. (The exception is a map compass, which is set into a clear plastic rule, that is quite good for feng shui.)

You cannot align a round compass parallel to a wall or a door, for the very good reason that round compasses don't have a flat side! You could simply stand in a doorway and simultaneously squint at the compass and at some imaginary point in the middle of the path leading from the door (assuming it is straight). Using this tactic you would be lucky to take a reading within 10 degrees of accurate. Of course, if there are any military types or geometricians out there, I'm sure you could devise some system to determine a sighting point, but for the rest of us it simply wouldn't work.

A TREKKING COMPASS IS
NOT IDEAL FOR FENG SHUI

The beauty of the lo p'an, or feng shui compass, is that you can simply place the flat outer edge against a wall or door, and turn the inner circular plate at leisure. I know that it's a little more complicated than this, but you get the idea that a circular trekking compass can only do so much.

Avoiding magnetic interference

In this modern world there is a lot of electrical equipment, such as computers and mobile phones, that can cause the needle of even the most stable compass to be deflected – a problem not encountered by the old feng shui Masters. The simple solution is to take at least three readings: Back away from the object being measured and take one reading on the door, one 3 feet from the door, and one 12 feet out. Make sure you are measuring the same thing by tying a (red) thread to the door and to a stake at right angles to the door, so that the readings are taken along the same alignment. Then average these three readings (add them together and divide by 3).

The complex solution (used by Master Tan in Singapore) is to use a theodolite (a stable table on tripod legs containing a telescope sight used by surveyors) which can be set up with the *lo p'an* some distance from whatever is being measured, well away from potential electrical interference. Traditional Chinese Masters go to great lengths for scientifically accurate readings, so try to be as careful as you can.

USING A THEODOLITE

■ **A feng shui Master** *uses a lo p'an and a length of red string fixed between two staves in the ground to judge the exact alignment of a site before construction begins.*

Looking at lo p'an rings

All *lo p'ans* have rings around the central needle well. These are called *tseng*, and there may be anywhere between seven and 39 such rings. I have not personally seen a compass with more or fewer rings than this range, though they may exist. In size, *lo p'ans* range from 2½ inches across to more than 3 feet across. There are certain key compass rings that are common to all compasses. In addition to these, there are special rings specific to particular schools of feng shui, or even to a particular feng shui Master. However, we can do much with just the basic six or seven rings.

Let's take a brief look at six of the inner rings of a typical *lo p'an*. At the center of the *lo p'an* is the "Heaven Pool," or the actual compass needle and well. The six rings leading out from the center are arranged as follows:

1 The rings immediately adjacent to the needle well contain the eight Trigrams, usually in the Former Heaven Sequence.

2 The "knotted cord" figures representing the numbers 1 to 9 (excluding 5 at the center), as they were shown in the original *lo shu*. This is why it is easy to see the *lo p'an* as a "round *lo shu*."

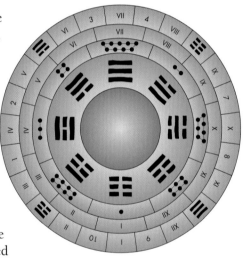

THE INNER FOUR RINGS

3 The 12 Earthly Branches. This is the "clock" part of the *lo p'an*, which can be used to relate direction to the 12 double-hours of the day, or the 12 solar months of the year, or the annual cycle of the 12 animal signs.

4 The 24 Directions, or Mountains, which we have discussed in detail, and which are used for Flying Star feng shui.

5 The ring showing the 24 seasonal ch'i, so that each direction has a connection with one of these 14–15 day micro-seasons throughout the year (see chapter 21). This is another good example of a *lo p'an* correlation between space (direction) and time (the seasons).

6 The 60 Sexagenary characters (see chapter 22), which on the compass (just to be a bit confusing) are called the 60 dragons.

The outermost ring

Finally, the outermost ring of a modern *lo p'an* should be instantly recognizable, as it is the 360 degrees of the compass. This ring is very useful. You can, if you want to "cheat" a little (and avoid Chinese characters altogether), just use this ring, plus the key table on page 345 to complete your basic readings.

Don't try to substitute intuition for accurate measurement. Please check your work.

Practice makes perfect

In this book we have reached the point where you have a working knowledge of Form School, Eight Mansion, and simple Compass School feng shui. We have also looked at the various cures and remedies, and how to apply them.

We have come a long way. This will suffice for you to make serious and correct changes in your own feng shui, but professional mastery of this wonderful and intricate subject requires long years of practice, preferably with a real Master.

A simple summary

✔ The *lo p'an* was originally a feng shui device dating from the 4th century BC.

✔ The 24 Directions ring is made up of four of the Trigrams, eight of the Heavenly Stems, and 12 of the Earthly Branches.

✔ To use a *lo p'an*, place it parallel with the alignment being measured and turn the disc till the compass needle head rests over the two dots in the needle well, then take a reading from the crosshairs.

✔ Avoid magnetic interference by averaging three readings.

✔ The *lo p'an* can have between seven and 39 rings. The most important, for our purposes, are the inner six rings.

✔ You should now have a number of perfectly workable feng shui formulas in your hands.

Quiz answers

The answers to the quiz on page 229 are shown below. On each diagram you can see the correct position of the *hsueh* spot or spots on the blank Water Dragon patterns. How did you get on?

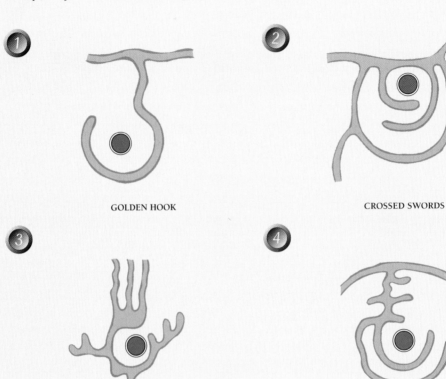

GOLDEN HOOK

CROSSED SWORDS

PHOENIX IN FLIGHT

RAINBOW SWALLOWING AZURE CLOUDS

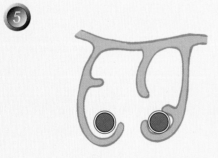

DOUBLE HOOK

DRAGON TURNING BACK

A simple glossary

Almanac, Chinese An annual publication that gives all kinds of advice, including the best/worst days for marriage, signing contracts, etc.

Arrowana So called "feng shui fish," used in feng shui aquariums because of the change in their scales from muddy carp-colored to golden (representing wealth), depending on diet. These fish are highly prized and rather expensive.

Bagua *See* pa kua.

Bazhai *See* pa chai.

Bird, Red Form School hill formation at the front of a house or site.

Branches *See* Earthly Branches.

Bright hall *See* ming tang.

Buddha Founder of Buddhism 566–486 BC.

Calendar, lunar A calendar based on the cycle of the moon.

Calendar, solar A calendar, like the standard Western calendar, based on the Earth's revolution round the sun.

Cardinal points North, south, east, and west.

Cash The name for old round Chinese coins with a square hole in the middle.

Celestial Animals, four Green Dragon, White Tiger, Black Tortoise, Red Bird.

Chai House.

Chen **Trigram** Trigram of thunder and spring.

Ch'i The vital energy of the universe, in man, the heavens, and earth, sometimes referred to as "cosmic breath."

Ch'i kung A martial art that concentrates ch'i energy in the body.

Ch'ien **Trigram** The Trigram of Heaven and late fall.

Chou I An old name for the *I Ching*, the *Classic of Changes*.

Chueh ming Severed fate or total loss location in house.

Classic of Changes *See* I Ching.

Coins *See* Cash.

Compass Chinese *See* lo p'an.

Compass School The Fukien School of feng shui that uses the compass to locate and diagnose ch'i flows. An early master was Wang Chih (*c.* AD 960).

Confucius Founder of Confucianism (551–479 BC).

Cosmic Breath *See* ch'i.

Daoism *See* Taoism.

Destructive Cycle The cycle of the Elements, which is ordered Metal, Wood, Earth, Water, then Fire.

Devil's Door The northeast, sometimes considered a bad direction to face a front door.

Direction One of the eight main Compass Points or,

in a more specialized sense, the 24 Divisions of the feng shui compass.

Double Happiness The Chinese calligraphy character for "happiness" repeated twice and interlaced.

Dragon, Green The Form School hills to the left of a house or site (looking out from the front door).

Dragon, Yellow The Celestial Animal sometimes associated with the central position.

Dragon Gate The gate through which successful scholars are supposed to pass, metaphorically turning from a carp into a dragon.

Early Heaven Sequence (*Hou t'ien*) A circular arrangement of the eight Trigrams, where the Trigram *Ch'ien* is in the south. Used on defensive *pa kua* mirrors, and for the feng shui of the exterior landforms.

Earthly Branches The 12 Divisions of the day, or the year, which are combined with the ten Heavenly Stems to form the 60 Sexagenary characters.

East Group The directions SE, N, S, E.

East/West system The system that divides people and houses into two types: the East Group and the West Group.

Eight House formula *See* Eight Mansion formula.

Eight Mansion formula The feng shui formula that associated the eight Aspirations with the eight Locations in a house or room.

Elements Water, Fire, Earth, Metal, and Wood. In Chinese, the *Wu hsing*.

Facing direction The front side of a building, often, but not always, the side with the front door.

Fang shih A master of Taoist magic.

Feng Wind.

Feng sha A noxious, ch'i-destroying wind.

Feng shui The Chinese system of maximizing the accumulation of beneficial ch'i to improve the quality of life and luck at a particular location. Literally "wind water."

Feng shui *hsien sheng* A professional practitioner of feng shui.

Flying Star feng shui A system of feng shui that takes into account time changes.

Flutes A wind instrument used in feng shui to convey ch'i, often away from an oppressive beam.

Form School Feng shui practice possibly originating in Kiangsi that uses landform structure to determine the positions of maximum beneficial accumulation of ch'i. Its most famous Master was Yang Yun Sung (AD 849–*c.* 888).

Four Pillars Your personal Chinese horoscope, specifically the eight Chinese characters and their associated Elements generated by determining the Stem and Branch of each of the year, month, day, and hour of your birth date.

Frog, one-legged A legendary creature that is supposed be able to bring wealth to your home. Often seen in Chinese homes.

Fu, Lou, and Shou The three Chinese domestic "gods" of Luck (including wealth), High Rank, and Longevity, respectively.

Fu wei House location that has mild good fortune.

Fuk, Luk, and Sau *See Fu, Lou, and Shou.*

Ganzhi system. See Kan shih *system.*

Geomancy An old mis-translation of "feng shui." In reality Geomancy is a completely different Arab system of divination by dots and sand originating in North Africa in the 9th century AD.

Goldfish Often suggested as a way of keeping the water moving in an aquarium and used for feng shui purposes.

Gravesites Location of an important part of feng shui practice, called yin feng shui.

Great Cycle of 180 years Nine cycles of 20 years. The current Great Cycle began in 1864.

Green Dragon *See* Dragon, Green.

Hai huo The accidents and mishaps or mild bad luck location in a house.

Heavenly Stems The ten terms that represent the cycle of the five Elements in their yin and yang form. They combine with the 12 Earthly Branches to form the 60 Sexagenary characters.

Hetu See ho t'u.

Hexagrams The 64 figures formed by placing one Trigram on top of another in every possible combination. A figure made up of six lines on top of one another, either broken or unbroken. The basis of the *I Ching.*

Ho hai See hai huo.

Ho t'u A square, like the *lo shu*, used with Former Heaven Sequence Trigrams.

Hsia calendar The Farmer's calendar, which is the basis for determining the Four Pillars, and the best/worst days.

Hsing See Elements.

Hsiu The 28 Chinese constellations often found marked on one of the outer rings of the feng shui compass.

Hsueh The lair, or site, of the maximum concentration of beneficial ch'i. A Form School feng shui term.

Hsun Trigram The Trigram of wind and early summer.

I Ching The Chinese *"Classic of Changes,"* a philosophical and divinatory book based on the 64 Hexagrams.

Intercardinal points NW, SW, NE, SE.

K'an The Trigram of moon and water and mid-winter.

Kan yu An old name for feng shui.

Kan shih system The 60 combinations of 12 Earthly Branches (*T'ien kan*) and ten Heavenly Stems (*Ti shih*), hence *Kan shih.*

Ken The Trigram of Mountain and early spring.

Killing Breath *See* sha ch'i.

Kirin A mythical creature, which is sometimes incorrectly translated as "unicorn," but looking nothing like it. Also spelled *qilin.*

Kua Trigrams and Hexagrams.

Kua number The annual number derived from your year of birth.

Kuei See kwei.

K'un The Trigram of Earth and late summer.

Kwan Kung A fierce god of wealth that should be placed facing the front door. Do not place a figure of this god in the bedroom or dining room.

Kwei Ghosts.

Landscape feng shui *See* Form School.

Lao Tzu Alleged founder of Taoism (6th century BC).

Laozi See Lao Tzu.

Later Heaven Sequence (*Hsian t'ien*) A circular arrangement of the eight Trigrams, with the Trigram *Ch'ien* in the NW. Used in assessment of the interior layout of homes or offices.

Li Trigram The Trigram of Fire and the south.

Liu sha The six curses or "six imps" location in a house.

Lo p'an The feng shui compass. The primary tool of Compass School feng shui.

Lo shu The magic square with nine chambers, whose numbers add up to 15 in any direction, connected with the Later Heaven Sequence of Trigrams.

Location *See* Direction.

Luck Something that can be accumulated by the right use of feng shui. Not the same as chance.

Lui sha Common but incorrect spelling of *Liu sha.*

Luk *See Fu, Lou and Shou.*

Lunar calendar *See* calendar, lunar.

Lung The Chinese dragon.

Luo pan. See lo p'an.

Luoshu See lo shu.

Mandarin ducks Famous for staying together as a couple, and therefore highly symbolic of marital fidelity. Used to activate the Romance and Marriage sector in the SW.

Mentor A guide or benefactor.

Ming gua See Ming kua.

Ming kua Destiny Trigram, or personal "kua number."

Ming tang "Bright hall," the open space in front of a building where beneficial ch'i can accumulate.

Mirror Used in feng shui to alter alignments and deflect *sha ch'i.*

Moon gate The omega-shaped gates that reduce ch'i loss from a walled area.

Nien yen The longevity location in a house.

Pa chai See Eight Mansion formula.

Pa kua Literally "Eight Trigrams," or more specifically, the eight-sided or circular arrangement of the eight Trigrams.

Pa kua mirror A mirror (flat, concave, or convex) surrounded by the eight Trigrams in the Former Heaven Sequence and designed to reflect *sha ch'i*.

Pagoda A multi-tiered Chinese tower designed as a feng shui landmark. Not functionally derived from Buddhist *stupas*.

Pine trees Symbol of longevity.

Pillars *See* Four Pillars.

Poison arrows *See* secret arrows.

Productive cycle The cycle of the five Elements, in the order Wood, Fire, Earth, Metal, Water.

Purple Planet A "god" related to the north pole, whose picture is often used as a protective device on wooden tablets.

Qi *See ch'i.*

Qi gong *See* ch'i kung.

Qilin *See* kirin.

Reductive Cycle of the Elements The cycle of the five Elements in the order Wood, Water, Metal, Earth, Fire.

Sau Seng Kong The god of longevity usually shown carrying one of the peaches of immortality and a staff and gourd, accompanied by a white crane, deer, and sometimes bats. *See Fu, Lou, and Shou.*

Secret arrows Cutting ch'i generated by a straight alignment of roads, trees, poles, or adjacent buildings.

Sector An area of a room or building corresponding to one of the cardinal or intercardinal points, i.e., N, S, E, W, NW, SW, SE, NE.

Sexagenary combinations The 60 combinations of 12 Earthly Branches and ten Heavenly Stems. *See also* Kan shih *system.*

Sha *See* sha ch'i.

Sha ch'i Cutting ch'i.

Shar *See* sha.

Sheng ch'i Strong or generating ch'i. Success and great prosperity location in house.

Sheng qi *See* sheng ch'i.

Shou *See Fu, Lou, and Shou.*

Shui Water.

Sitting Direction Where a house "sits," the opposite of the Facing Direction.

Solar calendar *See* calendar, solar.

Ssu ch'i Stagnant or torpid ch'i.

Stems *See* Heavenly Stems.

Hsun The Trigram of wind and early summer.

T'ai chi The Great Ultimate from which everything else came. The "tadpole" symbol, showing its division into yin and yang.

Taiji *See* t'ai chi.

Taoism One of the three great religions of China, dating from Lao Tzu (6th century BC). Concerned with the Tao and the natural flow of energy through all things.

Ti Earth.

T'ien Heaven or, in one sense and literally, the sky.

T'ien i/yi The "Heavenly Doctor" or health location in a house.

Tiger, White The Celestial Animal of the West, symbolic of yin.

Tong Shu *See* Tung Shu.

Tortoise *See* turtle.

Trigrams The eight possible figures made of combinations of three yin (broken) and yang (whole) lines.

Tsai Shen Yeh A fierce god of wealth shown riding on a tiger. Do not place a figure of this god in the bedroom or dining room.

Tui The Trigram representing lake and mid-fall.

Tung Shu The Chinese Almanac.

Tung Sing *See* Tung Shu.

Turtle One of the four Celestial Animals, associated with the north. A yin creature.

Tzu North (the 15 degrees centered on magnetic north).

Tzu wei Polar astrology system, which shows the 12 Palaces, 37 Major and Minor Stars, their Auspices and Degrees of Influence, and the cycles of Greater Limit and Lesser Limit.

West Group The people or houses whose best locations are NW, SW, W, NE.

Wind chimes Used as a cure to slow down rapidly moving ch'i.

Wu hsing Five Elements.

Wu kuei The "five ghosts" location in a house.

Wuxing *See* Wu hsing.

Yang Active male energy, the opposite of yin.

Yang chai The houses of the living.

Yang Yun Sung Perhaps the greatest early Master of the Form School of feng shui (AD 849–c. 888).

Yellow Emperor Huang Ti (2697–2597 BC), perhaps the greatest of the legendary Emperors. Not to be confused with Chin Shih Huang Ti (the first Ch'in emperor who "burnt the books").

Yi Jing *See* I Ching.

Yin Female passive energy, the opposite of yang.

Yin chai Literally "dark house," meaning tomb or grave-site.

Yin/Yang symbol *See* t'ai chi.

Zhou yi An old name for the *I Ching*, the *Classic of Changes*.

Zi wei *See* tzu wei.

Feng shui on the Web

ACCORDING TO WWW.GOOGLE.COM, *there may be over 185,000 websites dedicated to feng shui. The following sites are a small selection, and are additional to those sites mentioned under Organizations on pages 359–60.*

www.aafengshui.com
Traditional feng shui site.

www.asiawear.com/fengshui.html
Feng shui meets fashion.

www.astro-fengshui.com/
Chinese astrology and feng shui. Chinese astrology uses stars to describe the probable path of fate.

www.bloomington.in.us/~9harmony
The site of the Nine Harmonies School of Feng Shui teaches Black Sect Tantric Buddhist feng shui as taught by Professor Lin Yun.

www.chinastudies.com
Professional feng shui Certification Courses. Intensive training in the US and China. Also includes a feng shui catalog.

http://chinesefortunecalendar.com/fsdir.htm
Feng Shui – Lucky Places in the House. Use this tool to find your "lucky place" in the house.

www.chineseroots.com
Build a family tree by tapping into a database with records of births and marriages in China going back over 1,000 years.

http://designforhealth.hypermart.net/
Personalized feng shui guides designed specifically for your home or office.

http://dialspace.dial.pipex.com/town/road/xlx80/
Online school of feng shui and related subjects. Also includes a list of workshops.

www.dragon-gate
Excellent feng shui emporium site.

www.elegantbank.com
Feng shui expert Rocky Sung Siu-kwong teams up with ornaments provider Elegant Bank to offer tips and online purchases.

www.fengshui.co.nz
The Feng Shui Institute of New Zealand specializes in feng shui for the Southern Hemisphere, with information on courses and workshops.

www.fengshui.net
Stephen Skinner's feng shui site features a specialist feng shui newsletter, with details of English translations of feng shui classics like the *Shui Lung Ching*.

www.fengshuiatwork.com
Feng Shui At Work helps clients achieve a greater sense of balance at work and at home.

www.fengshuicdn.com
Canada's Feng Shui Institute offers feng shui certifications, seminars, consultations, training.

www.fengshuidirectory.com
Articles from all schools of feng shui.

www.feng-shui-essentials.com
Feng shui accessories, books, and tips for feng shui practitioners, students, and interested individuals.

www.fengshuigate.com/index.html
Dr. Stephen Field's Feng Shui Gate. Scholarly essays on feng shui and its origins.

www.fengshui-magazine.com
Feng Shui for Modern Living magazine offers subscriptions, up-to-date magazine details and feng shui software.

www.fengshuitimes.com
Online feng shui newsletter. Traditional approach written by reliable authors.

www.fengshuiww.dial.pipex.com
Online Feng Shui School and Astrology. Promotion and learning of feng shui and all related subjects. How to live in harmony with your environment.

www.fourpillars.net/newsl.html
Well worth a look if you are into Four Pillars horoscopes.

www.geocities.com/fengshui_us/flyingStar3.html
Chinese astrology covering feng shui, Four Pillars of destiny, and *zi wei dou shu* astrology.

www.geocities.com/fengshui_us/index.html
Chinese astrology, feng shui tutorials, and examples.

www.geofengshui.com/
The GEO Geomancy/Feng Shui Education Organization provides education in feng shui in the Black Sect (BHS) tradition.

www.geomancy.net
Excellent site by Cecil Lee offering feng shui resources, articles, books, courses, reports, advice, and consultation. Computerized tools for users to perform their own audit.

http://goodfortunefengshui.com
The Feng Shui Institute of Physics and Energy offers feng shui practitioner training and private consultations for homes and businesses.

www.harmonioushome.com
Hand-tooled feng shui enhancements for the home using colors, stones, and talismans.

http://homearts.com/depts/home/03fengb8.htm
Simple, inexpensive remedies for common office problems with feng shui.

http://home.hkStar.com/~starvsn/fsgeoinf.html
Temporal Location Theory. Information on *kan yu*, the ancient Chinese theory of site location (feng shui).

www.kathlyne.com/cafe.cfm
Kathlyne's Feng Shui Café offers articles on feng shui and insight into harmony in life.

www.lillian-too.com
Lillian's Too's feng shui site promises wealth, health, prosperity, personal happiness, satisfying family, love, relationships, and success.

www.madcool.com/kkds/fengshui.htm
KKDS Feng Shui Information. Introduction to feng shui, covering origins, principles, and feng shui analysis.

www.masterkwchan.org
Master Chan Kun Wah's site provides initiated Yeun Hom feng shui material.

http://maxpages.com/fengshuischool
This site, run by a Chicago-based feng shui school, offers consultations for home or business.

www.mjgdesigns.com/
Feng Shui jewelry, crystals, aromatherapy, and windchimes, plus a free newsletter. Feng shui consultations and workshops available.

www.9starki.com
The Blooming Grove Studio explores Nine Star Ki and the Macrobiotic theory which stem from the same roots.

www.qi-whiz.com
Feng shui facts as vigorously interpreted by Cate Bramble, minus the psychobabble.

www.spiritweb.org/Spirit/feng-shui.html
Comprehensive set of articles on feng shui and ch'i from SpiritWeb written by Jenny Liu.

www.thebook.com/mingli/ch.htm
Advanced *Ming Li* fate calculations.

www.thefengshuiconsultancy.co.uk
The Feng Shui Consultancy provides consultations for homes within the UK.

www.traditionalfengshui.com
Feng shui articles, practitioner listings, and links to feng shui educators.

www.urbanmerchant.net
Beautiful contemporary and traditional feng shui products for the urban home, office, and landscape.

www.wind8water.com
Specializes in individual feng shui consultations for home and office, group lectures, and workshops.

www.wofs.com
The World of Feng Shui site features an Aunt Agga column, tips by Lillian Too and other experts, seminar dates, and articles.

www.ychfengshui.com
Master Yap Cheng Hai's site.

www.zhouyi.com/
A brilliant site that lists many of the best sites dealing with the *I Ching*.

Other resources

Books

Applied Pa Kua and Lo Shu Feng Shui
Too, Lillian,
Kuala Lumpur: Konsep, 1993.

Chinese Astrology
Walters, Derek,
London: Aquarian Press, 1987.

The Complete Illustrated Guide to Feng Shui
Too, Lillian,
Shaftesbury: Element, 1996. *

Feng Shui
Rossbach, Sarah,
London: Hutchinson, 1983.

Feng Shui, the Ancient Wisdom of Harmonious Living
for Modern Times
Wong, Eva,
London & Boston: Shambhala, 1996. *

Feng Shui Before and After: Practical Room-by-Room
Makeovers for Your House
Skinner, Stephen,
Boston: Tuttle Publishing, 2001.

Feng Shui and Destiny
Lo, Raymond,
Tynron Press, 1992.

The Feng Shui Handbook: A Practical Guide to Chinese
Geomancy
Walters, Derek,
London: Aquarian Press, 1991.

Feng Shui for Modern Living (the book)
Skinner, Stephen,
London: Cima/Cico Books, New York: Trafalgar,
2000.

Feng Shui: Perfect Placing for your Happiness and
Prosperity
Walters, Derek,
London: Pagoda, 1988. *

Feng-shui: or the Rudiments of Natural Science in China
Eitel, Ernest,
Cambridge: Cokaygne, 1973.

Feng Shui, the Traditional Oriental Way
Skinner, Stephen,
Bristol: Parragon, 1997. *

Land of the Dragon: Chinese Myth
Allan, Tony & Phillips, Charles,
Amsterdam: Time-Life, 1999.

Living Earth Manual of Feng-Shui: Chinese Geomancy
Skinner, Stephen,
London: Penguin/Viking, 1982. (written 1976)

The Principles of Feng Shui
Sang, Master Larry,
California: American Feng Shui Institute, 1994.

The Shorter Science and Civilization in China
Ronan, Colin & Needham, Joseph,
Cambridge: Cambridge University Press, 1980.

Yi Jing. (The I Ching)
Wu Jing-Nuan,
Washington: Taoist Center, 1991.

* gives a well-rounded view of feng shui

Magazines

Feng Shui for Modern Living

This monthly magazine was the first glossy feng shui magazine, founded by Stephen Skinner and previously published worldwide from London. Surprisingly, it even had a Chinese language edition, published in Taiwan, exporting feng shui back to Chinese readers.
Fax: +44 (0)20 8740 4315
Internet: www.fengshui-magazine.com
Email: info@fengshui-magazine.com

Feng Shui Newsletter

A monthly newsletter of more serious feng shui material, including articles by well-known Masters and translations from Chinese feng shui classics.
Internet: www.fengshui.net
Email: info@fengshui.net

Qi magazine

Tse Qigong Centre, Box 15807, Honolulu, HI 96830.
Tel: (808) 528 8501
Fax: (520) 441 6578
Email: tse@wildgooseqigong.com

Organizations

168 Feng Shui Advisors

PO Box 11203, Burbank, CA 91510-1203
Tel: (818) 841 4135
Fax: (818) 841 9867
Email: info@168fengshui.com
Internet: www.168fengshui.com

American Feng Shui Institute

Master Larry Sang, 108 North Ynez Ave, Suite 202, Monterey Park, CA 91754
Tel: (626) 571 2757
Fax: (626) 571 2065
Internet: www.amfengshui.com

American Healing Arts Institute

Val Biktashev & Elizabeth Moran,
269 S. Beverly Drive, Suite 280, Beverly Hills, CA 90212
Tel: (323) 852-1381
Internet: www.aafengshui.com

DeAmicis School of Feng Shui

321 Avon Street, Philadelphia, PA 19116-3207
Tel: (215) 464 5149
Internet: www.FengShuiandtheTango.com

Denise Linn Seminars

PO Box 75657, Seattle, WA 98125-0657
Email: denise@qed-productions.com
Internet: www.qed-recording-services.co.uk/denise1.htm

Earth Design Inc

Jami Lin, PO Box 530725, Miami Shores, FL 33153
Tel: (305) 756 6426
Fax: (305) 751 9995
Email: earthdes@gate.net
Internet: www.gate.net/~earthdes

Feng Shui Chicago Center Inc

3745 West Montrose, Chicago, IL 60618
Tel: (773) 478 8878
Fax: (773) 478 2179
Email: fengshui@megsinet.net
Internet: www.fengshuichicagocenter.com

Feng Shui Designs Inc # +

Helen & James Jay, PO Box 399, Nevada City, CA 95959
Tel: (530) 470 9215 or (888) 701 8999
Email: info@fengshuidesigns.com
Internet: http://fsdi.com and www.fengshuidesigns.com

Feng Shui Institute of America

PO Box 488, Wabasso, FL 32970
Tel: (407) 589 9900
Fax: (407) 589 1611

Feng Shui Living #
Nancy Pond-Smith, 17878 N. Bay Road, Suite 601,
N. Miami Beach, FL 33160
Tel: (305) 935 9393
Fax: (305) 935 9394
Email: FengShuiLiving@hotmail.com
Internet: www.FengShuiLiving.com

Feng Shui Warehouse Inc * +
James Moser, PO Box 6689, San Diego, CA 92166
Major US supplier of feng shui products and organizer
of regular US conferences.
Tel: (800) 399 1599 and (619) 523 2158
Fax: (619) 523 2165
Email: fengshuiWH@aol.com
Internet: www.fengshuiwarehouse.com

Fortunate Blessings Foundation Inc
William Spear, 24 Village Green Drive, Litchfield,
CT 06759-3419
Tel: (860) 567 8801
Fax: (860) 567 3304
Email: info@fortunateblessings.org
Internet: www.fortunateblessings.org

International Feng Shui Research Center
1340 Marshall Street, Boulder, CO 80302
Tel: (303) 939 0033
Fax: (303) 939 0044
Email: fengshui@fengshui2000.com
Internet: www.fengshui2000.com

Karen Kingston Promotions
Tel: (301) 251 5122
Fax: (301) 217 9528
Email: USoffice@spaceclearing.com
Internet: www.spaceclearing.com

Lin Yun Temple #
2959 Russell Street, Berkeley, CA 94705
Tel: (510) 841 2347
Fax: (510) 548 2621
Internet: www.yunlintemple.org

Metropolitan Institute of Interior Design
13 Newtown Road, Plainview, NY 11803
Tel: (516) 845 4033
Fax: (516) 845 8787
Internet: www.met-design.com

Nancy Santo Pietro & Associates
1684 80th Street, Brooklyn, NY 11214
Tel: (718) 256 2640
Fax: (718) 232 8054
Internet: www.fengshui-
santopietro.com/about_nspa.html

Nine Harmonies School of Feng Shui
4271 Indian Hill Road, Nashville, IN 47448
Tel: (812) 988 0873
Internet: www.nineharmonies.com

New England School of Feng Shui
Waterbury, Connecticut
Tel: (203) 268 9483
Fax: (203) 268 9479
Email: amymims@aol.com
Internet: www.neschoolfengshui.com

New York School of Feng Shui
Janus Welton, PO Box 86, Woodstock, New York,
NY 12498-0086
Tel: (518) 448 8600
Email: fengshui_des@earthlink.net

Smiley's Holistic Feng Shui Institute
2209 Ross Road, Silver Spring, MD 20910
Tel/Fax: (301) 565 9453

Western School of Feng Shui
437 South Highway 101, Suite 752 Solana Beach,
CA 92075
Tel: (619) 793 0945
Internet: www.wsfs.com

* = Major supplier of feng shui equipment
+ = Major feng shui conference or travel organizer
# = Major feng shui teaching organization

Movies

Unfortunately, there are no movies specifically about feng shui, but a number of recent releases get close to working in some of the associated beliefs.

The Last Emperor (Director: Bertolucci, 1987)
This magnificent movie traces the last days of the Ching dynasty (1644–1911). It covers its fall and the life of the last Ching Emperor, P'u Yi, first under the Chinese Nationalists, and then under Mao's People's Republic of China. This is not a movie about feng shui, but should be seen by anyone who would like to see what the Forbidden City (the Emperor's palace) in Beijing was like. It is also useful to get an overall appreciation of the subsequent developments in China, where many of the old customs, such as feng shui, and their custodians, were ruthlessly suppressed.

The Emperor and the Assassin (Director: Chen Kaige, 2000, China)
This is one of the most extraordinary movies to come out of the People's Republic of China. It was probably the first Hollywood-style epic to be made there, and is certainly the most expensive Asian movie made to date at $20 million.

The movie is set in the 3rd century BC, at the end of the Chou (Zhou) dynasty (1027–221 BC) and the start of the Ch'in dynasty (221–207 BC). The Emperor concerned was Ying Zheng who later became the Emperor Ch'in Shih Huang Ti. He burned many of the books that existed before his reign, and unified a lot of warring states into what was to become China, a country named after the Ch'in dynasty. As an insight into the period it is quite extraordinary. The director filmed at some of the original sites, but he also reconstructed an entire palace, with huge battle scenes using 6,000 extras supplied by the Red Army. Look out for the ancient maps of the Empire, which are rolled out on the floor of the palace – they are in fact replicas of real ancient Chinese maps. Also note the extraordinary moving pathway across a deep pool.

A Touch of Zen (Director: King Hu, 1969, Hong Kong)
An important two-part movie set in the Ming dynasty (AD 1368–1644) that incorporates a lot of Chinese beliefs into a sword and sorcery format. Make sure you see both parts in the right order. Watch out for visual hints and clues.

Big Trouble in Little China (Director: John Carpenter, 1986)
A movie that's not to be taken too seriously. A bit of fun based on Chinese magic. One of the main characters is called Lo P'an, who, according to the plot, was cursed by no less a figure than the Emperor Ch'in Shih Huang Ti.

The Golden Child (Director: Michael Ritchie, 1986)
Eddie Murphy ensures that this movie is very funny, but in amongst the bunkum runs a serious thread of Chinese magic and belief, confused a bit by the introduction of the Persian demon Pazazu. Watch out for the female snake-bodied immortal and the wall-eyed Chinese magician masquerading as a street merchant in Kathmandu.

Software

Andrew Ballantine Technology Ltd,
Worting House, Basingstoke, Hampshire
RG23 8PY, UK
Tel: +44 (0) 12 5635 5350
Fax: +44 (0) 12 5681 1876
Internet: www.aballantine.com

Supplies *Software for Feng Shui*, which is a complete program that calculates Eight Mansion feng shui and Four Pillar horoscopes (including compatibility between partners), gives *I Ching* predictions, shows a *lo p'an* to enable exact facing degrees to be selected, does Flying Star calculations, and provides lucky and unlucky day calculations for months and years ahead. In fact, it covers just about everything featured in this book, and more.

Chinese dynasties and feng shui chronology

Traditional Emperors	BC	Significant feng shui event
	4000	Neolithic grave containing feng shui symbolism
Fu Hsi	2852–2737	Invented the eight Trigrams, discovered the Ho t'u and Early Heaven Sequence of the Trigrams.
Shen Nong	2737–2697	
Huang Ti (the Yellow Emperor)	2697–2597	Reputedly invented the compass and a primitive calendar based on 60-year cycles of Stems and Branches, which began in the year 2637 BC.
Shao Hao	2597–2513	
Chaun Hsu	2513–2435	
Ti Ku	2435–2365	
Ti Ch'i	2365–2356	
Yao	2356–2255	Set up astronomical observatories to help regulate the calendar.
Shun	2255–2205	Attempted to regulate the rivers.
Yu	2205–2197	Discovered the Lo Shu and Later Heaven Sequence of the Trigrams, and succeeded in regulating the floods.

Historic Dynasties

Hsia (Xia)	2150–1557	*Hsia* solar calendar devised.
Shang	1557–1027	60-day cycle devised from ten Heavenly Stems and 12 Earthly Branches.
Chou (Zhou)	1027–221	King Wen discovered the 64 Hexagrams & wrote the *Chou I*, part of the *I Ching*.
Spring and Autumn Period	770–476	Confucius edited the *I Ching*. Lao Tzu wrote *Tao The Ching*. Feng shui formed from the Compass + *I Ching* + calendar.
The Warring States Period	476–221	Chou Yen (350–270 BC) mentions the five Elements.
Ch'in (Qin)	221–206 BC	Burning of the books.
Han	206 BC –	*Kan-yu* (the old name for feng shui) becomes a profession.
	AD 220	Many books on feng shui known, for example *Golden Kan-yu Thesaurus* by Ching Wu, Master Blue Raven.
	AD	
Three Kingdoms (Wei, Shu, Wu)	220–265	Kuan Lo (209–256) writes classic feng shui text. *Chi-men tun-chia* style of feng shui introduced by Chu-kuo Liang.
Chin (Jin)	265–420	Kuo P'o (276–324), 'father of feng shui', writes the *Burial Classic*.
Southern & Northern dynasties	420–589	Wang Wei (415–443).
Sui	589–618	
T'ang	618–906	Feng shui flourishes. Yang Yun Sung (849–c.888) brings Form School together.
Five Dynasties & Ten Kingdoms	906–960	
Sung (Northern)	960–1127	Wang Chih founds the Fukien Compass School based on Trigrams, Stems, and Branches. *Lo p'an* established with 17 rings.
Northern Kin & Southern Sung	1127–1279	Chen Hsi-I founded *tzu-wei tu-su* feng shui.
Yuan (Mongol)	1260–1368	Chao Fang writes about the *lo ching*, or feng shui compass.
Ming	1368–1644	First Ming Emperor (Chu Yuan Chuan 1368–98) kills many Taoist feng shui masters, and issues false feng shui books. Establishment of *San Yuan* feng shui. *Lo p'an* expanded to 36 rings.
Ch'ing (Qing) (Manchu)	1644–1911	Use of Four Pillar horoscope integrated with feng shui.
Republic of China	1912–1949	Feng shui suppressed in mainland China (1927).
People's Republic of China	1949–present	The Cultural Revolution (1966–76) closes down most of feng shui in People's Republic of China. First 20th-century book on feng shui in UK written (1976). First book on feng shui published in Chinese in communist-era China (1989). First worldwide full color feng shui magazine *Feng Shui for Modern Living* published (1998).

Index

Acknowledgments

Author's acknowledgments

I would like to thank the Chinese feng shui practitioners and Masters whom I met in Hong Kong and Singapore in the 1970s and who first showed me where to look for the dragon's breath.

Publisher's acknowledgments

Dorling Kindersley would like to thank Neal Cobourne for designing the jacket, and Melanie Simmonds and Hayley Smith for picture research.

Packager's acknowledgments

Cooling Brown would like to thank Kate Sheppard, Patricia Coward, and Janet Swarbrick for editorial assistance; Barry Robson for illustrating the dogs and bringing them so vividly to life; Peter Cooling for producing computer-generated images; and Pauline Clarke and Chris King for illustrations.

Picture credits

The Art Archive/British Museum: 54; **Ashmolean Museum:** 195, 245b; **British Museum:** 285; **Pauline Clarke:** 48, 62, 64, 199, 200, 202, 233, 240, 242, 247t, 250, 280, 282, 284; **Paul Goff:** 208; Trump Tower, 725 Fifth Avenue NY ©**Michael Moran:** 36; **Photodisc:** 14, 16, 20, 22, 24 (and jacket), 26 (and jacket), 29, 30, 31, 33, 39, 41, 44, 45, 46, 52, 56, 57, 58, 66, 71, 76, 78, 83, 84, 85, 87, 88, 89, 90, 92, 98, 99, 104, 106, 110, 114, 116, 123, 132, 134, 138, 139, 140, 141, 142, 143, 145, 146, 152, 153, 154, 156, 160, 162, 165, 172, 176, 178, 180, 181, 182, 183, 185, 187, 190, 196, 197t, 198, 204, 206, 213, 216, 217, 218, 223, 232, 241, 252, 254, 263, 269, 272, 275, 290, 294, 296, 301, 304, 306, 307, 308, 310, 312, 315, 318, 323, 326, 331, 334, 335, 348b; **Science Museum:** 96; **"Sitting Pretty":** 171; **Stephen Skinner:** 6, 12, 13, 25, 28, 50, 60, 68, 70, 125, 174, 188, 192, 231, 243, 247b, 248, 264, 271, 274, 276, 278, 286, 287, 288, 289, 291, 292, 298, 324, 338, 341, 342, 346, 349.

All other images © Dorling Kindersley. For further information see: www.dkimages.com